"A provocative, pragmatic, and didactic take on a topic that is top of mind for corporate leaders around the world. A rich tapestry of insight, *Shocks, Crises, and False Alarms* is thought-provoking in its rejection of simplistic economic narratives, instead advocating for a balanced, grounded perspective that acknowledges the limits of economics. This work is a valuable resource and a compelling read for anyone seeking a deeper understanding of the intricacies of macroeconomics in an ever-changing global context."

—**ANDRE MACIEL,** Global CFO, Kraft Heinz

"Carlsson-Szlezak and Swartz combine a deep understanding of global financial and economic systems to offer a highly readable guide to coming risks and offer insightful approaches to help investors interpret and respond to future challenges."

—**MARY LOVELY,** Anthony M. Solomon Senior Fellow,
Peterson Institute for International Economics

"*Shocks, Crises and False Alarms* refreshingly argues that it is misplaced to believe in single, silver-bullet frameworks and models to predict and manage macroeconomic risk. Instead, the reader benefits from engaging analyses to demonstrate that business leaders must use their experience, open-mindedness, and decision-making to navigate whatever comes their way. With this book, everyone can learn to navigate what may come."

—**ALI DIBADJ,** CEO, Janus Henderson

"A terrific read that gives business leaders the tools to build confidence in our own judgment of macroeconomic risk. It reinforced my optimism that the bar for economic breakdown is much higher than the media make us believe and that the potential for a 'good macro' environment is real."

—**LUCY PILKO,** CEO Americas, AXA XL

"A valuable framework to improve decision-making in an uncertain world. The authors replace the false precision of point forecasts with an analytical focus on the economic drivers that shape risk and outcomes. The book encourages investors and business executives to overlay their judgment to define narratives that are adaptable to change."

—**TOM LUDDY,** former Chief Investment Officer,
J.P. Morgan Investment Management

"*Shocks, Crises, and False Alarms* brings great clarity to the macroeconomic realities leaders need to understand and operate under. It brings the authors' classic moves together in one good read: clarity of the facts, historical context, and a warning not to overreact to hype or doom. But most important for me are the tools and scenarios to help me think and plan ahead. The world is ever-changing, but this book helped to ground my thinking after the extraordinary shock of Covid and to navigate the global uncertainties that remain."

—**MIKI TSUSAKA**, President, Microsoft Japan

"A tour de force! With a perspective that spans decades to centuries and economic crises to geopolitical tensions, this book offers investors insights that will challenge their perspectives and bring the economic world into sharper focus. The authors combine the skills of economist, Wall Street analyst, and historian to bring a unique perspective to the issues that drive global economies. This book is a stunning rundown of the root drivers of economic growth and crisis—and an enjoyable read to boot!"

—**COLIN McGRANAHAN**, Global Director of Research, Sanford C. Bernstein & Co.

"*Shocks, Crises, and False Alarms* is an essential read in today's world of global macroeconomic uncertainty. Far from preaching infallible predictive models, it approaches the world's complexity with refreshing humility, busting plenty of doom-mongering myths along the way and offering a framework to ground decision-making in sound judgment."

—**ALEX DRUMMOND**, Chief Strategy Officer, American Express

"Tailored to executives, this excellent book serves as a compass for navigating economic, financial, and geopolitical risk, emphasizing the enduring importance of judgment over prediction. A must-read for those seeking a nuanced understanding of macroeconomics and a guide for leaders shaping strategies in an unpredictable world."

—**HON. BILL MORNEAU**, former Minister of Finance, Canada

"A great book that helps business leaders interpret macroeconomic risks and derive implications for their businesses. In particular, its focus on looking past headlines to underlying drivers to form judgment I found to be very impactful."

—**THOMAS SWEET,** former CFO, Dell Technologies

"A vital guide to thinking about macroeconomic risks for those executives—and policymakers—who have to make judgments about how to respond to a world that is likely to continue to generate new surprises."

—**BRAD SETSER,** Whitney Shepardson Senior Fellow,
Council on Foreign Relations

"Carlsson-Szlezak and Swartz offer a richly researched and timely analysis of how leaders can improve their understanding of macroeconomic risks and use these lessons to shape strategic thinking and action. If Warren Buffett says to be greedy when others are fearful, the authors break down macroeconomic fears so you can be a more effective leader."

—**DAVID M. VAN SLYKE,** Dean, Maxwell School of Citizenship
and Public Affairs, Syracuse University

"This incredibly readable book helps executives build a calm, commonsense approach to making balanced judgments about economic risk rather than model-driven predictions likely to fall flat. Helpfully eclectic and facts-based, it avoids certainty in either its excessively pessimistic or optimistic form."

—**GUY MOSZKOWSKI,** founder and former CEO,
Autonomous Research US; Director, Santander Holdings USA

"*Shocks, Crises, and False Alarms* is the antithesis to much of today's literature on the economy and financial markets, which makes simplistic, confident, and often dire predictions. It's a must-read for CEOs and business leaders in search of meaningful insights about the risks shaping the global economy. Timeless, compelling, and thought-provoking, the book also provides a framework for strengthening your own judgment."

—**FRANK BROSENS,** member of the Board of Directors,
Peterson Institute of International Economics; cofounder and
Chief Investment Officer, Taconic Capital

SHOCKS, CR!SES, AND FALSE ALARMS

SHOCKS, CR!SES, AND FALSE ALARMS

HOW TO ASSESS
TRUE MACROECONOMIC RISK

PHILIPP CARLSSON-SZLEZAK
and PAUL SWARTZ

HARVARD BUSINESS REVIEW PRESS
BOSTON, MASSACHUSETTS

Library of Congress Cataloging-in-Publication Data

Names: Carlsson-Szlezak, Philipp, author. | Swartz, Paul, author.
Title: Shocks, crises, and false alarms : how to assess true macroeconomic risk / Philipp Carlsson-Szlezak and Paul Swartz.
Description: Boston, Massachusetts : Harvard Business Review Press, [2024] | Includes index.
Identifiers: LCCN 2023051860 (print) | LCCN 2023051861 (ebook) | ISBN 9781647825409 (hardcover) | ISBN 9781647825416 (epub)
Subjects: LCSH: Macroeconomics. | Risk assessment. | Financial crises.
Classification: LCC HB172.5 .C3687 2024 (print) | LCC HB172.5 (ebook) | DDC 339—dc23/eng/20240122
LC record available at https://lccn.loc.gov/2023051860
LC ebook record available at https://lccn.loc.gov/2023051861

ISBN: 978-1-64782-540-9
eISBN: 978-1-64782-541-6

To those who share a sense of rational optimism in an uncertain world

CONTENTS

PART THREE

GLOBAL ECONOMY

From Convergence Boom to Divergence Gloom

CONCLUSION

!

INTRODUCTION

Good Macro at Risk

In the past 40 years or so, a confluence of tailwinds delivered a benign business environment for corporate leaders and investors alike. In the financial sphere, high and volatile inflation declined to structurally low and stable levels, pulling interest rates down with it, and boosting the valuation of equities and other assets. In the real economy, the longevity of expansions grew, and profit margins widened. In international relations, a process of geopolitical convergence unfolded, giving rise to a web of institutional arrangements and stable global rules that made possible growing cross-border value chains and access to dynamic markets. Taken together, this environment encouraged business leaders to take risks and expand their operations.

We call this environment the *good-macro* operating system of the global economy encompassing a dozen or so macroeconomic foundations.[1] It has profoundly shaped the mindsets and expectations of today's generation of leaders. They have grown their businesses and careers on a global stage that could treat macroeconomics as a friendly backdrop, not as proliferating risk to be managed. This is not to say there were no cracks in good macro—there were, chief among them the global financial crisis of 2008. But as policymakers averted a structural meltdown and went on to deliver the longest US expansion on record, the perception and belief were reinforced that the economy's operating system was inherently benign and resilient, particularly for firms.

Today, faith in good macro has been shaken. Over the past few years, a rapid succession of shocks and crises have rattled the foundations of the economy's operating system. In the financial realm, leaders have faced menacingly high inflation and rapidly rising interest rates for the first time in a generation. In the real economy, pandemic-induced physical disruptions, supply-chain bottlenecks, and labor shortages have introduced previously unheard-of risks. And the global institutional framework, built on expectations of hegemonic US leadership and inexorable political convergence, is fraying as a bipolar world reasserts itself. A war in Europe has even put great-power conflict back on the risk distribution.

Even so, the impact of shocks is rarely linear. As we will see throughout this book, macro risks have proliferated and must be taken seriously, but the darkest predictions rarely materialize—and are routinely overstated. Indeed, for every true crisis, there are many false alarms. Meanwhile technology, which struggled to lift growth during the past two decades, has renewed its promise to deliver a tailwind in the form of artificial intelligence. Pessimists beware: missing out on macroeconomic upside is also a form of risk.

Executives in charge of the strategy and long-term success of businesses or investment portfolios cannot ignore these risks to the real, financial, and global foundations of the business environment. Value creation was hard enough even when the good-macro operating system defined how the economy worked. But if the foundations themselves wobble, the task of value creation changes. Like it or not, after decades in the background, macroeconomics has moved center stage and is now firmly anchored on the CEO agenda.

This book is about helping leaders navigate such risks.

Navigating Shocks, Crises, and False Alarms

When assessing macroeconomic risks, or when risks turn into actual shocks, executives have a difficult call to make. Are the disruptions transient gyrations, permanent inflections, or just false alarms? Will the operating system be resilient and revert to what we've known, or could the shock leave a legacy by changing how the system works? Knowing that complacency can be costly, leaders often feel pressured to take action of some kind. But often a shock harbors at once the possibility of true crisis and false alarm. Consider this string of false alarms during just the past four years:

In 2020, when the Covid-19 pandemic caused extreme uncertainty, a narrative of a new Great Depression took hold. Invoking the 1930s, the narrative predicted an economic collapse worse than the global financial crisis of 2008: a deep, multiyear recession complete with a US sovereign-debt crisis and, later, a dollar collapse.[2] Yet the fearsome *intensity* of the Covid shock said little about the damage it would do structurally, or about the ability and willingness of policymakers to lean against it. By the first quarter of 2021, economic output had bounced back to its pre-Covid level. By late 2021, the US economy was nearly back to its prepandemic trend. And by early 2023, real (that is, inflation-adjusted) output stood 5% higher than its prepandemic peak, accounting for more than an extra $1 trillion in output.

In 2021, after the vigorous recovery had caught many doomsayers off guard, the popular narrative veered in the opposite direction. Hubris and doom are close cousins, so a narrative of repeating the Roaring Twenties suddenly emerged. Now, the digital enablers of the lockdown economy—think Zoom and Teladoc—were expected to deliver a tremendous boost to productivity, to the tune of 100 basis points or more.[3] The pandemic was to be the catalyst that finally delivered tech's long-elusive growth impact. Yet little of that transpired. And investors who bought into boom valuations of the pandemic enablers were left nursing losses.

In 2021 and 2022, when postpandemic inflation peaked higher and later than many expected, the false alarm of a structural break in the inflation regime sounded. Predicting a permanent shift to much higher and more-volatile inflation, the narrative equated postpandemic inflation to that of the 1970s, an ugly period when inflation expectations were unmoored and inflicted structural damage on the economy. Though inflation will very plausibly exhibit upside risks in the future, the postpandemic price spike did not signal a structural shift in expectations. Rather, it reflected a cyclical and idiosyncratic mismatch of supply and demand that gave firms a window of pricing power. Collectively, that made for an inflation spike—not a structural inflection. Sure enough, US inflation subsequently declined by 6 percentage points in less than a year, putting to rest the idea of a runaway 1970s-style problem.

In 2022, as the Federal Reserve raised interest rates at the fastest pace in decades to fight inflation, the false alarm of emerging-market (EM) crisis and contagion took hold. Popular predictions were that higher US rates and a strong dollar would put EM currencies under pressure and make EM debt repayment harder, thereby triggering defaults and capital flight. But many EMs have successfully weaned themselves off dollar-denominated debt. Their economic management has improved as seen by the decision of some EM central banks to raise interest rates ahead of the United States. And many simply did not face the same challenges as rich Western economies. As a result, even as the top of the US rate cycle came into view, there was no evidence of systemic EM crises.[4]

Starting in early 2022 and into 2023, a narrative of imminent and inevitable rich-country recession took hold. Prominent leaders spoke of an economic hurricane, and forecasters' models showed sharply higher recession odds. Fast-rising interest rates had derailed the equity market and were seen as doing the same to the economy. Pundits claimed that inflation could not moderate without much higher unemployment, the key determinant of a recession. And though the idea that there will be a next recession is always true, the fact remains that toward the end of 2023, 18 months after those alarmist calls about an imminent and inevitable recession, US unemployment remained near record lows, even as the Fed had made convincing progress in bringing down excess labor demand and inflation.

Unless they develop an understanding of the forces that are challenging good macro, executives will have a hard time keeping their balance as economic conditions, and the narratives around them, seesaw in this violent manner. Shocks and crises pose a real threat, yet so does overreaction to false alarms. Understanding macroeconomic risk—the potential for both positive and negative change, as well as the distinction between cyclical and structural change—is essential to grasping these threats.

Consider the experience of automakers who cut their semiconductor orders in early 2020 in the belief that the Covid recession would look more like the "Greater Depression" that many predicted.[5] When instead a rapid recovery unfolded, they found themselves at the back of the line, resulting in auto-supply bottlenecks, unmet demand, and a price squeeze that materially contributed to postpandemic inflation. Similarly, investors who got carried away by the so-called Zoom economy in 2021 paid frothy valuations for the pandemic darlings of the stock market, only to be laid low by sharp devaluations in 2022. False alarms can be costly macroeconomic traps.

Besides such dollar costs, there can also be leadership costs. Macroeconomic volatility undermines leadership if executives transmit it to their organizations. Abrupt reversals in strategy, operations, and communications are distracting for employees. There can be a personal toll from chasing the headlines.

Hence, there is value in navigating macroeconomic risk effectively. But standard macroeconomics does not help executives with this essential task. For all its scientific veneer and Greek-letter equations, the discipline offers no precise instruments for business leaders to rely on. None of the false alarms discussed above were captured by sophisticated macroeconomic models or announced by blinking dashboards. If anything, the discipline contributed to the problem by inviting knee-jerk reactions to volatile data flow.

Executives must embrace a more grounded approach to macro risk. As we will see, macroeconomics is about *judgment*—not prediction. And as we argue in this book, judgment is the basis of better decision-making (avoiding costly traps), and it can reduce experienced volatility (enabling smoother leadership). Nobody controls economic volatility—but leaders can choose what they focus on.

The bad news is that macroeconomic shocks will continuously present themselves and leaders will have to make difficult decisions. The good news—and the promise of this book—is that better macroeconomic judgment can be learned.

Let's see how.

How to Assess True Macroeconomic Risk

Can false alarms be avoided? Were the examples above written simply with the benefit of hindsight? Readers should understand that getting it right consistently in macro is not possible. Indeed, a key theme of this book is that we must let go of the false pretense of scientific certainty. Still, with the right analytical habits, leaders stood a fair chance of calling each of the false alarms discussed above. The key is an approach that values contextual flexibility over theoretical rigidity and judgment over prediction. In the face of so much doomsaying and so many false alarms we also need more optimism— not the Panglossian kind, but rational optimism.

We use an eclectic approach that treats macroeconomics as a set of narratives. It is built on judicious use of data combined with context and history. It aims to arrive not at a settled truth but at situational judgment. A mindset more than a theory, it is also skeptical of reflexive doomsaying, engaging with risk optimistically yet rationally. We think effective macroeconomic risk assessment consists of three strong habits. We sketch each in the following and offer a detailed exposition in chapter 2.

First, one must reject a master-model mentality. Don't frame economics as a system for generating an *output*—it's a debate. The track record of macroeconomic models' forecasting is so poor that they are rarely a source of insight and often one of false alarms. Surprisingly, a common belief that sophisticated models yield precise answers has persisted even as misguided predictions have piled up. Models are unreliable because macroeconomic dynamics are context dependent, and because the models rely on (very) small sample sizes. The United States, for instance, has seen only 12 recessions since World War II, each the result of a highly idiosyncratic constellation of drivers. As a result of these idiosyncrasies and limitations, supposedly scientific modeling is often remarkably unscientific. This does not make models obsolete, but leaders should not treat them as a reliable source of insight.

Moreover, forecasts are least reliable when they are most needed. In times of crisis, executives are understandably desperate for guidance as to what might happen next. But crises—by definition—generate extreme data prints. Thus, in situations where predictions would be most valuable, the models need to make extrapolations outside their known empirical range. To put this on a more technical footing, figure 1.1 shows the 70-year range of

FIGURE **1.1**

Covid's data whiplash was well outside the 70-year range, so there was no empirical basis for models to interpret the crisis

Highs and lows of change in economic indicators during Covid and their 70-year pre-Covid range

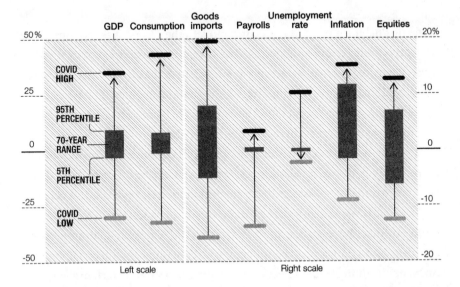

Note: GDP and consumption (both real) are Q/Q annualized. Imports (real) are Q/Q. Payrolls, equities (S&P 500), and inflation (CPI) are M/M (unemployment M - M in percentage points); inflation (CPI) is M/M annualized. Data since 1950; 70-year range through 2019.
Source: BEA, BLS, S&P, analysis by BCG Center for Macroeconomics

changes in major macroeconomic variables (gray bars represent the 5th to 95th percentile of change) as well as the highs and lows of the Covid whiplash (the lines above and below the bars). The extreme data generated by Covid is far outside the range experienced hitherto. The idea that a recovery path could have been modeled, when the models had essentially never seen these shifts before, is laughable.[6]

The whiplash in labor-market data (think payrolls and unemployment) deserves special mention, because models often anchor on unemployment as a proxy for recession and macroeconomic weakness. As unemployment soared from 3.5% to near 15% in just two months in early 2020—surpassing the peak of the global financial crisis of 2008 by nearly 5 percentage points—the predictions of a depression-like recovery seemed plausible. But as clear as the signals of structural break might have seemed, they were a false alarm.

Assessing economic risk is more about judgment than forecasts. And
unless leaders learn how to form their own judgment, they are buying into
a forecast whether they know it or not.[7]

· · ·

If the first habit is a rejection of master models, the second is skepticism of the
macroeconomic doom-mongering that public discourse leans into. Leaders
must navigate a constant whiplash of negative headlines that routinely
translate all manner of gyrations into doomsaying outcomes. The false alarms
of the last few years, as sketched above, are far from exhaustive. Remember, for every true crisis there are many false alarms.

Why the negative bias? Simple: doom sells. Economic and financial journalists rarely get to write about sex, crime, or celebrities. But crises and collapse are reasonable substitutes in a competition to attract eyeballs and generate
clicks. That is particularly true of mainstream and specialist TV, print, and
online media. But even the most respectable titles reliably dial up negative
coverage, as do pundits and commentators.[8] Economic and financial journal-
ism is not immune to the infection of turning news into entertainment.[9]

Thus, false alarms are amplified as the microphone is reliably passed to
the loudest pessimists in the room. They, in turn, know to grab airtime by
self-confidently portraying valid if long-shot risks from the edges of the distribution as being at its very center. Again, without judgment of their own,
executives have little protection against pervasive doomsaying.

· · ·

This leads us to the third and most important habit: economic eclecticism.
By that we mean a mindset that frees itself from a preeminent theory, school
of thought, or philosophy that presumes to offer a single, reliable lens with
which to assess risks. Instead, an eclectic mindset is situationally aware, focused
on causal persuasiveness and coherence in narrative. The inputs are opportunistically broad and come not only from economics but also from adjacent
disciplines. Sometimes thematic frameworks help us understand risks; sometimes historical episodes illuminate; sometimes even closed-form models can
be helpful. And throughout this book, we refer to what we call *regimes*—
narratives of how the economic system works.

As we make our way across the risk landscape, readers will see how we draw pragmatically and opportunistically on whatever we think delivers insight. Economic eclecticism allows us to assess macroeconomic risk by studying its drivers, its context and patterns, and its distribution. An advantage of this approach is that we acknowledge that dynamics and drivers may change. So, throughout the book we focus on *what it would take for true crises to happen*—not simply on the question of *whether* they will happen.

Consider again the false alarm of a Covid depression when a 15% unemployment rate led macro models astray. What delivered the strong recovery? A messy confluence of drivers. Policymakers and politicians acted aggressively to protect liquidity and balance sheets. Consumption shifted online rather than collapsing. Science was faster and better than anticipated in developing vaccines. And societies learned to live with the virus—in classrooms, at airports, in offices. Seeing the potential for recovery was less about models and more about narratives and judgment.

So, it is true that macroeconomics lacks the analytical elegance of a solo performer, like physics. But it plays well in a band. We must bring in a broader set of perspectives and methods to make it shine. As we argue at greater length in chapter 2, this eclectic approach is accessible and suitable to those with curious minds—a group that, in our experience, includes many business executives and investors. Equipped with curiosity and judgment, leaders should not feel intimidated by number crunchers and model-based forecasters, whose grasp of risk and context may be far weaker than theirs. Economic eclecticism doesn't seek to shut down debate, the way model-based "truths" do. It encourages debate, because debate is the foundation of good judgment.

Leadership is about navigating uncertainty. If the future were readily predictable, there would be nothing special about leading—it would be mere execution. Assessing macroeconomic risks is no different. It involves a mix of knowledge, skill, and experience—in short, judgment.

What You Will Get Out of This Book

For many years we have published research and advised corporate executives and institutional investors on the macroeconomic risks covered in this volume. Our approach, themes, and arguments translate the arcane world of global macroeconomics for curious leaders who have devoted their careers to bigger themes than interpreting the macro space—yet who have discovered the growing need to engage with it.

This book brings these conversations to a broader audience: readers who face similar challenges as they navigate the risks of the macroeconomy. As one will notice, this book aims to deliver on two objectives at once. First, a *how* objective—giving readers the analytical instruments to assess a broad range of macroeconomic risks. Second, a *what* objective—articulating our perspective on key risks and the future of the macroeconomic system, that is, the question of whether good macro will persist. Specifically, we hope that readers will benefit across the following dimensions:

- *Develop new analytical skill.* Across the chapters we aim to develop the skill of foundational macroeconomic analysis, always remembering that the operating system of any area matters more than the shock it is experiencing. This provides the basis for distinguishing between credible structural risks and false signals.

- *Navigate the macroeconomic risk landscape with confidence.* Collectively our chapters cover a comprehensive range of macroeconomic risks and their interactions with the business environment. Leaders must be fluent in the real, financial, and global risks that abound—and be able to translate what those mean for their businesses.

- *Think like a rational optimist.* Executives should never belittle risks (and neither do we in this book). That's why they need effective skills to quickly calibrate threats and debunk doom-mongering. The walls of negativity that surround us can feel claustrophobic. Though systemic risks cannot be dismissed, typically the bar for a breakdown is far higher than assumed. Hence the case for a rationally optimistic mindset. We know that doomsaying all too easily conveys gravitas, while optimism can be construed as naivete. Leaders should ignore all that and focus on insight.

- *Hear our views.* We are acutely aware of how difficult it is to write a book about risks and the future. We make no pretense that we can know or nail it. But we believe readers can benefit from watching us apply our practice systematically and comprehensively. New shocks and crises will arise, and facts will change. While our assessments of risks may therefore also change in the future, we think the way we conduct assessments will prove durable. Readers can gather insight both when they agree with us and when they have a different take. The goal is to foster critical and thoughtful engagement with macroeconomic risk.

What isn't in this book? First, it does not offer comparative analysis of major economies and their relative potentials. Instead, we offer thematic analysis of macroeconomic risks that are relevant to many economies. Though we draw on examples globally, we tell the story predominantly through the lens of the US economy, because of its centrality to the global system—be that in interest rates, technology, or global institutions. It is also the most natural common denominator in a debate that is both global and fragmented. Further, the US economy offers a rich availability of long-run data, which matters to our approach. And it is the economy that we happen to know best. All these factors make the United States the strongest baseline for globally relevant narratives.

Second, some readers may wonder why there are no dedicated chapters about key topics: artificial intelligence (AI), climate change, and the Chinese economy spring to mind (as well as industrial policy, competition policy, and so on). They all feature throughout this book—yet they intersect with, rather than explain, the workings of the economic system. AI we see broadly through the lens of productivity growth addressed in chapters 5, 7, and 8; climate change through the lens of capital formation, inflation, debt, geopolitics, trade, and even bubbles (chapters 5, 12, 13, 15, 16, 18, and 19); and China through the lens of the gravity of growth, geopolitics, and trade (chapters 6, 17, 18, and 19).

Traversing the Landscape of Risk with Us

Can good macro persist? Are we exiting the essentially benign macro backdrop against which a generation of leaders built their careers? Following a deeper discussion of *how* to analyze risk in chapter 2, this book breaks the question into three interacting components: the real economy (risks to growth), the financial economy (financial risks), and the global economy (geopolitical risks). Parts 1, 2, and 3 reflect this three-way partition of the risk landscape. In each part we deconstruct the three components further into discrete risk topics, each chapter tackling one. There are 18 topics in all. Readers can traverse the landscape of macro risk sequentially—seeing how we build up the map—or they can choose to jump around.

In part 1, Real Economy: Growth Risks and Growth Boosts, we take on cyclical risk by looking at how recessions can unfold and how recoveries happen (chapters 3 and 4). We then analyze long-term growth prospects by confronting hubris, defeatism, and magical thinking (chapters 5 and 6). Finally, we consider the growth promise of technology and particularly AI (chapters 7 and 8).

In part 2, "Financial Economy: Good Strains and Systemic Risks," we start with an analysis of why the United States is addicted to all manner of stimulus (chapter 9), the risks to the government's ability to deliver stimulus in times of crises (chapter 10), and the challenges to the government's use of tactical stimulus to goose the economic cycle (chapter 11). We then proceed to distinguish between structural breakdowns and cyclical surges of inflation (chapters 12 and 13) and round out the financial-risk debate by looking at three consequences of our earlier analysis: higher interest rates (chapter 14), debt sustainability (chapter 15), and the risk posed by bubbles (chapter 16).

In part 3, "Global Economy: From Convergence Boom to Divergence Gloom," we trace the rise and fall of the convergence bubble of the past 30 years (chapter 17) and analyze why geopolitical risk rarely translates linearly into macroeconomic impact and how to approach this challenge (chapter 18). We then consider the economic impact of changing trade patterns (chapter 19). Last, we explain why we consider predictions of the end of the dollar's status as the global reserve currency a classic example of a false alarm (chapter 20).

. . .

We close the book not with a classic synthesis—actionable conclusions on *how* to analyze risk are located within the chapters—but by articulating our strategic narrative of the economy. In chapter 21, looking across the real, financial, and geopolitical arenas, we argue that the remainder of the 2020s will still feature a good-macro system that underpins a favorable business environment. In brief, it will be an era of real-economy tightness that delivers stronger, if still relatively modest, growth as well as financial strains that force more-disciplined capital allocation. The concurrent and geopo-litically driven reallocation of global productive capacity reinforces those (positive) trends in the medium run while representing a loss of potential in the longer run. The risks that come with this reading are many, genuine, and sometimes systemically threatening. Big resets can and do happen in macroeconomics. Yet, we are unwilling to move them to the center of our assessment unless we can tell a clear and persuasive narrative about why such outcomes have emerged as the likeliest. We remain rational optimists.

CHAPTER 2

How to Assess True Macroeconomic Risk

B efore traversing the landscape of macroeconomic risks in the 18 chapters ahead of us, we invite readers to reflect more deeply on the three habits we introduced in chapter 1: letting go of master-model mentality, discounting doom-mongering, and practicing economic eclecticism. What motivates this approach to macroeconomic analysis and how can we make the habits actionable? Some may be tempted to skip directly to the risks analyzed in parts 1, 2, and 3, but we encourage readers to stay with this chapter to hear how we think about macroeconomics. What follows is not a preview of the risks, analyses, and findings—it is a deeper exposition of the analytical mindset we believe aids effective macroeconomic risk assessment.

Our approach is a deliberate counterweight to how macroeconomics typically presents itself, which is as a highly technical, codified field with high barriers to entry, even for those who are trained in other areas of research. Here we seek to demonstrate that creating insight and value for decision-makers is not about gaining membership to the world of academic economics. That world has its own uses as well as remarkable scholarship—its role is to advance the frontier of knowledge. It is also arcane and mostly disconnected from the challenges and questions leaders face.[1] Knowing this world is certainly helpful, but having a dynamic stochastic general equilibrium model at your fingertips is not essential to developing sound macro judgment—it is often an impediment. As we often stress, the idea of an economy that reverts to known equilibria is important for modeling. Outside the world of academia, however, the economy continuously moves from one disequilibrium to another.

In this spirit, we refrain from offering our own unifying approach, method, or theory—and certainly not a singular model. Business books, much like academic publications, often provide a silver-bullet approach—a new perspective or trick—to overcoming a problem. Those typically come with catchy names and perhaps an analytical process, often reduced to a seductively small number of simple-sounding steps. In contrast, we ask readers to do the opposite and adopt an open mindset. The messy reality of macroeconomics calls for a broad and adaptable lens, not one that collapses reality into narrow inputs and outputs. We should understand macroeconomic risk as a series of shifting narratives, each steeped in context and history. Remember, we are not seeking settled truth. We aspire, more realistically and more humbly, to situational judgment.

Though there isn't a trick we can learn and apply to all the macro risks we'll encounter, we can articulate the mindset that underpins a productive engagement with them. Our view of economics is, at heart, a more honest relationship with uncertainty.

Voltaire, the 18th-century French philosopher, captured the need for a more realistic relationship with uncertainty when he wrote, "Doubt is not a pleasant condition, but certainty is an absurd one."[2] Though he wrote this just before macroeconomics emerged, his insight addresses a critical problem about how we engage with the discipline today. We treat it as a system for removing doubt and delivering certainty because certainty is pleasant. In the process we forget how absurdly unattainable that is. As we saw in chapter 1, and contrary to the scientific veneer the discipline projects, macroeconomic outcomes simply cannot be predicted with reliability, not even a few quarters out. Forecasts must give way to perspective; theory to narrative; and certainty to judgment.

In other words, leaders should not give into the temptation to tame uncertainty with models—leadership is about navigating uncertainty and striving for good judgment. This requires a nimble and eclectic mindset. That may be harder than a narrower approach but will be more rewarding. Mac-

FIGURE **2.1**

Four quadrants of macroeconomic risk:
Firms face downside but also risk missing out on upside

	Cyclical (tactical)	Structural (strategic)
Downside	**Downturns** E.g., recessions, shocks	**Breaks** E.g., deflationary depression, inflationary break
Upside	**Tailwinds** E.g., recoveries, accelerations	**Upshifts** E.g., productivity shift, capital stock deepening

Source: BCG Center for Macroeconomics

roeconomics fits this challenge perfectly. There are no fixed answers—only dynamics, drivers, and tendencies—and to navigate macro risk effectively, leaders must accept this reality.

Some clarification about *risk*—a versatile word in macroeconomics as summarized in figure 2.1. Often, it refers to big structural downsides: the possibility of a deflationary depression, the chance of an inflation regime break, the threat of a systemic debt crisis. But we also discuss structural upsides, such as technological tailwinds to growth—and the risk of missing or misjudging those. To practitioners, they are all macroeconomic risks. Similarly, though we cover many risks that are structural in nature and that have the potential to durably change the economic operating system, we also discuss tactical risks pertaining to the cycle. Tactical macro risk, too, is typically about downside (recession), but upside risk remains—like when a recovery is stronger than anticipated.

Though we are confident that following the three good habits enhances the assessment of macroeconomic risk, we would not be surprised if some conclusions about future macroeconomic outcomes in this book, which we make at a particular point in time (fall of 2023), turned out to be wrong. (We'd be more surprised if they all turned out right.) But we would be disappointed if the frameworks we used to make these conclusions failed to shed light on why. The difference is that we cannot know the conditions and context in which future shocks and crises play out. But we can understand drivers, how they interact, and the risks they pose—and we can be empowered to watch their ongoing evolution and adjust as they develop. Unlike with the fixed context of a book, readers can continuously and incrementally refine and update their risk assessment.

Letting Go of Master-Model Mentality

Master-model mentality (MMM) is how we referred in chapter 1 to the overpowering desire in macroeconomics to find a definitive answer—an output—that closes the debate. It ascribes the rigor of natural science to economics, suggesting that certainty is a reasonable proposition because we can follow the science.[3] By-products of MMM are precision forecasts and other trappings of hard natural science—think universal models, reams of data, and computing power projecting precision.

Nearly 50 years ago, Friedrich von Hayek (and Ludwig von Mises before him) criticized macroeconomists' jealousy and imitation of physics as dangerous: "It seems to me that this failure of the economists to guide policy more successfully is closely connected with their propensity to imitate as closely as possible the procedures of the brilliantly successful physical sciences—an attempt which in our field may lead to outright error."[4]

So-called physics envy has only gotten worse.[5] But the reality remains that economics is too uncertain, too nonstationary, and too multidisciplinary to pass as a natural science. This isn't said with shame. It is said with some pride—macroeconomics in its complexity will remain challenging (and, we think, more interesting) as the rules will stay in flux. Its idiosyncrasy can be both bewildering and captivating.

In chapter 1 we established that models are weakest when they are needed the most: in times of crisis. But the weakness of MMM goes beyond limited empirical data. Even if a broader empirical base were available, model design would remain an obstacle. For example, before the global financial crisis of 2008, models of the real economy commonly assumed away the workings of the financial system—a simplification that proved fatally flawed.[6]

In truth, the expectations of scientific rigor and precision in economics are entirely unreasonable. Consider that disciplines that stand on much firmer scientific ground—such as epidemiology—are no better at handing reliable predictions to decision-makers. The onset of the pandemic in 2020 was an accidental race between epidemiologists and economists to read the future.

Epidemiologists' predictions of many millions more Covid deaths were wide of the mark—making economists almost look good by comparison.[7] In both cases, the unknowns and instability meant that using models to make point forecasts wasn't realistic. Master-model mentality ignores all this—and demands a specific answer. When those narrow answers were given and utilized, their failures undermined credibility. Leaders must know what is possible, in what circumstances, and why. They must reject the narrowness and brittleness of artificial precision.

Analysts often find MMM appealing because it loves new data points. Such data supplies the scientific veneer of quantification and measurement. And the audience loves it because to measure is to control. Yet when something can't be quantified but is measured anyway, the result is misjudgment that can be detrimental to decision-making. Consider what Secretary of Defense Robert McNamara said about Vietnam: "Every quantitative measurement we have shows we're winning."[8] The United States wasn't winning, regardless of the numbers. Little has changed. Modern geopolitical discussion in boardrooms (see chapters 17 and 18) often looks to reduce uncertainty rather than embrace it. Similarly, in crises, it's easy to find data to back up what doomsayers proclaim. To paraphrase McNamara, at the start of Covid every quantitative measurement we had pointed to a deep depression. But the foundations of the US economy were not imploding, regardless of the collapsing data across the board (see figure 1.1, on Covid's data whiplash).

To be clear, it's not that we think models are useless. On the contrary, they can be useful, and we will at times invoke models in our own analysis. But they are an aid at best, not the engine—they don't provide a final answer. MMM does not like to confess to the inability to provide a precise answer, or to the idiosyncratic and situational nature that makes many risks impossible to model. This is to be rejected.

What can be done to resist the powerful allure of certainty and MMM? We follow three actionable practices.

- *Be skeptical of theory.* None of the risks we encounter in this book can be seen through a single and reliable theory. Each is the subject of never-ending debate. Instead, understanding the drivers of risk is key to conquering complexity. Consider the monetarist mantra hammered into generations of economics students that "inflation is everywhere and always a monetary phenomenon."[9] As chapter 13 demonstrates, monetary forces are but a (valuable) piece of a complex topic. In the postpandemic inflation squeeze, it provided little insight into either structural-regime risks or cyclical inflation dynamics. The Phillips curve, another theory of inflation with a storied history, did not perform better.[10] We must pursue coherent narrative that is ready to change, not static theory looking to reign.

- *Discount point forecasts.* That is, unless you know how to make and use them. There is a meaningful use case for economic forecasting where it's understood to be a form of communication, a compressed version of today's available information in the snapshot of a single set of numbers.[11] But unless you operate in this world where forecasts are made and implemented accordingly, they will only deceive and frustrate you. They are not designed to have a shelf life, so they can't be stable inputs into business or investment strategy. It's in forecasting that the physics envy of MMM shines through most clearly. The problem is that the rules of physics are laws. They don't change. Those of economics do.[12] To treat economics as stable isn't sophisticated. It's risky and foolish.

- *Handle the data flow with care.* Incremental data points are the fuel that MMM runs on. Knowing the data is important. (And those who know it well know the weaknesses of every time series.) But the ability to make worthwhile inferences from incremental data is modest, and the attention that data receives amplifies the risks inherent in MMM. Incremental data flow is no substitute for the judgment required to understand what the data means. Consider the obsession with mobility and with footfall data in the early days of the pandemic. The data said everything about a drop in people spending time and money in shopping malls, movie theaters, and airports. And it said nothing about everyone going online and delivering the biggest shift in consumption patterns on record. Footfall data was at once an obsession and a red herring, merely confirming with numbers what shelter-in-place orders had made inevitable. An unquestioning focus on the data flow sent many economic analysts astray (pointing, in error, toward deeper downturns and weaker recoveries). Data is critical—but it alone will not provide an insight that closes the debate.

Our criticism of closed-form models isn't ours alone or even new. In fact, it has been present across the spectrum of economic thought. Some four decades before Hayek, John Maynard Keynes had also taken issue with modeling. Though we'd quibble with the first part of Keynes's statement, we think his position resonates: "Economics is a science of thinking in terms of models joined to the art of choosing models which are relevant to the contemporary world. It is compelled to be this, because, unlike the typical natural science, the material to which it is applied is, in too many respects, not homogeneous through time."[13]

It's these imperfections that led us to articulate the dos and don'ts above, each to be taken with a grain of salt: be skeptical of theory, discount forecasts, and handle the data flow with care. When Keynes said "choosing," we think "judgment." When he said "not homogenous," we think "nonstationary."

Most executives and investors instinctively know that their craft is one of judgment, not implementing truths and certainties. We're simply striving to persuade readers that macroeconomics is no different. When entering the land of macro, they need to retain these instincts.[14]

Discounting Doom-Mongering

The second habit is about confronting ever present doom-mongering. In chapter 1, we made the case about the pervasive and persistent negativity in public discourse. It's rational to consider risks from the edges of the risk distribution. It is not rational to *assume* that those risks are at its center. Treating news as entertainment distorts the debate and the public consciousness of macro risks. Precisely because many risks are grossly overstated, the rate of false alarms is high. For every true crisis there are many false alarms.

In this book we will encounter many risks—and belittle none. There is little doubt that the global macro backdrop is less benign than it was during the past few decades and that we cannot dismiss systemic risks. But a habit of assuming the worst and then making the analysis fit that mental model does not help us spot true risk.

The doomsaying is so ubiquitous that we have grown numb to it. In chapter 1, we already encountered the recent string of false alarms about a Covid depression, an inflation regime break, a cascade of emerging market crises, and inevitable recession. But it's worth reminding ourselves of the forcefulness and ubiquity of the false alarms in some more detail:

Regarding the false alarm of a Covid depression, *Project Syndicate* captured the predominant sentiment with "A Greater Depression?" (March 24, 2020). Even as extraordinary stimulus measures were on the way, *Bloomberg* asked "How Bad Might It Get? Think the Great Depression" (April 22, 2020). And the first shoots of a recovery were clearly visible when *Time* leaned into extraordinary pessimism with "The Next Global Depression Is Coming and Optimism Won't Slow It Down" (August 6, 2020). Of course, none of these takes on the Covid recession held up.

Regarding the false alarm of structural inflation, *Forbes* declared, "Energy Crisis Threatens Return of 1970s Inflation" (October 19, 2021). *Bloomberg* said, "This Is What Living with Long-Term High Inflation Feels Like" (April 18, 2022). And *Bloomberg* piled onto the structural inflation narrative a month later with an article titled "Forever Inflation" (May 13, 2022). All these headlines were too confidently pessimistic.

Regarding the impact of higher interest rates on emerging markets, *Al Jazeera* warned early that "Looming Fed Rate Hikes Have Emerging Markets Dreading Déjà Vu" (January 25, 2022). As rate hikes progressed, dread turned to misplaced certainty. *Bloomberg* suggested that a "Historic Cascade of Defaults Is Coming for Emerging Markets" (July 7, 2022), while the *Washington Post* concluded, "Strong Dollar Always Clobbers Developing Nations" (July 29, 2023). Yet, there was no cascade of emerging market defaults.

Regarding a 2023 recession, public discourse dispensed with doubt altogether, leaning heavily into the idea of its inevitability. *Bloomberg* explained, "The Fed Has Made a US Recession Inevitable" (March 29, 2022). *Barron's* concurred: "There Will Be No Soft Landing. Why a Recession Is Inevitable" (April 29, 2022). Even as economic resilience persisted into late 2022, *The Economist* strove to explain "Why a Global Recession Is Inevitable in 2023" (November 18, 2022). But the recession did not come; instead, a strong economy forced forecasters to revise their gloomy predictions higher and higher—by an enormous 2 percentage points as 2023 progressed.[15]

These and other doomsday narratives reliably appear on stage as part of a gloomy macro play, especially in times of crises. Yet these dire predictions thrill and mislead rather than enlighten. To be sure, there is nothing in our telling that rules out such outcomes. The Covid recession could have grown into a depression. Inflation could have become entrenched. Rising interest rates could have driven contagious damage across emerging markets. And recession risk *was* elevated in 2023. But none of these outcomes was inevitable. Constantly presenting such outcomes as being at the center of the risk distribution is fallacious.

There are natural and unnatural origins of this culture of doom-mongering. We have already encountered the latter in chapter 1—news as entertainment—but we must also understand the natural origins of doom-saying if we are to rationally lean against them.

The long-run journey of the macroeconomy is shaped by crisis. For example, the global financial crisis of 2008 delivered an era of structural labor market slack as well as enduring change in financial regulation. Though the world economy since 1945 is a remarkable story of growth and prosperity, crises deliver setbacks that can have lasting impact. This is one reason why being able to discern true crises from false alarms is so important. This is compounded by the reality that if things go well, the upside is typically slow and incremental—in portfolios, in growth, in employment. Yet, if things go poorly, the downside can happen quickly and can be extreme. Macroeconomics and markets do have a negative skew, particularly in the short run.

So, what to do? Here are actionable practices:

- *Choose your clicks wisely.* Leaders need not be pulled into the muck of every negative news cycle. Almost every negative data release is spun into a tale of crisis. Housing starts, manufacturing surveys, initial unemployment claims, GDP trackers, and so much more can all be seen to offer warning signs, and any negative tick may be presented as the evidence of a coming crisis. Leaders should avoid being hooked by a feed of negative narratives—sometimes generated by algorithms to cater to our own personalized worries. News cycles will come and go—and then repeat. Build a healthy information diet that is composed of a variety of thinkers—including those with negative outlooks. Such variety can give a high-quality picture of risk.

- *Remember who is speaking.* Where you stand depends on where you sit.[16] In the 2010s, think tanks on fiscal responsibility were unlikely to say that debt piles were sustainable even if interest rates were structurally lower than growth rates, because reassuring the public would have undermined their objective of building pressure for a healthier budget (an admirable objective in our view). Similarly, pundits who have long predicted a dollar collapse will seize any new opportunity to repeat their warnings. Aggressive use of geoeconomic sanctions or any tactical dollar weakness enables confirmation bias—while contrary evidence is ignored. And who amplifies the doomsaying narratives? A press that needs to fill the air 24-7 to generate advertising revenues. This is not to begrudge their business model, just to recognize it.

- *Don't reward the success of a broken clock.* When a crisis does strike, someone will claim to have seen it coming. But don't give credit for "resulting" unless it was accompanied by coherent causal and driver-based arguments about why the crisis happened.[17] Having called the 2008 crisis in housing and the banking system doesn't count if the doomsayer also predicted a half dozen other meltdowns that somehow haven't occurred over the past 15 years. A broken clock is right twice a day. The doomsayers don't bear the cost of false alarms, as public discourse does not hold them accountable. Those who act on those false alarms, however, do bear a cost.

- *Focus on drivers.* Probe if narratives of doom can pin down the path to the dark outcome. "What does it take?" is the litmus test, not "When will it happen?" or even "Why will it happen?" And "It will happen eventually" doesn't cut it. If they are going to hold the microphone, doomsayers must present an internally consistent and plausible path with signposts along the way that explain why we will end up where they claim we will. Drivers and dynamics are required, not just dour predictions. Eventually something will go wrong, but if you want credit, you should have to show your work.[18]

Resisting the allure of sophisticated pessimism is hard to do. Nobody wants to look like the simpleton.[19] Everybody wants to be the prophet who saw it coming. Even rational optimism is easily spun into naivete, whereas pessimism tends to convey gravitas. And because public discourse doesn't keep a record of false alarms, thereby holding their purveyors to account, the incentive is to prophesy doom. To have a chance of navigating the gloom in a world that is full of risks and challenges requires a calm and sober take— perhaps even reading a book, rather than just headlines.

Practicing Economic Eclecticism

If we let go of master-model mentality and learn to decode doom-mongering, we've made room for the third and most important habit: economic eclecticism. Recall, by this we mean assessing macroeconomic risk with a broad array of approaches and doing so situationally, pragmatically, and opportunistically. It is a natural habit if we admit that there is no universal theory or model, that what we're analyzing is not linear or rigid but represents the messy reality of economies. Thus, we should not lament the absence of a singular framework but celebrate the rich tapestry of approaches we can use as the basis of our judgment.

Recall, the objective is not to arrive at settled truth but at good judgment that facilitates better decision-making. This is done by deconstructing causal drivers of the macroeconomic operating system while treating them as nonstationary components.

As sketched in the introductory chapter, this eclectic approach draws on macroeconomics and also on related disciplines—including finance, history, political economy, international relations, and beyond. In consequence, we employ a patchwork of quantitative and qualitative methods. This includes everything from frameworks, case studies, models, historical analogies, and whatever else can help—while also recognizing that regimes can shift and that an old and trusted approach may no longer work, and that a new one has taken over.

Economic eclecticism, therefore, is less rigid than relying on a singular theory, as the eclectic approach allows for the possibility of multiple drivers and radical change. At the same time, the approach is less idiosyncratic than a case study because it strives to show patterns and proclivities. Each topic we cover in this volume is approached with this in mind— building a view on drivers to understand and assess risks to the business environment.

In figure 2.2 we provide an overview of the macroeconomic risks covered in this book and the eclectic mix of approaches we use to analyze them. They can be applied not just to today's circumstances but also to future circumstances as they point toward tendencies and biases, not absolutes; toward what it takes, not what will happen; toward probabilities and scenarios, and away from forecasts and base cases. Ultimately, all of this gets us closer to something we can sum up in a single word: judgment.

. . .

Where to start when the approach is so broad and each arena is so idiosyncratically narrow? Consider these actionable practices:

- *Always look for a narrative*—or construct one yourself. A good narrative is constructed of plausible and coherent (internally consistent) drivers and likely outcomes. It tries to persuade and nudge without denying different possibilities.[20] If you think in terms of narratives, you are well on your way toward economic eclecticism and have avoided the trap of MMM. Conversely, if you think in terms of data points, you've ceded the essential role of judgment to a methodology (which for leaders won't work).

- *Ask what drives risk*—not what the outcomes are. Beneath the surface of analytical complexity typically lurks a penetrable constellation of drivers that shape risk and outcomes. We must seek to understand those drivers. Remember that shocks and crises command the most attention, but risk is equally about how the system absorbs or amplifies them, how policy responds, and how repercussions unfold. Data helps you watch the state of the system, but it does not help you understand the system's dynamics.

- *Ask what it takes.* If we use a narrow analytical lens, we're more likely to focus on, and get stuck at the edges of, the risk distribution. With an eclectic lens, we're more likely to see a broader part of the distribution. Tellingly, doomsaying tends to cut straight to questions like "When will it happen?" and "How bad will it be?" But it's more rational to ask: What does it take? What are the drivers? How high is

FIGURE **2.2**

Economic eclecticism: Approaches used in this book

	Macro topic	Approach	Key tenets to assess macroeconomic risk	Ch.
Real-economy risks	Recession	Cyclical risk profile	Recession types and their prevalence in the modern cycle allow for better understanding of cycle risk than top-down recession probability	3
	Recovery (or not)	Supply-side damage	Recession intensity says little about recovery; the degree of recovery is about the battle between the impact on the supply side and the policy response to contain overhangs	4
	Mature growth	Factor potential	Low growth in rich economies can be a sign of maturity, not stagnation; growth is harder at the frontier but reacceleration of growth factors remains possible	5
	Developing growth	Gravity of growth	Fast catch-up growth invites fear and envy of new growth models, but growth rates will succumb to the gravity of growth as the drivers shift from capital accumulation to innovation	6
	Productivity growth	Tech-cost-price-income cascade	Spurts in productivity growth are about at-scale labor (cost) reduction (not predominantly product innovation), which drives down prices, boosts real incomes, and spurs new spending	7
	Productivity timing and sizing	Labor-market tightness	Though technology is the fuel of productivity growth, it requires the spark of tight labor markets that forces firms to substitute capital for scarce labor	8
Financial risks	Compulsive stimulus	Willingness and ability	The ubiquity of all manner of stimulus is the result of structural trends toward greater willingness and ability to deploy it	9
	Systemic stimulus	Crisis enhancement	Deep crises enhance stimulus willingness and ability, making system collapse a high bar for the United States	10
	Tactical stimulus	Situational constraints and enablers	The capacity to protect or goose growth is situationally determined by political and financial drivers of willingness and ability	11
	Structural inflation	Volcker inheritance	An inflation regime break is a process, not an event, requiring sustained policy errors in the face of broken inflation expectations, and remains a high bar	12
	Cyclical inflation	Upside and downside bias	Cyclical inflation cannot be reliably predicted, but its biases and the policy response that it triggers offer guidance	13
	Interest-rate regime	Absolute and relative rates	The interest-rate regime is shaped by the structural inflation backdrop as well as cyclical inflation bias; they determine the relative position of the policy rate and the neutral rate	14
	Debt crises	g-versus-r spread	Debt levels say little about sovereign-debt risk, and there are no fixed breaking points; debt sustainability is about the interplay of nominal growth and interest rates, a matter of degree	15
	Bubbles	Risk taxonomy	Bubbles are an inevitable by-product of the modern cycle and can even be good; as the ability to spot and stop them is poor, the focus must be on de-risking systemically threatening ones	16
Global risks	Geopolitical flux	Convergence bubble	A confluence of security, political, economic, and financial tailwinds inflated a global "convergence bubble," i.e., exalted expectations that amplify the perception of geopolitical decay	17
	Geopolitical impact	Transmission channels	The pass-through from geopolitics to macroeconomic impact is never linear, often neutral, and sometimes counterintuitive; impact comes through real, financial, and institutional linkages	18
	Trade decay	Trade architecture	Global trade is remarkably resilient—its composition is what changes—and evolving trade architecture demands investments that will add to economic tightness	19
	Dollar demise	Privilege and burden	Reserve currency status is a competition, not destiny; the winner enjoys privileges and faces burdens that not all economies are willing or able to carry	20

Source: BCG Center for Macroeconomics

the bar? Running through these questions helpfully forces users to entertain multiple outcomes—including ones opposite of their own.

- *Seek context and history.* Recall that one flaw of MMM is that sample sizes—from recessions to debt defaults—are too small to allow for the quantitative testing of models. In other words, macroeconomic risk is largely idiosyncratic. The flip side of this insight is that context and history matter a great deal. A knowledge of history, humbly applied, can provide the context needed to rein in wild extrapolation and excess simplification. History can also open the imagination to how dynamics progress, how drivers work, and what to watch along the way.

Remember, It's All about Judgment

Readers should not be intimidated by the technical foundations of MMM or by the noisy narratives of doom-mongering. They should have an eclectic analytical mind and make their own judgment—there is no need to parrot forecasts or headlines. Remember the economic emperor has no clothes. Be the child that calls that out.

Economic eclecticism, and our broader view of macroeconomics, is not poor-man's macro. In fact, it is a stronger approach. Excessive pessimism isn't sophisticated, and rational optimism isn't naive. Artificial precision removes the art from economics and tries to pass economics off as a science. It is a mistake. Knowing what economics can do and what it can't and using it appropriately is better than pretending it is something it is not. In contrast, being grounded and humble helps one do what can be done, as well as it can be done.[21]

As readers make their way across the landscape of macro risks, they will encounter, over and over again, the three habits outlined above: rejecting the certainty embodied in MMM, discounting the doom-mongers in public discourse, and employing the skill of economic eclecticism. Together these habits form a sound basis for macroeconomic judgment.

PART ONE

REAL ECONOMY

Growth Risks and Growth Boosts

Cyclical Growth Risks

Long-Term Growth

Technology and Productivity

CHAPTER 3

How Cycles Die

Few economists saw the 2008 crisis coming. The 2020 recession struck without advance warning. In 2022, many rushed to call the next recession—albeit incorrectly. The following year, a US recession was described as inevitable in countless headlines—yet it failed to land in 2023. The lack of predictability, even a few short months out, is stark.

Realistically, the only certainty about future recessions is their uncertainty. Learning from prediction failures, ever better data, and growing analytical sophistication have still not moved us closer to the goal of reliably forecasting downturns. Executives and investors must be clear-eyed that this isn't going to change.

Yet leaders don't have the luxury of ignoring these debates. In fact, the risk of a recession is often top of mind when the economy is growing. And while executives won't be able to call the next downturn with precision, they can develop an understanding of the underlying drivers and risks.

This chapter introduces readers to the economy's *cyclical risk profile*. Rather than engaging in binary framing (will there be a recession or not?) or top-down probabilities (for instance, 61% risk of recession over the next 12 months—near the consensus probability for much of 2022 and 2023), we show readers how to assess, isolate, and compare the drivers and dynamics of recession. It doesn't provide a reliable forecast, but it is the first step to developing that power of judgment that we emphasized in chapters 1 and 2.

A cornerstone of the cyclical risk profile is the recognition that recessions are not homogenous but come in three types. By differentiating among real recessions, policy-induced recessions, and financial recessions, we can build a structural risk profile that is relatively stable across cycles. It helps us shift our perception of recession risk away from top-down predictions and toward causes, relative probabilities, and narratives. This approach provides a baseline of, and proclivities for, recession risk and can be used to evaluate tactical prospects for a recession in the near term. And as we'll see in chapter 4, it also helps in assessing prospects of recovery.

The Risk Profile of the Modern Cycle

On any given day one can obtain current recession probabilities. Some of these come from statistical probit models based on financial-market inputs. For example, the yield curve probit, a popular recession gauge, derives recession risk from the difference between short-term interest rates and longer-dated ones.[1] Other forecasts use data from surveys of consumers and managers, movements in commodity markets, or measurements of the opinions of economists. The idea that we can collapse the whole spectrum of influences and risks into a single number is seductive. But one trouble is that such measures are hopelessly volatile. We can check the numbers one day and find that they have swung wildly the next. They are not a reliable input into strategic planning or tactical decision-making. As a result, top-down recession probabilities are often a source of frustration for executives and investors alike.

Instead, we should approach recession risk analysis with simple questions: What is the background risk of recessions? How common are recessions? Where do they come from? Do they differ substantially? How do cycles die? In other words: more understanding, less predicting. The goal is to generate a narrative, an explanation of what could *cause* a downturn and what that downturn would look like.

Figure 3.1 makes a start on these questions. It shows the long-run structural change in the US economic cycle, expressed through a barcode visual where each bar represents a recession. Over the past 40 years or so, during the era we call the modern cycle, the recession barcode thinned noticeably. The time spent in recession fell from about 30% in the prior 80 years to just

FIGURE **3.1**

The modern cycle: Scanning the recession barcode

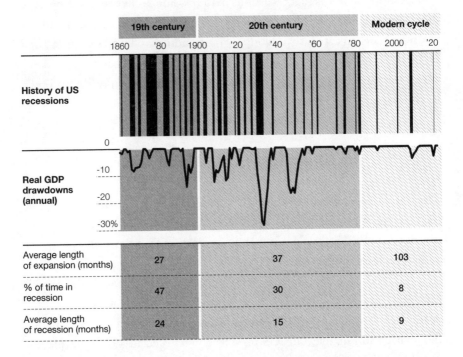

Note: GDP drawdown measured in per capita terms; 19th century: 1860–1899; 20th century: 1900–1982; modern cycle: since 1983. Average length of modern cycle doesn't include ongoing post-Covid expansion. % of time in recession through 2022.
Source: NBER, Louis Johnston and Samuel H. Williamson, Sanford C. Bernstein, analysis by BCG Center for Macroeconomics

8% in the last 40. This was driven by shorter and less frequent recessions. The average duration dropped to nine months, while the time between grew to an average of 103 months. Average drawdowns in (per capita) GDP have become more modest when compared with large GDP declines before the late 20th century—even as recent recessions have seen larger drawdowns.

Though it may not feel that way to readers, the fact is that we have been living in a more benign cyclical environment in the last few decades than in earlier periods, an important aspect of the good-macro regime. This modern cycle doesn't rule out recessions, even ugly ones, but its relative moderation is an important starting point when thinking about recession risk—and prompts more questions: What accounted for the decline in frequency and change in impact? Are these forces structural—and thus reliable?

Do they allow us to say anything about future recessions? And why, if the cyclical regime is more benign, does it not feel this way?

The short answer is that recessions have become far less frequent because the underlying *risk profile* has changed structurally. Specifically, the incidents of three recession types (real-economy busts, policy-induced recessions, and financial recessions), as well as their relative importance, have changed. To see all this, we need to look at the idea of the cycle's risk profile, and then its component drivers, more closely.

Infections, Heart Disease, and Cancer

The notion of a cyclical risk profile, comprising different risk drivers, and their changing prevalence may sound abstract. In fact, the concepts are intuitively familiar. The evolution of human death risk follows an analogous, and more familiar, pattern.

A hundred years ago, infections were the leading cause of death.[2] Simple infections, beginning with as little as a blister, could easily lead to sepsis and death even for the most privileged—as happened with Calvin Coolidge Jr., the teenage son of the 30th US president, who died in 1924 after playing tennis on the White House lawn. It was the discovery of penicillin just four years later and its gradual popularization in the middle of the 20th century that sharply reduced human death risk. But the fading of infections meant that the next-most prevalent causes of death grew their share of mortality risk. Heart disease and cancer have become the two dominant drivers of human mortality since then.

Knowing the risk profile has many benefits. Even if death is inevitable and its timing unknowable, a better understanding of each risk type and its relative share allows more focused and effective risk assessment. An appreciation of which types of risk are most prevalent helps us to know which ones to watch out for. And understanding rather than guessing or believing offers reassurance and some peace of mind.[3]

Recession risk is analogous to mortality risk from infections, heart disease, and cancer.[4] We've already seen that the time spent in recession dropped sharply over the past 100 years. Figure 3.2 reiterates this point and then explains it. The declining incidence of recessions is not a random occurrence but driven by structural changes in the relative prevalence of the three

FIGURE **3.2**

The cyclical risk profile: The long view

Recession risk over time

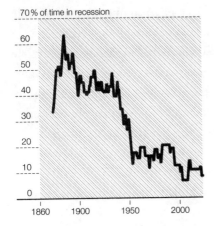

Share of risk by recession type

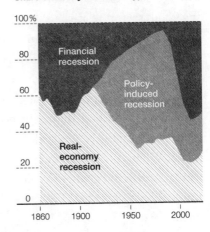

Note: Data through 2022. Driver shares (right) are time-decaying averages of the relative incidence of recession, tagged by our own recession classification. Driver shares do not indicate probability of recession.
Source: NBER, analysis by BCG Center for Macroeconomics

types of recession risk, which are shown on the right-hand side of figure 3.2. Real-economy recession's share showed a marked downward trend. Policy recession's risk share grew, and then shrank. And financial recession's risk share fell, and then increased.

This compositional shift has enormous consequences. And understanding why this shift occurred and how the mix could change again provides a narrative of recession risk that can be called upon at any time.

Why Real Recession Risk Has Declined

What lies behind the shifting importance of various risk drivers in the right-hand graph in figure 3.2? Real economy recessions occur when exogenous shocks or endogenous production volatility drags the economy's growth rate below zero. A key reason real recessions have become less prevalent is that the inherent volatility of the real economy has gradually declined. A century and a half ago, the weather could and did end cycles, because the economy was significantly agrarian. Weather hasn't moderated (the opposite is true), but agriculture's economic significance has. Similarly, in the middle of the 20th century, the unwind of investment booms in industry, inventory mismanagement, or even labor strikes, could trigger a recession. But a shrinking goods sector (relative to services), reduced physical investment demand, and better inventory management have all contributed to less real risk.

Above all, the rise of services in the economy has moderated the cycle's natural volatility. Services deliver a relatively stable contribution to GDP, and as they represent a growing share of the economy, accounting for about 70% of private-sector output, it becomes harder for volatile physical production to dominate the cycle.[5] Consider the fracking boom of the early 2010s. When it collapsed in 2015, the investment decline that followed was similar in size to declines that corresponded to recessions in the past. Many feared a recession then, but the economy pulled through without experiencing one.

To be sure, real risks are not gone—exogenous shocks (such as the pandemic) can still trigger a recession by interrupting firms' spending and households' consuming. But the shocks have to be rather large, and in general, today's highly diversified economy is far more resilient than its antecedent.

Why Policy Recessions Still Matter

Just as heart disease took a larger share of deaths when infections waned, policy-induced recessions grew in prevalence when real recessions receded.[6] Policy recessions happen when (monetary) policymakers try to slow the economy, typically by raising interest rates, and end up triggering a recession.[7] Such policy recessions take one of two forms. The first is accidental: that is, policymakers drive interest rates too high, tanking the economy rather than merely cooling it; or policymakers hold interest rates too low, allowing the economy to overheat and setting the stage for a painful correction. The second form of policy recession is intentional: that is, policymakers deliberately induce a recession to bring down structural inflation.

Policy-induced recessions have a wide variety of impacts. They can be colossal, as when monetary policy fails to act and thus contributes to a deflationary depression. The Fed's failure to dampen the boom of the 1920s, coupled with its failure to cut interest rates aggressively after the 1929 crash, set the economy up for the Great Depression of the 1930s—an era of structural slack and overwhelmingly high unemployment rates. Or policy-induced recessions can be merely very painful, as when monetary authorities deliberately deliver a recession to combat elevated structural inflation (as in the early 1980s). Or they can be only somewhat painful, as when policy-makers try to slow down the economy in the hope of a soft landing but move too aggressively, leading to a recession instead. That said, monetary tightening can also succeed, avoiding a policy-induced recession, and deliver a soft landing.

In figure 3.2, policy-induced recessions begin to gain share after the creation of the Federal Reserve in 1913.[8] This is not to say that the central bank always adds to cyclical risk—but it took time to be effective. The Great Depression was initially a financial crisis, but it was the Fed's persistent policy failure that turned it into a deflationary depression; the structural break of the inflation regime in the late 1960s and early 1970s was also the result of persistent policy errors (policy rates were too low).[9]

From the 1980s on, the risk of policy errors declined significantly for three reasons. First, central banks have learned from their mistakes and have used that knowledge to guide a modern approach to policymaking that includes inflation targeting and enhanced communication. Second, they have benefited from an easier environment of structurally anchored inflation (that is, healthy long-term inflation expectations; see chapter 12). The secular decline and anchoring of inflation have allowed policymakers to run longer cycles.[10] And third, inflation was biased downward after the global financial crisis of 2008, allowing policy to remain persistently easy.

Of these three drivers, the first two—the learnings of modern central banks and anchored structural inflation—remain, but the third has likely flipped durably (see also discussion on cyclical inflation in chapter 13). Though still structurally anchored, an era of tightness is likely to keep cyclical inflation upwardly biased. That means monetary policy will need to be restrictive more often, raising the risk of policy-induced recessions (and their risk *share* in the cyclical risk profile) above that of the 2010s.

The appropriate level of interest rates is difficult to know, so the risk of policy-induced recession is always present. And the postpandemic economy is a powerful reminder that policy risk is two-sided. A dovish error forced the Fed to move rates aggressively higher to catch up with inflation in 2022.

And as inflation quickly moderated the Fed ran the risk of a hawkish error of keeping rates too high for too long. Yet despite the fast move to restrictive policy, the strength the economy and moderation of inflation in 2023 showed that a soft landing was far from impossible; rather it was well advanced.[11]

Financial-Recession Risk Remains Key

Last, financial recessions are akin to cancer, the emperor of all maladies.[12] Their origin, progression, and remedies are all less well understood than is the case with other types of recessions. Just as cancer is a leading cause of mortality for humans, financial recessions are the leading cause of downturns—the structural proclivity for them is high.

Financial recessions occur when problems in the financial system weaken the entire economy. This happens when cascading losses cripple credit flows, particularly when the capital of the banking system is impaired. Or, financial-asset bubbles pop, delivering shocks to confidence and to balance sheets—shocks that drag down economic activity and deliver long-lasting damage (see chapter 4).

In the last few decades, financial recessions have dominated. The sample is small, but the 2000s dot-com bubble was an asset-price financial bust. The real-estate and banking bust of 2008 brought the financial system to the brink of systemic collapse.

Why have financial recessions loomed larger? As economies become better at avoiding real and policy-induced recessions, the financial kind have naturally assumed a larger relative significance. Further, the increasing longevity of growth cycles provides more opportunity for financial imbalances to accumulate. Figure 3.1 highlighted that the average length of an expansion grew dramatically, from just 37 months in much of the 20th century to 103 months in the modern era. Another reason is the increased financialization of the economy and a culture of compulsive stimulus where policy encourages froth in finance to boost the real economy, something we analyze in chapter 9.

Though financial imbalances are often visible, they are, frustratingly, not easy to interpret or manage. For example, it is not at all clear that higher interest rates would have materially changed the path of the dot-com bubble or the subprime bust of the 2000s (see chapter 16 on bubbles for details).[13] And more recently, the collapse of Silicon Valley Bank (and related casualties) spurred fears of financial recession, but those fears didn't materialize as policymakers intervened successfully.

Its greater share of the baseline risk profile and tendency toward severity (with overhangs of elevated unemployment and structural slack) make financial-recession risk critical to focus on. And while the financial system is opaque, and risk can emerge from unseen corners, vulnerabilities can be monitored—even if knowing when a crisis will strike is impossible.

Using the Cyclical Risk Profile

Understanding the different kinds of recession—real, policy, and financial— cannot give us a precise measure of recession risk. But unlike a top-down recession probability of, say, 28% or 55%, this perspective allows us to differentiate risk types (drivers) and to understand what may be coming—a narrative of the cycle more than a narrow prediction.

Consider the summer of 2022 when recession was the received wisdom, and prominent leaders suggested that an economic hurricane would hit before the end of the year. This ominous narrative was less than helpful, seemingly extrapolating from negative news and data flow driven by the Ukraine war, energy prices, and inflation. Not only did it prove wrong, but it augured a dark turn without providing a causal basis for it.

It is more helpful to view recession risk through the lens of the risk typology we have discussed (figure 3.3 summarizes the three recession risks along with their typical impact on the economy). In 2022, the framework highlighted the following insights, even as perceptions of risk moved higher and stayed high: (1) real-economy risk remained low, underpinned by exceptionally healthy labor markets and other factors; (2) a policy-induced recession was plausible given the rapid tightening, but was far from a certainty given the robust position of consumption and hiring—not to mention the idiosyncratic nature of the economy still in the shadow of the pandemic; and (3) financial risks—which even in apparently calm times can never be dismissed lightly—rose but did not look to undermine credit creation holistically or threaten systemic institutions. Leveraging the economy's risk profile in March 2022 we argued all three of these positions.[14] Each offered a causal

FIGURE **3.3**

Recession typology and typical macroeconomic impact

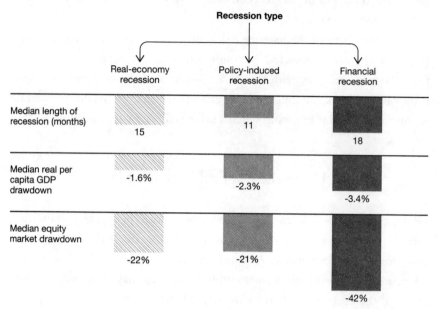

Note: Impact profile shows US historical data. Real GDP drawdown based on annual since 1857; equity market drawdowns are one-year rolling; DJIA: 1900–1928; S&P 500: 1929–2020.
Source: NBER, Bloomberg, BEA, Louis Johnston and Samuel H. Williamson, analysis by BCG Center for Macroeconomics

narrative decision-makers could internalize, rather than just top-down probabilities. Together, they argued that avoiding recession was likely. The same framework also helped resist narratives of inevitable recession in 2023.[15]

Beyond calibrating recession risk meaningfully, thinking in terms of the risk profile offers additional insight. The impact of recession types is not homogenous. Though there is a relatively wide range of experiences within each type, they have tendencies, as shown in figure 3.3. Financial recessions—the emperor of all maladies—are typically deeper, longer, and have more-significant overhangs (as they damage balance sheets and policy often responds too slowly; see chapter 4). Real recessions can be deep, but they are typically short as the shock passes and policy response tends to be faster. And the typical policy-induced recessions tend to be milder as well.[16] Thus, even for the pessimists who expected a recession in 2022 or 2023, the risk profile would have pointed toward a moderate one.

Is the economy's risk profile stable? Are these insights durable? The forces that have delivered the proclivities of risk are structural: they can change but tend to do so slowly. As a result, cyclical proclivities will also change slowly over time, much as we showed in figure 3.2. For example, the economy's vulnerability to real recessions likely falls when the economy's trend growth strengthens because it is better able to absorb shocks, whether domestic or global. The risk of policy-induced recessions will change with the inflation challenges faced by policymakers. Those challenges will be greater as the era of tight labor markets persists (see chapters 13 and 21); it also implies that the risk of policy-induced recession is higher relative to the 2010s, when it was very low. Financial risks will also change based on the health and complexity of credit intermediation. Many chapters in this book offer detailed discussions of the regimes that shape these risks.

Remember, the Next Recession Is Always Coming

Economics is far less precise and reliable than the natural sciences. And even medicine, from which we borrowed our risk analogy, is far from precise. A thorough health checkup today does not rule out death by heart attack tomorrow; cancer may not be spotted or be treatable. And don't forget shocks. A virus could come out of nowhere and kill both you and the cycle.

As we argued at the start of this chapter, recession risk gets a lot of attention, as it should, but the debate more often confuses than illuminates. These are the key recommendations to escape that confusion:

- *Don't focus on probabilities.* Outside of headlines many analysts are working diligently to estimate the probability of a recession. While the odds are not meaningless, their supposed precision deceives us by implying that recessions are homogenous things. Yet the recession of 2001 differed sharply from that of 2008, which differed sharply from that of 2020.

- *Think in terms of risk types.* Understanding the cyclical risk profile shifts attention away from top-down odds and toward recession types, the foundation of judging cyclical risk. It helps reveal building risks, existing vulnerabilities, the potential for effective response, and ultimately what the nature of the downturn will be if—or rather, when—it comes.

- *Internalize recession types.* Each recession type has its own history, context, and relevance. To appreciate the breadth of dynamics across— and within—types, some knowledge of cycle history and cycle dynamics is important.

- *Don't anchor on headlines.* They play to our fears by peddling a sense of sophisticated gloom. Headline prominence says little about actual risk— but it does drive clicks. The next recession is—always—coming.

- *Think in scenarios, not forecasts.* A framework approach to cyclical risk can be used for scenario planning by executives in ways that recession odds, even if they are right, simply cannot.

As it turns out, understanding the risk profile of real, policy, and financial drivers is not only helpful for gauging recession risk. It is also critical for understanding recession severity and recoveries—to which we turn to in the next chapter.

CHAPTER 4

How Recoveries Happen

I n March 2020, when the pandemic stopped the global economy in its tracks, many automakers reacted by canceling orders for the semiconductors that power their vehicles. Like many other firms, investors, and commentators, theirs was a response to the intensity of the unfolding crisis. For one, the unemployment rate was surging to a modern record of 15%, far above its 2008 crisis peak, so they hunkered down for what was expected to be a slow and painful recovery.[1]

When the Covid recovery played out very differently, and the output of the US economy took on a tight V-shape, many automakers were caught off guard. Now at the back of the line, they did not have enough semiconductors to meet the exploding demand for autos. This hurt not only their own businesses. The resulting spike in vehicle prices was borne by consumers and contributed materially to the postpandemic inflation surge.

For automakers, and many others who feared the worst, it did not have to be this way. As we demonstrate in this chapter, anticipating the shape of recovery is decidedly more feasible than calling the recession itself. The key to anticipating recoveries is to understand the *structural impact* of the recession. The intensity of shocks and the extreme data points they generate grab headlines, but insight comes from assessing how the economy's productive capacity will be impacted relative to its prerecession trend. This requires a recovery framework. All recessions reflect a weakening of demand and thus growth. But not all recessions damage the supply side of the economy—its productive capacity. It is such damage that translates into structural over-hangs and weak recoveries.

In future shocks—and they will happen—executives and investors can anticipate recoveries by focusing on the interplay between two countervail-ing forces: the potential impairment of the economy's supply side versus the success of economic policies in limiting such damage. It is this tug-of-war that determines the nature of recovery.

A Shock with Three Recoveries

We can get to know recovery types and their drivers by looking at the 2008 global financial crisis, a shock that produced three distinct shapes. Figure 4.1 shows the diverging experiences of Canada, the United States, and Greece in the years after the global financial crisis. For each of the recovery shapes—which correspond to the letters V, U, and L—we must ask two questions:

1. Did the *level of output* return to its prerecession trend (that is, to the gray trend lines in figure 4.1)?[2]

2. Did the *growth rate* recover (that is, did output parallel the trend line)?

Canada exhibits a classic V-shape—that is, the full return to its preshock output path and the return to its former growth rate (the slope of the out-put line). The recession was overcome with no lasting structural damage.

The US recovery followed a U-shape. It managed to regain its old growth rate (the slopes are parallel), but output never returned to its pre-2008 trend. The gap between the old trend and realized output represents a permanent loss that accumulates over time—a *structural downgrade*.

Greece returned neither to its old output level nor to its growth rate over the following 10 years—an L-shaped recovery that barely deserves the name. Here the structural downgrade is not only cumulative but is grow-ing over time. That is, the percentage downgrade increases.[3]

This demonstration of recovery shapes and their two conditions (trend and slope recovery) is not specific to 2008 but offers a broadly applicable frame-

FIGURE **4.1**

A typology of recovery shapes based on damage to real GDP levels and growth rates

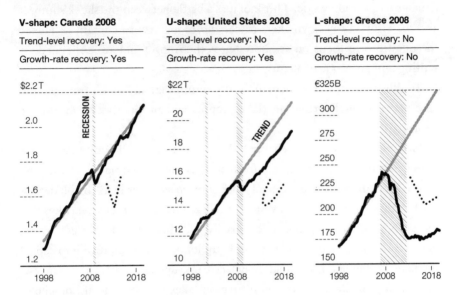

V-shape: Canada 2008	U-shape: United States 2008	L-shape: Greece 2008
Trend-level recovery: Yes	Trend-level recovery: No	Trend-level recovery: No
Growth-rate recovery: Yes	Growth-rate recovery: Yes	Growth-rate recovery: No

Note: Data through 2018. Real GDP in 2012 Canadian dollars, in trillions; 2012 US dollars, in trillions; and 2015 euros, in billions (Greece).
Source: Statistics Canada, BEA, Hellenic Statistical Authority, NBER, analysis by BCG Center for Macroeconomics

work to assess recoveries. Once drivers are understood, they provide a powerful tool to anticipate the nature of a recovery, regardless of time and place.

The Battle for the Economy's Supply Side

What determines the recovery shapes? All recessions are slumps in demand and activity, but some recessions have long-lasting legacies, as in the U-shape discussed above. That happens when the demand slump spills over onto the economy's supply side—that is, to the productive capacity that is the basis for longer-term performance. Capital investment, labor supply, and productivity can all take a hit in recessions (see also our discussion of supply-side factors in chapters 5 and 6). It is the extent of the spillover from demand to the supply side that will define the structural legacy of a recession—that is, the shape of recovery.

Fortunately, economic policies can be deployed to prevent or to limit damage to the supply side. Think of it as a battle between the shock's impact and the efforts of policymakers (fiscal and monetary) to contain it. Hence the questions to focus on are how big is the impact and are policymakers willing and able to lean against it?

To illustrate, figure 4.2 schematically summarizes a shock's transmission channel to capital formation (labor inputs and productivity can also be damaged).

First, the real-economy channel. A recession creates liquidity strains for households (unemployment) and for firms (revenues). As household and corporate investments decline, capital stock growth slows or halts. If the drop is brief, perhaps higher future investment will make up for it, but the risk is that the economy's future productive capacity will be lower. It can get worse, however. If protracted or unchecked, liquidity problems can turn into capital problems. Firms and households may face bankruptcies, in which case investment slumps further, and capital formation takes a serious hit. If households and firms must slowly repair their balance sheets, capital stock growth may never make up for the early setback. This is the basis of a U-shaped recovery. The economy may well regain its old growth rate, but it now travels along a

FIGURE **4.2**

Supply-side damage: How capital formation can be disrupted

	Real-economy channel	Financial-system channel	Role of policy
Liquidity problems	Shock or recession triggers cash-flow problems for households and firms, driving down investment (and consumption)	Shock or recession drives liquidity and/or funding problems for financial institutions, hampering credit intermediation and reducing investment	• Policy can contain, counteract, or offset damage in both the real and financial channels • Different tools are required for different shocks and different quadrants of the matrix • Role for policy is systemically important when liquidity issues threaten to turn into capital problems
Capital problems	Households and firms repair damaged balance sheets, delaying or canceling investment	Capital problems shutter the credit channel to the real economy, undermining investment	

Source: HBR, BCG Center for Macroeconomics

diminished trend growth line. This lower trend line reflects the period of downgraded capital formation—a permanent legacy.

Second, the financial-system channel. Far worse can happen to the economy's capital formation if the banking system is impaired. If banks experience liquidity problems, they will slow down credit intermediation to the real economy—households and firms won't have the finances to keep investing.[4] The problem is multiplied if banks' liquidity challenges turn into capital deficiency. Bank bankruptcies not only shut the credit channel to the real economy but put it in reverse (by selling assets and refusing to roll over loans). This spreads balance-sheet damage throughout the economy as asset prices fall and delivers a serious hit to capital formation that shifts down the path of potential (trend) growth.

The global financial crisis demonstrated all these dynamics (see figure 4.3). Real-estate prices collapsed in the United States, leaving the balance sheets of households and small businesses severely damaged. Household and small-business efforts to repair them were a drag on consumption and investment. In Canada, by contrast, household and firm balance sheets were not nearly as

FIGURE **4.3**

Structural damage? Falling home prices left scars on US balance sheets, but not so much in Canada

US and Canadian home prices, indexed to precrisis peak at 100

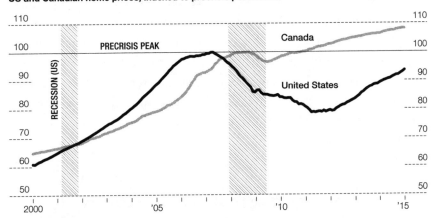

Note: New house prices (Canada); purchase-only index (United States). Data through January 2015.
Source: Statistics Canada, Federal Housing Finance Agency, NBER, analysis by BCG Center for Macroeconomics

impacted, because the housing market did not collapse. Canadian households and firms did not have to repair their balance sheets and thus resumed strong consumption and investment much more quickly.

On the financial side, the US banking system was crippled by cascading capital losses from the housing bust, which shut down credit flow and left an indelible legacy on the growth path of the US economy (thus creating a U-shaped recovery, without trend-level recovery). The Canadian banking system, by contrast, remained healthy, contributing to that country's V-shaped experience.[5]

Even so, the initial shock is not destiny and does not write the ultimate outcome of a recession. As already mentioned, it remains a tug-of-war between the shock and the policy response. Whether it's the real or financial channel (typically both, as they interact) through which supply-side damage occurs, timely and well-designed policy can mitigate it—and influence the shape of recovery.[6] Sometimes fiscal stimulus can tide over firms and households. At other times, it is monetary policy that provides liquidity to banks or capital markets (see chapters 9, 10, and 11). (To be clear, the purpose of such stimulus is not to provide blanket insurance for firms that are unviable but to stop macro-induced systemic destruction.)

What about Greece? Its L-shaped recovery after 2008 followed a particularly pernicious confluence of damage across the entire supply side (not just capital formation), driven by policy's lack of ability. L-shaped recoveries are born from exceptional circumstances. Their key drivers are recessions that overwhelm the ability of policymakers to respond. These downturns are accelerated by policy failures and imply not just missed investment for a time but declines in the capital stock; not just unemployment for a time but joblessness that results in the demotivation and deskilling of workers and therefore a decay in labor supply; not just a slip into suboptimal ways of doing things but the potential of a sustained deterioration in efficiencies and productivity. It typically takes sovereign default or institutional failure for things to go so terribly wrong.

Understanding the Pandemic Recovery

Readers may wonder if we write with the benefit of hindsight. We don't. Further, anticipating the recovery path remains one of the more feasible predictive tasks in macroeconomics. Focusing on the experienced intensity of the downturn will likely lead you astray, but focusing on the strength of an economy's supply side during the recovery phase will offer a fair chance to get it right.

Go back to the near-universal doom that spread in February and March 2020, when a little-understood virus first paralyzed the globe. The US unemployment rate would approach 15% the following month, and GDP fell 30% (annualized) in the second quarter. This collapse in economic activity provoked dark predictions about an eventual recovery. Like many others, the economist Nouriel Roubini sketched a "greater depression"—that is, a 1930s-like outcome that could send "the global economy into persistent depression and a runaway financial-market meltdown."[7] Put in the language of shapes, the United States was destined, per Roubini and many others, for something between a severe U-shaped recovery and perhaps even an L-shaped one.

But in an article in *Harvard Business Review* in March 2020, we focused on the likelihood of the crisis impairing the economy's supply side. Our argument was that the intensity of the decline was not a strong indicator of the recovery shape and that strong policy innovation could deliver a V-shaped recovery. Then, as in nearly any future crisis, policy had a chance "to prevent a full-blown U-shape, keeping the shock's path closer to a deep V-shape."[8]

And policy did prevent and protect, immediately delivering massive liquidity injections, followed by overwhelming fiscal support to both households and firms in ways not seen before to address challenges not seen before. The call of a V-shape, in March 2020, was the right one to make and a foreseeable one if looking at necessary drivers.

The success of the recovery—see figure 4.4—was aided by the fact that the recession did not come with any in-built overhangs (for instance, excess investment), and the crisis itself spurred unique political unity to deliver timely, sizable, and innovative stimulus. (See chapter 10 for stimulus during systemic crisis. See also our discussion on stimulus ability and willingness in chapter 9.)

Not Destiny but Tendencies

As our earlier characterization of a battle between supply-side risk and policy response hinted, the shape of recovery is not deterministic but one that evolves. In the case of Covid, stimulus was renewed and expanded, vaccines discovered and distributed. In other words, the recovery path was plotted

FIGURE **4.4**

Despite greater intensity, Covid has a much smaller legacy than a global financial crisis

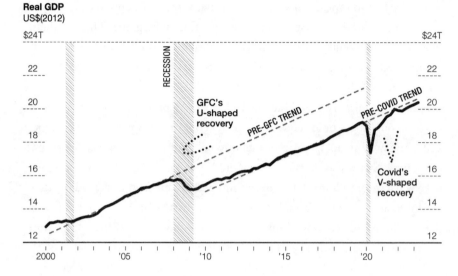

Real GDP
US$(2012)

Note: Data through Q2 2023.
Source: BEA, NBER, analysis by BCG Center for Macroeconomics

against the potential of structural damage on the supply side—and it could have turned out differently.

That said, there are tendencies. They are rooted in the origin and nature of the recession, a topic we covered in the preceding chapter. Recall, there are real-economy busts, policy mistakes, and financial crises that can trigger and drive a recession. These dynamics provide useful hints about the likely recovery shape.

Real-economy recessions lean toward V-shapes, particularly if they are driven by exogenous shocks. In the case of a (relatively) small shock, such as the oil-price spike triggered by the first Gulf War in 1990, the shock passes, and output can return to old levels swiftly, as happened after 1990. In the case of a large shock, policy is likely to be proactive in responding to unfair economic problems. In the case of endogenous shocks, such as an unwinding investment boom and/or slow policy response, a mild U-shape becomes likely as balance sheets are impaired and demand takes a while to recover—and spills over into supply-side damage as some capital formation is foregone forever.

Policy recessions, particularly when driven by a fight to contain cyclical inflation, lean toward mild U-shapes, although V-shapes are plausible. Why? If policy's objective—the containment of inflation risk—is achieved swiftly, then policy can ease, and a V-shaped rebound is plausible. But a small U-shape is more likely, as policy is driving the downturn and thus not likely to support growth until inflation falls—leaving time for spillovers to the supply side. If policy needs to drive a severe recession to wring out entrenched inflation expectations, then a deeper U-shape is likely.[9]

Financial recessions lean toward U-shapes because they always damage balance sheets. In mild cases the damage is kept out of the banking system, leaving growth sluggish but the downturn not necessarily deep. In more-severe cases (for instance, 2008 in the United States) the financial system's capital base is impaired leading to deleveraging and balance-sheet carnage. This will deliver both a deep recession and a sluggish recovery, with material damage to capital formation and labor-force trends. The potential for recovery is worsened by the reality that policymakers don't like to step in to bail out asset markets (and often they shouldn't) and despise having to bail out the banking system. Thus, policy responses are often too meager for too long.

Remember, Intensity Is Not Legacy

While consistently calling the timing of a recession is impossible, understanding its nature is possible, and foreseeing the shape of recovery even more so. Here are our key takeaways to think strategically about recovery:

- *Don't conflate recession intensity and recovery.* The macro data that describes a downturn, such as collapsing demand or employment, must be monitored, but it says little about eventual recovery. An intense shock can see a swift recovery, and a mild shock a protracted one. The initial impact and data flow will not tell you the recovery shape.

- *Focus on output trend and growth rate.* Shocks will have a permanent legacy if they push the economy off a growth trend and/or downgrade its future growth rate. The recovery shape is determined by those two matters, irrespective of the recession's intensity (that is, the depth or speed of a shock).

- *Assess impact on the economy's supply side.* A sluggish recovery and permanent legacy require the shock to spill over to and downgrade the economy's supply side. Focus on the emergence of liquidity and capital problems as damaged balance sheets lead to long overhangs in demand and investment. Evidence of diminished growth in capital stock, labor supply, or productivity are valuable indicators.

- *Don't forget policy.* The drop in economic activity dominates the debate but is only half the story. How policy responds matters as much in the battle to contain supply-side damage. Seeing what policymakers are doing, when they are doing it, how they are doing it, and gauging the impact are all critical to assessing the prospects for recovery.

- *Don't assume the worst.* Pessimism is contagious. But it takes time for a crisis response to materialize, so resist jumping to conclusions. Ultimately, policymakers' ability and willingness to act will be significant (see chapters 9, 10, and 11). Don't be infected by negativity—remember "it'll be better than you think" is a less natural headline than "this is the worst ever."

For many, the cycle dominates day-to-day concerns about the economy. In times of positive growth, the focus is often on the next recession. And when recession strikes, the focus is typically on the risk of a poor recovery. This and the prior chapter offered frameworks for assessing each. Yet growth is not only a cyclical theme. We turn to its long-term nature next.

CHAPTER 5

Between Defeatist and Hubristic Growth Narratives

Economic growth is not only about the cyclical fluctuations and risks analyzed in chapters 3 and 4. The economy's underlying capacity for growth across cycles, or trend growth, also matters to business leaders and investors. And though each can influence the other, trend growth matters more in the long run because it powerfully impacts the path of prosperity. At 1% growth, it would take the US economy about 70 years to double in size. At 2%, just 35 years. At 4%, only 18.

Hence, when executives devise long-term strategies, and investors finance them, they must have a view on attainable long-term growth. But there is little consensus. In fact, there are competing narratives that often veer into the extremes of defeatism and hubris. On the side of defeatism, proponents can draw on well-established evidence of structural deceleration. US trend growth, as captured by 20-year realized growth in figure 5.1, appears to be under the spell of the gravity of growth, seemingly pulling the line ever closer to the floor. Since the mid-2000s, the moving average has fallen well below 3% and has been trending closer to 2% in recent years.

FIGURE **5.1**

The gravity of growth: A destiny?

Real US GDP growth

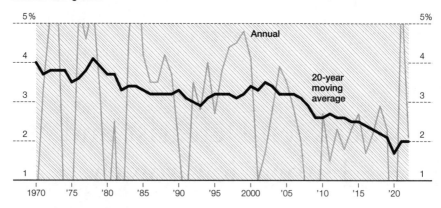

Note: Y/Y. Moving average implies average growth over prior 20 years (e.g., 2015 data point is average of 1996–2015). Y axis truncated for scale. Data through 2022.
Source: BEA, analysis by BCG Center for Macroeconomics

This structural slowdown not only lends itself to pessimistic predictions of a future of sub-2% growth. It also feeds a narrative that the economic model itself is obsolete. Such declinism goes hand in hand with the idea that other economies have discovered new and stronger growth models destined to deliver durably better growth prospects (see chapter 6).

On the side of hubris, slow growth is seen as unacceptable and easily fixable, precisely because of the expectations created by what was once achieved. Politicians, who have a habit of making exuberant promises, often fixate on 4% growth.[1] To hit that magic number, they often talk up silver-bullet policies (stereotypically tax cuts on the political right and spending or redistribution on the left).[2]

Technologists, though for different reasons, are also prone to rosy narratives of higher growth.[3] And though there is good reason to believe technology will lift growth again, a topic we discuss in detail in chapters 7 and 8, the fact that the last 20 years of rapid technological progress failed to arrest the slide seen in figure 5.1 should at least make us skeptical.

Our examination of long-term growth prospects spans this and the subsequent three chapters. In this chapter, we introduce readers to what we call the gravity of growth, the structural growth regime. Though imperfect, the analytical instruments are good enough for developing sound judgment about the ability of specific drivers to accelerate or decelerate long-term trend growth. We also employ these tools to debunk the extreme versions of exuberance and declinism: neither 4% growth (salvation) nor growth far below 2% (pessimism) hold up well against scrutiny.

But that leaves additional claims about future growth to be examined on both sides of the argument. In chapter 6 we demonstrate why the declinist fascination with alternative magical growth models does not add up: as they mature, all economies are eventually subject to the gravity of growth. We then take a detailed look at the promise of technology and productivity growth, the most credible upside growth narrative. Needing to carefully calibrate what can truly deliver macroeconomic impact, we devote chapters 7 and 8 to this topic.

Collectively the four chapters argue that a material reacceleration of US trend growth is possible and likely—even if the dreams of a 4% economy will remain out of reach.

The Gravity of Growth

It's tempting to think growth is always about demand. Cyclically that is generally right. But in the longer term, trend growth is about the supply side of the economy.[4] Think how much stuff can be made and how many services can be provided. It is our ability to produce that determines our level of prosperity, not our ability to consume. And the economy's productive capacity comes down to the supply of labor (available hours of work), stock of capital (number of machines, facilities, software solutions, etc.), and level of productivity (how good we are at turning these inputs into outputs).

These three lenses are the components of growth accounting, a simple, tried-and-tested workhorse of macroeconomics. Like all models, it has imperfections. Reflecting on them, the intellectual godfather of this approach, Robert Solow, once concluded that it could be abandoned "as soon as something better comes along."[5] But nothing better has come along. And the approach is good enough for pressure testing—indeed, as we will see, to derail—some claims of both the optimists and the pessimists. Certainly,

FIGURE **5.2**

Growth narrative: 4% requires rosy glasses; 1.8% requires gray

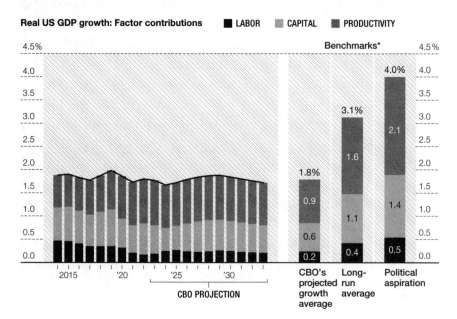

Real US GDP growth: Factor contributions   ■ LABOR   ▨ CAPITAL   ▨ PRODUCTIVITY

*Sums do not always add up because of rounding.
Note: Using potential real GDP. Factor contributions (percentage points) assume shares according to CBO's decomposition of nonfarm business potential real GDP. Long-run average = 1950–2019.
Projected average = 2024–2033.
Source: CBO, BLS, analysis by BCG Center for Macroeconomics

their more extreme versions—growth of 4% or far below 2%—wither under its scrutiny. Let's see why.

A good starting point is the nonpartisan Congressional Budget Office's deconstruction of US trend (or potential) growth. In figure 5.2, the CBO's estimates over the past and coming decade are shown. The growth in labor, capital, and productivity will add up to 1.8% on average, a nearly linear extrapolation of the growth in the prior decade—and well below the historical average of 3.1%. This pessimism apparently pulls forward a decade in the shadow of the global financial crisis—one where investment was weak, the labor market full of slack, and productivity growth meager.

Is a repeat of the 2010s really the best and most persuasive view of what is achievable? Also shown in figure 5.2 is the more aggressive perspective of 4% growth—a perennial political aspiration. But if 1.8% looked too timid, this looks remarkably hubristic, exceeding not only the last many years but also, to a significant degree, the long-run historical average of 3.1%.

Consider what it would take to return to long-run annual growth of 3.1%. Assuming that the three growth drivers contributed the same share as in the baseline of 1.8%, labor's contribution would have to rise from 0.2% to 0.4%, capital's from 0.6% to 1.1%, and productivity's from 0.9% to 1.6%. For the 4% aspiration, the increases are greater: to 0.5% (labor), 1.4% (capital), and 2.1% (productivity).

These are prodigious improvements in driver growth. Of course, to deliver these ambitions for trend growth doesn't require these exact configurations—if one driver outperforms, others won't have to carry as much weight, and vice versa. But figure 5.2 illustrates the magnitude of the challenge.

Though we comfortably suggest that 4% is too high, we also consider 1.8% too low (if not nearly as outrageous a suggestion). To navigate the space between these disappointing and elevated suggestions, we must look at each of the three drivers in more detail to consider their potential.

Labor: No Upside

Labor-input growth is about quantity of hours worked. There are many pieces, but in the long run, it is meaningfully driven by growth in the working-age population. Figure 5.3 shows population growth has slowed down over a long period, which strongly suggests that future labor growth will not be as robust as in the past.

To better understand this factor, consider what drives population growth. First, there are internal factors—the net of births and deaths. Birth rates have declined, and an older population will see more deaths, relatively speaking. And even if birth rates suddenly moved higher, they would impact labor supply with only a lag of about two decades—the time it takes for a newborn to become a new worker. Second, there are external factors—net migration. Here there are often assumptions that a labor-market tailwind would result if only cogent policy could be agreed on. And while that would be welcome, a reasonably optimistic view would suggest only a modest extra contribution—not a reversion to historical averages.

FIGURE **5.3**

Labor force follows population growth (with a lag), without which it is hard to see a surge in supply

Population and labor-force growth
Five-year moving average of annual growth

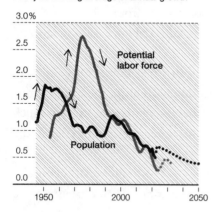

Contributions to population growth
Five-year moving average of annual growth

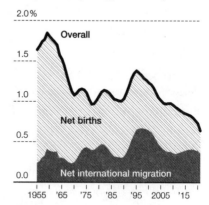

Note: Actual annual data through 2022.
Projections through 2032 and 2050.
Source: BLS, CBO, analysis by BCG Center for
Macroeconomics

Note: Annual data through 2021.
Source: World Bank/United Nations,
analysis by BCG Center for Macroeconomics

But the labor supply isn't only about population growth. The degree to which the population is working matters, too. In the United States there was structural growth in the share of the population at work in the second half of the 20th century as more and more women entered the workforce and more than offset the gradual decline in male participation, as seen in figure 5.4. That trend ended over 20 years ago, and now the combined participation rate is trending down.

Taken together, we should not expect increases in the supply of labor to drive significantly higher long-term growth.[6]

Capital: Modest Upside

Some look at capital growth as the key to a quick and easy boost in growth. The argument is that tax cuts will boost corporate estimates of the after-tax return on investment. Higher returns mean more investment; more investment means more capital stock growth; more capital stock growth

FIGURE **5.4**

Growth in women's participation more than offsets men's falling participation until about 2000

Labor-force participation rate
Ages 16–64

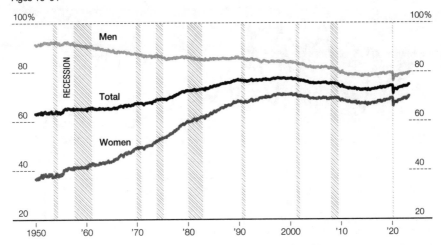

Note: Data through May 2023.
Source: BLS, NBER, analysis by BCG Center for Macroeconomics

means more economic growth. This story is too micro and too textbook—it is not consistent with macroeconomic reality. Yes, tax policy—particularly when targeted and sizable—will induce investment. But total investment levels are far more influenced by business perceptions of strategic need and growth opportunities than by taxes. Investment's cyclical moves are easy to see in figure 5.5—but one would be hard-pressed to identify the effect of tax-code changes.

An additional challenge is that *net investment*, and thus growth in capital stocks, is decelerating. That is illustrated in figure 5.5, where despite a healthy share of national income being dedicated to investment, the growth rate of the capital stock is slowing. Why does steady investment yield slower and slower growth of the capital stock?

First, the capital stock is simply bigger. There are many bridges, roads, factories, and buildings. When the capital stock is bigger, depreciation of that stock will be bigger as well. More investment will be needed to keep the existing capital stock steady. It is a separate, but complementary, argument

FIGURE **5.5**

New investment doesn't necessarily grow the capital stock; it must overcome depreciation to do so

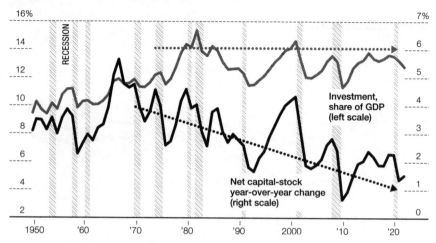

Note: Investment and capital-stock data through 2021.
Source: BLS, NBER, analysis by BCG Center for Macroeconomics

that when the capital stock is large, the benefits of growing the capital stock diminish. The first city airport has greater impact than the third. While new generations of technology can provide new opportunities to invest, the highest-impact investments have likely already been made.[7]

Second, not only is the capital stock larger, but its modern composition also depreciates faster (figure 5.6). Today's investments are more often in intellectual property (IP—think software) and less often in structures (think buildings) and equipment than in the past. Physical structures typically depreciate slowly, adding to the capital stock for multiple decades—but software may last for four or five years, meaning no effect on the capital stock after that period (right panel of figure 5.6). This mix-shift adds to the challenge of needing to run faster just to stand still.

An additional challenge is that many critically important investments—such as decarbonization technology for the energy transition—may be replacing rather than supplementing capital. For example, shutting down a coal-fired plant and replacing it with wind turbines amounts to a complete depreciation of that portion of the capital stock.[8] Other technologies, such as carbon capture, may target costs that are not accounted for in GDP (the

FIGURE **5.6**

Running faster to stand still: Investment has shifted toward capital that depreciates more quickly

Share of nonresidential fixed investment

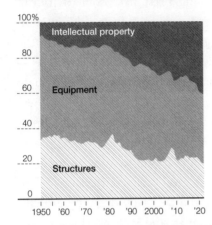

Average life of assets (years)

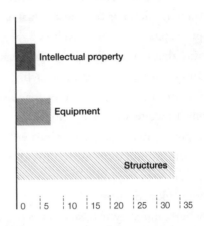

Note: Data through 2021 (shares). Average life of assets based on the inverse of the depreciation rates (1/depreciation rate). Depreciation rates are averages for 2000–2020.
Source: BEA, analysis by BCG Center for Macroeconomics

externality of pollution in this example). While these are necessary—and though they will add to investment—they will not always be fully additive to the capital stock and thus to long-term growth prospects.

In all, it is hard to see how trend growth reaccelerates significantly because of capital growth. A modest tailwind driven by an economy near its potential and in need of more investment is quite plausible—but that is unlikely to sustainably shift growth to a higher trajectory.

Productivity: Real Upside

If labor and capital are unlikely to give us significant upshifts in trend growth, then hope must hinge on productivity growth. And, indeed, here we find better reasons for optimism. The gravity of growth is not absolute, and even mature economies can lean against it.

Productivity's contribution to growth is far more complex than labor's or capital's. Labor means more bodies; capital means IP and machines. What

economists call multifactor (or total factor) productivity is literally the residual. Definitionally it is making more value per unit of input. Think of it as
simply doing things better. Of course, that doesn't make its growth particularly intuitive.

Despite the conceptual difficulty of being a residual, productivity can
stake its claim as the most valuable form of growth. It fuels, without cost,
per capita incomes as well as aggregate growth. It isn't constrained in the
way that labor and capital are. Eventually we cannot add more workers—
and eventually one more machine doesn't help very much (even if there
remain many opportunities for wise investment, and often there are new
machines to invest in). But if we can discover better ways of combining
inputs to make outputs, things will get better—forever.

But productivity growth is also commonly misunderstood. Aggressive
predictions abound, often based on technological progress. Because of this,
we're devoting two chapters—chapters 7 and 8—to productivity growth,
where and why it hasn't delivered in the past, and why we think it will
deliver more in the future. Part of the story is about tight labor markets driving gains. When firms can't easily hire, they are nudged to reinvention and
technological adoption.

While we are confident in a boost to productivity growth over time, particularly if a tight economy can persist, we also have a sober view on how it
works and on its magnitude. Big productivity gains are not about new products; they are typically about removing costs in the production of goods
and services we already consume. And the next big shift will need to touch
the service economy—much of which has struggled to see meaningful productivity growth. Additionally, even when hurdles are overcome, the question of magnitude will remain—and those hoping for adding much more
than 1% to growth on a permanent basis are too exuberant in our view, as
we detail in chapter 8.

Remember, Cassandra and Pollyanna Dominate the Debate

Widely divergent growth narratives are constantly thrown around with conviction. But having examined the three drivers of the gravity of growth,
we are better prepared for our next encounter with a Cassandra and a

Pollyanna.[9] Hubris is the right label for narratives about 4% growth, a claim without credible analytical foundation, while a destiny of far below 2% is too timid, anchoring on a decade in the shadow of the global financial crisis that is now truly in the past.

Yet, narrowing the space above 1.8% and below 4% trend growth is only the beginning. We are yet to assess the defeatist narrative of relative decline—the idea that better growth models outshine US growth on a relative basis (see chapter 6). And we must still assess whether a tech-driven growth transformation is imminent and if it can deliver big upside (see chapters 7 and 8). For now, we wish to capture the insights derived so far:

- *Focus on growth drivers.* Cassandra and Pollyanna both owe us more than claims; they must back them up with views on labor, capital, and productivity growth. Nobody asks for precision—just reasonable arguments and judgment. Though growth accounting is not precision surgery, it is not a black box either.

- *Slow growth can be a sign of success.* The gravity of growth is deceptive. The harder growth that sets in when the capital stock has been built and when the existing stock of innovation has been implemented is often a sign of economic success, not failure. As growth gets harder, the slower rise in the level of output can be evidence of a good-macro world.

- *The gravity of growth can be suspended.* Growth is pulled down as factors pass from easier to harder phases of growth—labor pools are exhausted, capital stock is built, innovation gets harder at the frontier. But it need not be a continuous straight line down. The drivers can improve from time to time—and seeing when a growth spurt may come requires judgment.

- *Know the differences among growth drivers.* The macro potential of labor, capital, and productivity differ materially. This is true both of their nature (labor affects aggregates, while the others have more impact on per capita growth) and of their cost (labor and capital are expensive; the doing-it-better part of productivity doesn't have to be). They also differ in their growth prospects: labor's are modest, capital's are a tad better, and productivity is a tantalizing promise (see chapters 7 and 8).

Next time you are confronted with claims of US growth above 4% or far below 2%, ask what growth driver is supposed to deliver such outcomes. And before you accept claims that other economies have found superior growth models that deliver higher growth forever, consider the evidence about magical growth models in the next chapter.

CHAPTER 6

The Enduring Appeal of Magical Growth Models

Defeatist narratives about US long-term growth prospects are misguided, we argued in the last chapter, as even mature economies can reaccelerate under the right conditions. We return to such credible prospects in chapters 7 and 8. But there is also a *relative* version of defeatism, the idea that the US economy is falling behind those with a superior growth model. In reality, as we shall see, no economy escapes the gravity of growth. Advantageous growth differentials reliably shrink as emerging economies approach the frontier.[1] But the fear (and envy) of supposedly superior growth models is curiously enduring.

Executives care about *relative growth* across economies for the same reasons they are interested in US trend growth—it influences global capital allocation, strategies for markets and products, production locations, and much more. But popular discourse about competing growth models complicates a clear view of long-run growth dynamics. Too often, declinist narratives of fear (of falling behind) and of envy (of faster, more dynamic growth abroad) take the place of sober analysis of growth drivers.

We should not conflate catch-up growth and mature growth. Catching up allows for high growth, as already proven technologies and business processes are adopted at speed, a process that usually involves big increases to the capital stock. But this growth model is not sustainable as the technological frontier is approached and the capital stock built out. Eventually the hard work of innovation is required. This is why no economy escapes the gravity of growth.

Why do narratives of "magical growth models" stubbornly persist? We explore this question with three case studies from the last 100 years: the Soviet Union, Japan, and more recently China, the last with unique characteristics. It is hard not to be impressed by fast-growing economies that were pulling hundreds of millions out of poverty, building impressive new cities and infrastructure, and shifting the geographic center of the global economy. But fast growth and sustainable growth are not the same. Aggregate growth and per capita growth are not the same. And the skill set for pushing growth at the frontier (on a per capita basis) versus pushing growth off the floor, or even in the middle of the income distribution, are different.

None of this suggests that the membership of high-income economies will remain static.[2] Nor does it imply that those at the frontier should never be anxious about competition. But it does demonstrate that magical growth models are not so magical after all.

Why Nobody Escapes the Gravity of Growth

Recall from chapter 5 the analytical building blocks that explain slowing trend growth in the United States. Labor, capital, and productivity are subject to the gravity of growth, though we argued that each factor has the potential for reacceleration, causing trend growth to rise periodically. What we want to argue now is that the same gravity of growth is internationally present. It is not a US-specific handicap. We can see this empirically in the experiences of Japan, South Korea, and China (see figure 6.1—there isn't enough data to show this for the Soviet Union, one of three case studies to follow; we use Korea in this figure to broaden the empirical evidence). All have been extraordinarily successful with catch-up growth, moving their economies toward the frontier—as seen in the rightward drift of per capita GDP. And yet, as incomes grow, we can see how labor, capital, and productivity growth become harder.

FIGURE 6.1

The gravity of growth around the world:
Impact of each driver diminishes as economies get wealthier

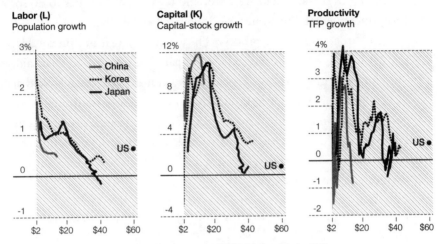

Labor (L)
Population growth

China
Korea
Japan

Capital (K)
Capital-stock growth

Productivity
TFP growth

Real GDP per capita, US$(2017) thousands, PPP

Note: TFP = total factor productivity; PPP = purchasing power parity. Capital stock in per capita terms. Lines chart six-year moving averages of each ordered pair. X axes cut off before $2,000 to reduce noise. Data point for the United States is six-year moving average through 2019.
Source: Penn World Table 10.01, analysis by BCG Center for Macroeconomics

This is not a coincidence but an expected pattern. Let's expand on the drivers seen in the prior chapter to see why the gravity of growth is a broadly applicable framework:

- *Labor-supply growth* slows as societies become wealthier because birth rates decline, resulting in a slump in population growth.[3] With a lag, that turns into fewer workers.[4] This downward trend is visible in the left–hand panel of figure 6.1.

- *Capital formation* slows as societies become wealthier, because larger capital bases cause the rate of growth in capital stock to diminish. This happens because depreciation is higher, so countries have to invest more just to stand still, and because the most compelling opportunities for investment have already been taken. This down-shifting pattern is visible in the middle panel of figure 6.1.

- *Productivity growth* slows as societies become wealthier because the easiest gains—the low-hanging fruit—have been harvested. Large productivity gains can result from adopting well-known best practices, but over time there are fewer and fewer opportunities to do so. Any incremental gains must be discovered rather than emulated—a much harder and slower process. Thus, a clear, albeit not inexorable, downshifting exists in the right-hand panel of figure 6.1. That said, productivity growth plays a special role, as it did when we looked at US potential in chapter 5. Productivity is the most sustainable source of growth, and it also flows directly into per capita growth. The performance of economies at the frontier will primarily be defined by their capacity to innovate, invest wisely, and turn inputs into outputs with increasing efficiency.

In sum, catch-up growth—moving along the three *x* axes in figure 6.1—is regularly impressive. New cities are built, populations move into those cities and are educated, learning curves are climbed—in short, economies pull themselves up out of poverty, sometimes at astonishing speeds.

While observing this ascent, it's easy to believe that something new has been discovered, that a better growth model is working its magic. But when a detailed look is taken at each driver of growth, as done above, it is clear that gravity will assert itself well before the frontier is reached. Any model of growth must face these challenges. There are no magical growth solutions. Growth at the frontier is hard, and slowdown will have settled in.

The Stages of Magical Growth Narratives

Even though the evidence should lead us to believe that the gravity of growth applies to all economies, magical growth models are an enduringly popular narrative. Taking in the last 100 years, we count three secular narratives about alternative growth models that delivered fear and envy into US public discourse. Why are such narratives so pervasive? We can start to answer this question by looking for patterns. Each of our brief case studies—the Soviet Union, Japan, China—follows four stylized stages.

Stage 1: Crisis of confidence. The US economy hits a bump in the road, struggles, or experiences an outright crash—a crisis of confidence in the growth model unfolds.

Stage 2: Challenger rises. A catch-up economy appears to sustain superior performance, making rapid gains in per capita GDP.

Stage 3: Fear and envy grow. A mix of fear (of being overtaken) and envy (of faster-growing markets) drives a narrative of gravity-defying sustainable growth. Some elements of top-down planning are pointed to, suggesting that the new model works, while the model experiencing the slump doesn't. Extrapolation of growth rates builds a belief that the faster growth is underpinned by a superior system.

Stage 4: Gravity of growth asserts itself. Over time the alternative model loses its luster, as the once superior performance—whether driven by systemic differences or not—succumbs to the gravity of growth.

The stages tend to play out when the aspiring economy isn't yet close to the frontier (in terms of per capita GDP)—yet the leader is still rattled. This is less surprising than it may initially appear. First, the fast-growing economy has new resources to allocate to new endeavors, while wealthy economies at the frontier may have more-difficult choices about allocations. Second, the fast-growing country is likely to successfully compete in specific areas, well before its per capita income catches up, generating a genuine competitive threat.

Let's explore three case studies.

The Soviet Union: "We Will Bury You"

As mentioned, the detailed macroeconomic statistics we use for the cases of Japan and China are hard to come by for the Soviet Union, but the story of magical growth is easy to see even if qualitatively. In 1956, Soviet First Secretary Nikita Khrushchev famously declared to an audience of Western diplomats, "We will bury you."[5] He was suggesting that the Soviet system would outstrip that of the West because capitalism was doomed to fail. To modern ears this sounds preposterous, but it didn't seem that way to Westerners for several decades in the 20th century.

Well before Khrushchev's tirade, the collapse of the 1930s had left wealthy capitalist societies reeling. The experience of the Great Depression elevated both fear and envy of socialist planning: fear that the old order would be overthrown, and envy that another economy appeared to retain high levels of employment during a depression. Lincoln Steffens, a prominent muckraking journalist at the time, captured a common envy (for many) and fear (for most everyone) when he said about the Soviet Union, "I have seen the future, and it *works*."[6]

Even after the West escaped the Great Depression, the fear and envy of Soviet growth persisted. The United States enjoyed significantly higher incomes, but Russia was perceived to be catching up quickly. In the military sphere, the so-called missile gap underscored politically potent fears of Soviet superiority. In the sphere of innovation and technology, the Sputnik satellite had the same effect. And even in the realm of economic prosperity, the competition seemed far from decided. Three years after that "bury you" comment, in 1959, Khrushchev took on Vice President Richard Nixon in the celebrated Kitchen Debate. Standing in a model of a home that formed part of a US cultural exhibit in Moscow, Khrushchev dismissed the display of newfangled domestic appliances and gadgetry as frivolous, rather than as signs of prosperity, and declared that the Soviet Union would soon match and then surpass the West.

Of course, that was not what happened. The internal decay of the Soviet economy had many drivers and has been widely studied.[7] However, the Soviet Union's high rate of capital accumulation, which appeared to deliver respectable per capita growth rates near 3.5% in the 1960s and early 1970s (Russia's was even stronger, near 5%), soon succumbed to the gravity of growth.[8] Estimates put it at sub 1% growth in the late 1970s and 1980s.[9] Well before the economy reached high income levels, the gravity of growth asserted itself.

Japan: "First Among Equals"

The 1970s brought a new crisis of confidence to the US and other wealthy economies. Global inflation, energy shocks, currency volatility, and high interest rates came with a period of stagflation (high unemployment and high inflation). The 1980s then began with deep recessions in the United States, ending an era of high inflation but also ushering in an era of deficits (both external and fiscal).

Japan, at this time, grew quickly, seeing its currency appreciate and its trade grow. Its burgeoning confidence on the global stage was exemplified by notable Japanese asset acquisitions, such as Rockefeller Center in New York City. And a new narrative of growth maintained that Japan had found a model of efficiency that would deliver it a seat at the exclusive table of global leaders. The dynamic created a sense of fear—in October 1989 more Americans viewed Japan as a threat than the Soviet Union.[10]

All this is epitomized in the influential 1989 book *The Japan That Can Say No: Why Japan Will Be First Among Equals*, by Shintaro Ishihara and Akio Morita, the cofounder and chairman of Sony at the time.[11] It argued that Japan was ready to take its place as a global leader—first among equals—and should be able and ready to say no to US dominance. Ishihara argued that the difference between "Japanese and American industry and business is not just in efficiency—production, distribution, and services—but is related to Eastern ways and values. Japan is both part of the capitalist world and Asian."[12] In other words, the authors believed that cultural characteristics underpinned a superior growth model. They predicted a world led by Japan and the United States, and rejected the view, common at the time, that there was a "penta-polar" world dominated by the United States, Japan, Europe, the Soviet Union, and China.

And it wasn't only Japanese nationalists who saw a reshuffling of the economic order on the horizon. The future Nobel laureate Paul Krugman wrote in 1990 that over the next 10 years, "by many measures the United States will have sunk to the number three economic power in the world."[13]

Then the Japanese bubble burst and growth stagnated as the gravity of growth worked against Japan. As figure 6.2 shows, labor's contribution to growth was already set to turn negative and capital's contribution had been in steady decline for a long time. And the alleged magic of Asian efficiencies disappeared as productivity growth vanished. Just as it was pulling level with the United States, Japan's progress reversed. While Japan remains a wealthy country, its mystique of having a growth model to be emulated has been lost for good.

FIGURE **6.2**

How the gravity of growth asserted its pull on Japan

Japan GDP growth decomposition
Five-year moving averages

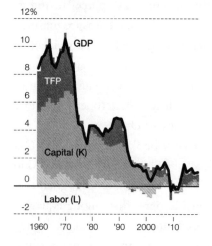

Japan total and per capita GDP
Ratio of US equivalent

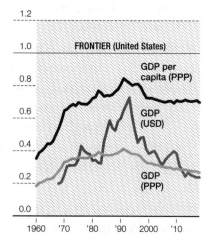

Note: TFP = total factor productivity. Total real
GDP through 2019.
Source: Penn World Table 10.01, analysis by
BCG Center for Macroeconomics

Note: PPP = purchasing power parity; in
US$(2011). Data through 2018.
Source: Maddison Project, OECD, analysis by
BCG Center for Macroeconomics

China: More Than a
"Moderately Prosperous Society"?

Since at least the early 2000s, China has emerged as the new face of permanently higher growth. This narrative, remarkably persistent, has taken a
hit only more recently in the context of an uneven recovery from the Covid
crisis.

And China does have unique characteristics that make it a particularly
impressive growth experience. Its own aspiration of being a "moderately
prosperous society" looks like an accomplished fact and may end up being
an understatement of its trajectory and potential.[14] Yet, even the most optimistic views of its path ahead cannot ignore the gravity of growth—a theme
well understood and articulated by China's leadership.

Though similar to the experience of other East Asian economies (so-
called Asian tigers), China's size and sustained high levels of growth make it

stand out. To keep growth up, China has adroitly and repeatedly adjusted its growth model. Before 2008, when Western economies were booming, it thrived on a model of export-oriented, currency-managed, capital-intensive development. But when Western economies stumbled in 2008 and their growth looked too risky, too fragile, and too debt driven, China successfully shifted to a growth model led by even greater (internal) investment, rapidly building out its infrastructure and capital stock. This allowed its economy to progress even as the wealthy world contracted sharply. And in recent years, a third shift, toward a consumption-based development model, seeks to rebalance growth while maintaining a strong pace.

Yet, since the stimulus-fueled run after the global financial crisis, growth has slowed. Gravity has begun to assert itself. Consider China's supply-side drivers (figure 6.3). Labor contribution has declined for a long time as population growth has slowed. The fact that the population has peaked will pose a sustained headwind to aggregate growth in the future. Capital growth

FIGURE **6.3**

China has defied the gravity of growth for a long time, but the pull is beginning to assert itself

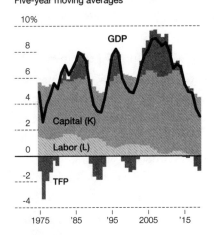

China GDP growth decomposition
Five-year moving averages

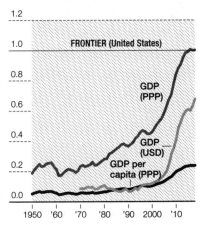

China total and per capita GDP
Ratio of US equivalent

Note: TFP = total factor productivity. Total real GDP through 2019.
Source: Penn World Table 10.01, analysis by BCG Center for Macroeconomics

Note: PPP = purchasing power parity; in US$(2011). Data through 2018.
Source: Maddison Project, OECD, analysis by BCG Center for Macroeconomics

continues to be an overwhelming driver due to extraordinary high gross investment. Yet, as in all maturing economies, efficient capital allocation at scale becomes more challenging as the capital stock builds. Measures of productivity growth have decelerated, too.

The deceleration is well understood by the Communist Party. In October 2022, Sun Yeli, spokesman for China's 20th National Congress of the Communist Party, declared that "the Chinese economy has entered a new normal, moving from high-speed growth to high-quality development."[15] The mentioned pivot toward consumption-led growth is an attempt to shift away from capital- and debt-intensive growth. But this strategy comes with less opportunity for top-down management; leaders will still be tempted to use investment levers if growth becomes uncomfortably slow.[16]

Nothing should be taken away from China's remarkable growth history. Sustaining extraordinary growth over several decades, pulling hundreds of millions of people out of extreme poverty, and creating a new source of global economic growth is remarkable. The approach has already delivered an economic superpower that in aggregate size is equal with the US economy in terms of PPP (purchasing power parity) GDP, about 65% in dollar terms, and about 25% in terms of PPP GDP per capita (right-hand side of figure 6.3). But it is also clear that China's extraordinary development has emphasized capital-stock growth, and now that the capital stock is substantially built, it will be harder to get growth from. This exposes China's history of weak productivity growth, as the future Chinese economy will increasingly rely on this factor (left-hand side of figure 6.3).

Despite China's imposing aggregate size, the country's per capita GDP remains modest, suggesting that substantial opportunities for catch-up growth with the frontier remain. Achieving that will require stronger productivity gains than in the past. Given China's size and willingness to direct its clout into investments, as well as the reality that specific areas of the Chinese economy are already at the frontier, China may be able to deliver productivity growth both by adopting best practices and by defining them. It remains a substantial challenge, but not an impossibility.

China was once an unquestioned story of forever high growth, but the gravity of growth has asserted itself there. Catch-up growth, fueled by factor accumulation, is fading, and a new stage of harder, slower, and riskier growth awaits. That reality, long foreshadowed by growth-factor analysis, is beginning to sink in.

Remember, All Growth Is Hard but Mature Growth Is Harder

In chapter 5 we showed readers that defeatist and hubristic growth narratives should be pressure tested and provided the tools to do so. In this chapter we offered the insight that stacking mature growth against catch-up growth produces a mirage.

- *There is no magical growth model.* Executives are right to hunt for growth in economies that are catching up, but they should avoid extrapolating beyond what the factors suggest. Growth narratives regularly overshoot the potential suggested by supply-side drivers. Any narrative of a superior growth model should be met with skepticism. And even if the timing of any slowdown is uncertain, remember that no one escapes the gravity of growth.

- *Changing the growth model is hard.* Up-and-comers should not be deceived by their own success, and those selling into fast-growing markets should have their own assessment of how growth can continue. What has brought new economies this far will have to be reinvented. The challenge is to see how long accelerated factor accumulation (particularly capital) can deliver elevated growth, without building too many imbalances and low-return assets on the back of debt. Being able and willing to adjust growth models is key but fraught with risks.

- *Remain confident.* For those at the frontier, this means not being afraid of those who are catching up. Wealthy countries should focus on their own challenges (of which there are plenty) rather than envying models that deliver a phase of growth that is unattainable in mature economies. The difficulties of slower growth at the frontier is more a sign of success than failure.

As we saw, for mature economies the key to better growth rests less with labor or capital and more with stronger productivity growth. This is where we turn in the next two chapters.

CHAPTER 7

When Technology Lifts Growth and When It Doesn't

Technological progress is a critical engine of growth. But their relationship is anything but straightforward, as we see in simplified form in figure 7.1.[1] Over the last 50 years, US productivity growth has decelerated unmistakably—even as investment in technology (particularly the intangibles like software) has grown steadily. Frustratingly, simple extrapolations from technological marvel to strong growth have not and will not work.

That disconnect is all the more pertinent as the advance of artificial intelligence has put us on the cusp of a new technological age. A few critical questions arise: When does technology lift growth—and when does it not? Facing a new generation of technology, should we expect higher trend growth, or a continuation of the paradox? And does the lack of growth suggest that technological investments are in vain?

The story of the humble taxi intuitively captures many of the arguments we make in this chapter. The rise of Uber, Lyft, and other such providers epitomizes much of the technology/growth paradox. Their snazzy apps offer better user experiences, and to many they represent what drives us forward,

FIGURE **7.1**

The growth paradox: Sagging productivity growth despite surging technology (software) investments

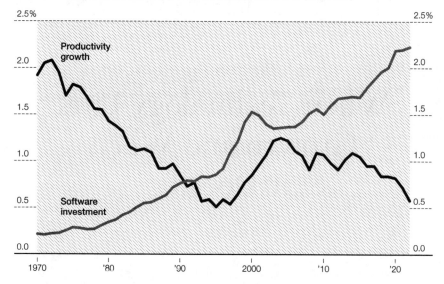

Productivity growth and software investment
20-year moving average (productivity growth) and annual share of GDP (investment)

Note: Productivity growth = utilization-adjusted total factor productivity (Y/Y). Data through 2022.
Source: BEA, FRB of San Francisco, analysis by BCG Center for Macroeconomics

literally and figuratively. Yet all this innovation has not changed productivity—the ratio of inputs to outputs. The capital and labor inputs (car and driver) are unchanged. The matching of driver and rider is somewhat better.[2] But as prices tend to be higher, there is scant evidence of a material productivity shift.[3]

We should not be surprised. As we argue in this chapter, big productivity boosts are not about product innovation but about at-scale labor-cost reduction that drives down prices and raises real incomes that consumers spend elsewhere in the economy. (As we argue in the next chapter, that process also generates new employment.) Until they can replace the taxi driver, Uber and its peers will offer dazzling product innovation that many are willing to pay for—but not meaningful productivity growth.

For executives, the technology-cost-price dynamics we analyze in this chapter represent a treacherous strategic challenge. Whereas productivity growth is an unalloyed positive for consumers (who enjoy real income gains from falling prices) and for the macroeconomy (which sees stronger growth), it can be threatening to firms and entire sectors. Firms have little choice but to engage in technology-driven cost competition where only relative gains produce advantage. Market structures are thrown into flux, and, where impactful technology becomes broadly available, the profitability of entire sectors may be competed away. Technology is always dazzling when viewed through the marvels of product innovation. But we see both promise and peril for firms when viewing technology through the macroeconomic lens of cost.

Why Technology Failed to Lift Growth

What explains the technology/growth paradox captured in figure 7.1? The decline in aggregate US productivity growth is really a story about a powerful compositional shift within the economy. Over the past 70 years, consumption has gradually shifted away from goods, where productivity growth has been relatively high, toward services, where it is low. Figure 7.2 captures this mix shift. It shows a 20 percentage-point decline in goods' share of consumption since 1950. It also shows that many goods sectors have experienced strong productivity growth. Meanwhile the share of services, which has risen 20 percentage points, is predominantly made up of sectors that have low productivity growth—think health care, education, and transportation.

In other words, technology has not generally failed to lift productivity growth. It has succeeded in the goods economy, while mostly having disappointed in the service economy. But because services make up a growing share of the economy, *aggregate* productivity growth is slumping. There have been periods, such as the late 1990s, when gains in productivity more than offset the drag from the shift to services, but these have been the exception, not the rule.[4] The secular trend has been a growing service sector coupled with falling productivity gains.

These macroeconomic observations need causal explanations. If we're looking to explain significant shifts in productivity growth, we need to focus on the reduction in labor cost—the large-scale displacement of workers. Reflecting on the technology available over the last few decades, it's clear it

FIGURE **7.2**

Rising but low-productivity services tilt the playing field against aggregate productivity growth

Services and goods' share of consumption

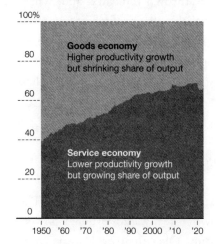

Annual productivity growth
1950–2021

Goods examples	2.1%
Agriculture	3.8
Manufacturing (durables)	3.5
Wholesale trade	3.2
Manufacturing (nondurables)	2.6
Retail trade	1.2
Construction	-0.1

Services examples	1.3%
Information	4.4
Professional services	1.6
Finance	1.4
Leisure/hospitality	0.0
Education and health	-0.1
Other services	-0.9

Note: Left: Data through 2022. Right: Given data limitations for sector productivity, growth in gross value added per worker is used to represent productivity growth.
Source: BEA, BLS, analysis by BCG Center for Macroeconomics

had the ability to replace mechanical and linear activities in the physical production of goods (think robots on assembly lines). But technology did not have the ability to replace workers in the service economy (think teachers, call-center workers, nurses, drivers, and so on). These are macroeconomic clues about what drives productivity growth; they suggest we need to take a closer look at the relationship between technology, labor cost, and productivity growth.

Snazzy Apps versus Gritty Costs

Ascribing productivity growth to large-scale cost savings hasn't always been popular. But we think the technology/growth paradox is often misunderstood because snazzy apps tend to steal the show—the impact of technology is too often seen through a lens of product innovation. How can economic growth possibly be so sluggish when there is so much tangible innovation all around us, the reasoning goes. Technologists have often brushed aside the evidence of disappointing growth rates, going so far as to suggest that productivity statistics fail to accurately capture technology's macroeconomic impact. (We return to this claim below.)

But we have long argued that productivity shifts are about the gritty world of cost, rather than snazzy apps.[5] We also believe that the *availability* of new cost-saving technology alone is not enough to drive productivity growth. It comes when firms are nudged or forced to embrace technology to bring down cost. It's no coincidence that phases of strong productivity growth coincide with tight labor markets when hiring is expensive and capital-for-labor substitution becomes more attractive. This cost-focused take on technology was seen as contrarian in recent years, but the maturing of generative AI as a credible laborsaving technology in the service economy has focused attention on it.

The role of labor cost can be seen in past productivity shifts. In figure 7.3 we use the history of manufacturing to demonstrate the relationship between falling labor inputs (costs) and productivity growth. Over the past 70 years, ever fewer workers were needed to generate $1 billion in manufacturing output—labor intensity collapsed, as shown in the top panel. The bottom panel shows the pieces of that ratio, worker count (input) and value added (output).

To be sure, labor-displacing technology doesn't necessarily mean a lowering of head counts. A closer look at different eras illustrates the multiple ways in which productivity growth can happen. Before 1970, aggregate output rose, as did the number of workers. This represents a more-with-more form of productivity growth, as output rose more rapidly than the rising worker count. Next, between 1970 and 2000, aggregate output rose, while the number of workers stayed roughly the same (or trended down somewhat)—a more-with-the-same form. After around 2000, the number of manufacturing workers fell, driving a boom in output per worker—a more-with-less form. This last shift is more complex, as it coincided with the outsourcing overseas of low-productivity tasks. However, because real domestic manufacturing output continued to grow in this period, outsourcing doesn't reverse the argument about falling labor intensity. It's fair to conclude that at-scale displacement of labor inputs has shaped the history of productivity growth in goods production.

Most services, unfortunately, have not shared any version of this history. Figure 7.4 compares how many workers it takes to generate $1 billion of real output in various sectors. Unlike in manufacturing, the decline in the service

FIGURE 7.3

The labor intensity of manufacturing drops and drops

Manufacturing labor intensity, output and input

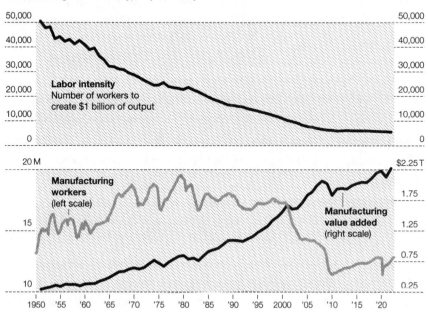

Note: Real gross value added (output) in US$(2012). Monthly data through August 2022 (workers) and annual data through 2021 (manufacturing value added and labor intensity).
Source: BEA, BLS, analysis by BCG Center for Macroeconomics

sector has been modest in aggregate; in several sectors it has moved sideways or gone up (right-hand side of figure 7.4). While not all service sectors are a disappointment (see the information sector in the chart), sectors such as education and health care are a particularly disappointing drag on overall performance because of their size.

Prices Tell the Truth about Productivity Growth

Some might quibble with the definition of productivity (yes, gross value added per worker is an indirect measure—though a reasonably good one) or with the true impact of offshoring (difficult to fully discern). But if additional evidence of the dynamics of productivity gains (or the lack thereof) is needed, we can look at prices—a powerful cross-check.[6]

FIGURE **7.4**

Unlike the goods economy, the service economy has seen little reduction in labor intensity

Number of workers to create $1 billion of gross value added

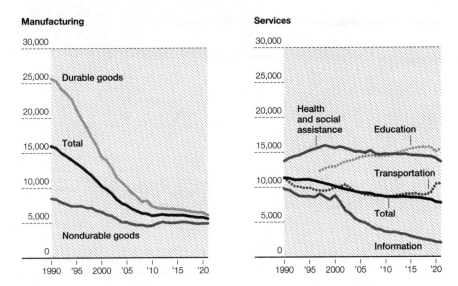

Note: Real gross value added in US$(2012). Data through 2021.
Source: BEA, BLS, analysis by BCG Center for Macroeconomics

Why? When a product (or service) goes through a strong productivity transformation, the cost basis of a unit will be slashed. That, in turn, will typically lead to falling prices for consumers, as the firms that are able to deliver at those lower prices fight for market share.[7] We call this the tech-cost-price cascade. While falling prices are not a prerequisite for productivity, they are evidence of productivity growth that is hard to refute.

Let's put this to the test by looking at the evolution of consumer prices. Figure 7.5 shows the prices of manufactured goods, driven lower by higher productivity as well as by global trade.[8] In contrast, services prices have risen steadily, particularly where productivity growth has been weakest, like education and health care.[9] Conversely, where services did experience productivity growth (information), prices are trending down.

Again, some enthusiastic technologists will push back, saying that the productivity gains in services are simply not measured correctly and that if they were, productivity growth would be revealed as strong. What should

FIGURE **7.5**

How have prices moved? Falling prices are powerful evidence of productivity growth

Price indices
January 2000 = 100

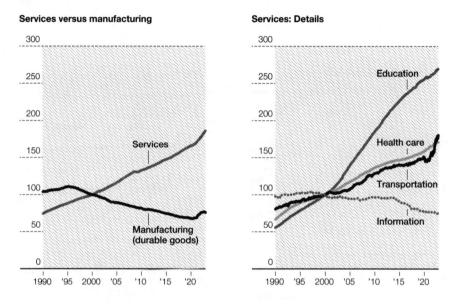

Services versus manufacturing

Services: Details

Note: Consumer prices from personal consumption expenditure (PCE) price index data. Data through 2022.
Information is the PCE price index for communication.
Source: BEA, BLS, analysis by BCG Center for Macroeconomics

one make of these claims—do productivity statistics underestimate the value of snazzy apps?

To be sure, the "mismeasurement" debate is real and tricky. The story goes that productivity in services is much higher than it seems, because the statistics fail to capture the value of qualitative changes in products and services fully. If those were accounted for accurately, the price index would be lower, real output higher—and there would be no productivity paradox. Why? Consider first a case where measurement is easy. If computing power doubles and the price stays the same, the price of computing power has fallen by half. If you spend the same in nominal terms on computing, you're now buying twice as much output. In this example, the accounting for the changing nature of output (so-called hedonic adjustments done by national statistical agencies) and, along with it, the measuring of productivity growth, is relatively simple. Yet for many things, particularly services—from the doctor appointment going digital, to the food order going through an app, to the consumption of music with personalized streaming—understanding the true change in real output is extremely difficult.

But this narrative misses the point. Of course, price deflators used to compute real output (and thus productivity growth) lack precision—most macro variables do. The question that matters is whether such mismeasurement is conceivably big enough to change the thrust of the macroeconomic narrative. And that we find to be an implausible suggestion.

Consider two mistaken arguments often invoked by technologists, and one cross-check. First, the alarm–clock fallacy. Sure, it may be true that an iPhone costs less than the sum of the components it could replace (alarm clock, camera, calculator, etc.), so it's tempting to think the iPhone saves us money. But it is shoddy economic accounting to treat a onetime cost the same as recurring costs: the replacement cycle of an iPhone is far shorter than that for an old alarm clock. If, say, 2% of the $800 iPhone's value is the alarm clock, then you spend $16 for that feature every time you buy a new iPhone—but how often do you replace a $10 alarm clock?

Next, the hedonic-adjustment trap. It is true and necessary that goods and services are quality-adjusted to determine inflation, real output, and productivity. But how to adjust when products change radically? Here some technologists want to account for a *quality-of-life* adjustment (for example, it's nicer to order an Uber than to hail a taxi in the street) rather than an *income* adjustment. However, that's moving outside of the realm of macro and productivity. Consider the polio vaccine, which undeniably improved the quality of life for populations. Yet it would be an odd argument that this should be considered a discontinuity in the national accounts and a jump in productivity growth. (And nobody does argue that.) What matters is if *incomes* change—not if the quality of life changes.[10]

Last, a simple back-of-the-envelope calculation. Let's assume that mismeasurement of productivity growth is a large and consequential problem; some have suggested a gap of as much as 1.4%.[11] If that were true in the 2010s, then real GDP growth did not average 2.3%, but was a fast 3.7%. Similarly, inflation did not average the lowish 1.7%, but a near-deflationary 0.3%. These numbers are not credible. Some mismeasurement seems likely, but not enough to rewrite the reality of sluggish real-income growth in the 2010s or enough to persuade us of near deflation. It flies in the face of everything we know about the 2010s economy.

Remember, Productivity Growth Is Promise and Peril

Collectively, our arguments in this chapter allow us to articulate a strategic framing of productivity growth. Technology lifts the economy's productivity growth rate when it can significantly drive down production cost, particularly labor cost. Of course, innovation in products and consumer experiences will continue to race ahead relentlessly, but the macroeconomic story of productivity growth will be driven predominantly on the labor-cost side of the service economy.

That dynamic represents promise or peril depending on whose perspective we take. We see technology as an unalloyed positive for consumers and the macroeconomy, but for firms it is a mix of promise *and* peril.

Starting on the side of technology's promise:

- *It's all about services.* The service economy has seen low productivity growth but claimed a growing share of total output, dragging down *aggregate* productivity growth. If services can emulate the production of physical goods, where tech has successfully displaced labor at scale, the service economy will see a growth boost.

- *Focus on the tech-cost-price cascade.* When technology can lower labor cost at scale, a cascade of effects follows: lower production costs will lead to lower prices as firms use cost advantage to gain market share. Productivity statistics will only confirm that a shift has happened. Downward pressures on costs and prices will be telltale signs. This process is mostly disconnected from the pace of product innovation.

- *Consumers are the winners.* The tech-cost-price cascade boosts consumers' real incomes—they are the ultimate beneficiaries of technology's deflationary nature. Rising real incomes will be spent on more of the same, or on new goods and services; it will also create new employment (see next chapter).

- *A realistic boost to trend growth.* After years of sagging *aggregate* productivity growth, the prospects of at-scale labor cost reduction in the service economy are consistent with an acceleration of US trend growth, calling into question the defeatist growth narratives we discussed in chapter 5. That said, we need to remain realistic about the magnitude and timing of such growth boosts (see next chapter).

Yet what promises to be an unalloyed positive for the economy and consumers looks decidedly more perilous for firms and entire industries. When it comes to the impact of technology on productivity growth, firms should be careful what they wish for and what strategy to pursue:

- *Cost leadership is not optional.* Once-stable sectors will see reordering when a cost-driven productivity shift is in motion. The cascade of technology, cost, price, profits, and market share will squeeze any firm that hasn't moved up the new productivity curve.

- *Only relative cost advantage counts.* Finding new ways of doing more with less may sound like a sure way to win in a competitive market. But this will hold only if the gains are relative. When productivity gains are widespread, sectors may descend into price wars. No firm can avoid it, but firms can make sure—by being at the edge of the cost learning curve—that they are in the best position to succeed.

- *Product innovation remains table stakes.* Though our analysis showed that productivity growth happens on the cost side, firms have no choice but to invest heavily in their product and user experience. That is only table stakes. As firms feel the burden of the investments required to stay in the game, they are at risk of deprioritizing productivity-enhancing cost leadership that has less appeal than the snazzy apps.

- *Productivity growth is not always profit growth.* Productivity can drive profits, but productivity and profits are not the same. Productivity gains that spread widely can drive competition that, ironically enough, leaves most or even all firms worse off than they were before as they compete down their margins. In retail, where the introduction of IT-based inventory management drove large productivity gains, only a few won, and many lost. Yet sitting on the sideline wasn't an option for any firm.

- *Scarcity is your friend.* Productivity growth tends to come not simply when technology is available, but when labor markets are tight and firms are forced to consider technological alternatives (see the next chapter). Counterintuitively, those wishing to spur adoption and ingenuity may benefit from scarce conditions and the incentives that come with them. Firms that persist in their willingness to transform have the best chance to stay at the forefront of the productivity curve.

Productivity growth is what matters most for the economy in the long run. It is built upon a foundation of technology, but not all technology facilitates productivity booms—just remember the story of the humble taxi. The technology that does will reduce production costs. So, when looking for the technological revolution, focus not on technology's whizbang but on its grit.

CHAPTER 8

Timing and Sizing the Next Growth Boost

I n the last few chapters, we argued that defeatist growth narratives ignored the potential for productivity shifts (chapter 5); that such macroeconomic acceleration happens because of the transformation of labor cost (chapter 7); and that a new wave of technology makes credible promises to deliver such labor-cost reductions in the service economy (also chapter 7).

But how much can productivity boost growth? And how soon? After two decades of disappointing growth impact from digital technology, readers are rightly skeptical about the often exuberant claims made by those at the frontier of technological change.

This chapter provides a guide for timing and sizing the next growth boost. Though we think an acceleration will happen, we caution against exuberance and hubris. The idea that deployment of AI amounts to flipping a macroeconomic switch that will deliver a step change in productivity growth is misguided in our view.

The question of timing is not only one of technology's availability. We view technology as the fuel, but tight labor markets are the spark that forces firms to adopt technology. Technological implementation is also a process that builds over time as obstacles are overcome—a process of incremental gains that compound and eventually deliver substantial impact, not a sudden step change.

On the topic of size, we also caution against the exuberant numbers that are thrown around. Instead of extrapolating from case studies, we should look at prior shifts and how they unfolded. We see a boost of 0.25–0.5 percentage points to trend growth over the next ten years as far more realistic than 1.5 percentage points. One should recall that in macroeconomics, small numbers can have large impact; even 0.25 percentage points would be significant, particularly when accumulated over time.

We also reject the doomsaying conclusion that so-called technological unemployment is on its way. That story has not held up over the very long run, it hasn't held up with automation over the last 20 years, and we don't think it will hold up now. This popular narrative actively ignores the deflationary nature of technology we laid out in the preceding chapter. Because technology can deliver cost savings, it also drives down prices, boosts real incomes, and drives spending—and employment—in new areas. Labor will be displaced—and reabsorbed, into a tight labor market. While that process can be disruptive and challenging, we do not believe in a world without work.

Timing: Fuel versus Spark

The popular narrative of technology, as we saw in the previous chapter, always focuses on the impressive nature of tangible product innovation. But just as that narrative obscures the reality that cost (labor) savings matter more than product innovation for macro performance, so too is the focus on product innovation unhelpful when trying to gauge the timing of a productivity boost.

We think of the availability of cost-saving technology as the fuel for productivity growth. The spark lies in a macroeconomic condition: tightness.[1] There are other drivers of technology adoption, but when labor markets are tight, firms are first nudged and eventually forced to adopt and utilize technology (both new and old) to figure out how to produce the same or more despite labor shortages. When there is slack, firms typically prefer to

FIGURE 8.1

Technology is the fuel, but tight labor markets are the spark for productivity growth

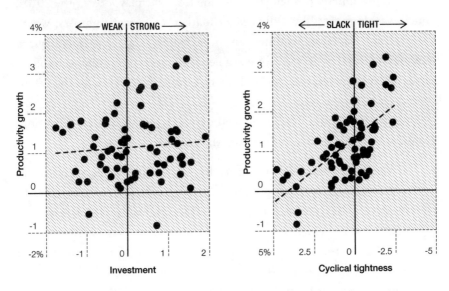

Weak link between productivity and investment ...   ... but strong link with labor-market tightness

Note: Productivity growth = five-year average TFP (total factor productivity) growth; investment = nonresidential fixed investment % of GDP minus five-year average; cyclical tightness is defined as the unemployment gap (unemployment rate minus neutral unemployment [u*] and is shown as the inverse on the x axis). Data starts in 1963.
Source: CBO, BLS, BEA, World Economic Forum, analysis by BCG Center for Macroeconomics

plod along with tried-and-tested production functions, linearly scaling their operations without concomitant productivity gains. When that is no longer an option, transformations abound.

Consider figure 8.1, which shows this empirically. In the left panel, we correlate investment strength (x axis) with productivity growth (y axis). The relationship between investment booms and productivity growth is trivial. In the right panel, we correlate labor-market tightness (x axis) with productivity growth (y axis). Here we find a stronger relationship. When firms are pressured to reinvent and transform their production processes, the fuel of technology meets the spark of tight labor markets and productivity growth pops.

We think this dynamic is welcome news, because as we show elsewhere in the book, the US economy is already in an era of tightness that we think will persist (see chapters 13 and 21). That will spark firms to reinvent the production process, and it has been visible in recent years as the labor market tightened—both since the pandemic and in the years immediately before the pandemic. When talking with executives, we've found that one of their most difficult challenges is moving from the playbook of the 2010s, which was dominated by a slack labor market, to one of tightness, where the need for capital expenditure and reinvention is greater. But they are moving. Add to that the availability of new and more-promising technology in the form of generative AI, and it's not difficult to see why the 2020s should see a growth boost.

Even so, we should not be seduced by narratives of sudden inflection. Consider four factors that will impact the timing of such gains:

Technological maturity. Is the technology ready to have impact at scale? Though technological breakthroughs often seem within reach, timelines are routinely overstated. Take the example of driverless technology—which we already encountered in our analysis of the taxi in the previous chapter. Driverless cars are many years behind schedule. In October 2016 Elon Musk made public claims about the self-driving capabilities of Tesla cars. As of 2023 these claims had not only failed to materialize but had also led to federal civil and criminal investigations.[2] Driverless taxis now operate in San Francisco and a few other cities, but the timeline for truly widespread adoption remains unclear.

Societal frictions. Will the new mode of production be accepted by society? This may seem straightforward, but there is a long history of resistance when it comes to a new way of doing things—including everything from elevators to electricity.[3] For instance, technology in education has the potential to be disruptive—particularly in adult education. However, the prestige and expectations of brand-name universities make it difficult to disrupt the market with new technology even when the quality of the educational attainment may be similar. Over time, norms and attitudes can change dramatically (for instance, consider women joining the workforce), but how a shift begins is unpredictable, and the effects of a shift often accumulate over a long time.

Regulatory frictions and lags. Often, new technologies need rules to facilitate adoption. Think of drones and their use in everything from agriculture to construction to delivery. Without clear guidelines and standards, it is difficult to have the confidence necessary to make significant investment.[4] Conversely, when standards promote interoperability, investment can be spurred as the fear of spending on the wrong standard dissipates. Without rules of the road, significant investment is less likely to happen. While regulators can be a powerful force for accelerating adoption, they are often well behind the technological frontier—leaving industry to nudge them ahead. Related, but less likely, there can be swift and significant regulatory backlash when public opinion turns against market practices.[5]

Technological costs. New technology can come with high costs. This is particularly true for businesses that add a digital layer without changing existing nondigital platforms. Consider the doctor who continues to see patients in the office, with the attendant fixed costs, but who now also sees patients virtually and is burdened with an additional set of costs (including merging online and offline processes). In the worst case, technology can reduce productivity rather than enhance it, even as the adoption of new products and platforms is necessary to stay competitive and meet consumer expectations and demand. And even if technology is making the user more efficient, if it doesn't cover the capital costs of investment, it is reducing productivity, not improving it.

In the years ahead, the conditions for technology to have macroeconomic impact are probably the best in a generation, but our expectations are still for a slow and gradual process, not a sudden inflection. Beware exuberance about immediate impact.

Size: Closer to 50 Than 150 Basis Points

The exuberance of technologists shapes perceptions not only of timelines but also of magnitudes. During the pandemic, it was fashionable to argue that greater digital penetration would translate into an impressive productivity boost. Because we learned on Zoom and talked to doctors on Teladoc, the story went, the economy was being reborn in a higher-productivity mode. Many rushed to declare a growth upshift, for example, an astounding extra "percentage point [of labor productivity] between 2019 and 2024."[6]

That hasn't happened. Macro just doesn't work that way, and we expressed our views in 2020 and again in 2021 on why we should not overstate the pandemic's effect on productivity growth.[7] We understand the temptation to take case studies of firm-level productivity gains, extrapolate from them, and add everything up—a bottom-up approach, much like the way one might go about identifying cost savings in a large organization. But such micro-to-macro extrapolations are treacherous. When uncertain changes are coming from countless tweaks, there will be a wide distribution of impacts— in both magnitude and timing—because the tweaks themselves vary widely in nature. Technology will work in some places but not in others. In some areas, it will gain traction quickly; in others it will take more time; in others still it will be tripped up by hurdles. On net, the impact will be much smaller than anticipated by a bottom-up sum.

Rather than take a bottom-up approach, we prefer to start with a macro lens on what happens when a general-purpose technology gains traction in a persistently tight economy. The ICT boom of the 1990s, when rapid advances in information and communication technology delivered a productivity surge in the United States, is a strong historical case. This episode offers important lessons that are captured in three numbers: 30, 100, and 10, illustrated in figure 8.2.

The number of years the 1990s ICT boom was in the making: 30. In the case of computers, productivity gains materialized only after the installed base reached critical mass and could be networked effectively. Computers were hardly new in the 1990s, but it took time (and the internet was a catalyst) for their systemic impact to manifest. Figure 8.2 shows the enormous investment in ICT starting in the 1970s that nonetheless left productivity growth as a flat line—until it shifted up in the mid-1990s. In an often quoted quip, the economist Robert Solow in 1987 lamented that "you can see the computer age everywhere but in the productivity statistics."[8] Yes, what is today referred to as the Solow paradox was on full display in 1987. But 10 years later, the productivity surge had arrived.

FIGURE **8.2**

The 1990s productivity boost:
30 years in the making, 100 basis point uplift lasting 10 years

Productivity growth
Potential total factor productivity (change, year/year)

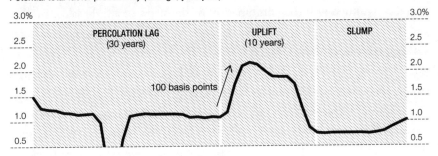

Information-processing-equipment investment
Share of GDP

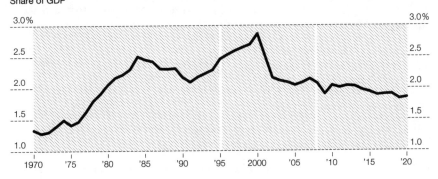

Note: Productivity growth for nonfarm business sector. Data through 2021.
Source: BEA, CBO, analysis by BCG Center for Macroeconomics

The magnitude of the productivity growth upshift in basis points (bps): 100. Relative to long-run trends in productivity growth—before and after—100 bps was a significant discontinuity. In a sign of how impressive this surge was interpreted to be, the upshift transformed the policy debate of the 1990s, driving belief in a permanently high-growth economy, persuading monetary policymakers to hold off on rate hikes, and equity markets to be exuberant.

The number of years the productivity surge lasted (roughly): 10. A productivity boost is likely to expire naturally. It's easy to forget that productivity growth is a change concept—it is not about levels. If productivity-enhancing innovations aren't followed up with new innovations at least as impactful, then the rate of productivity growth will drop.

So, how much will the combination of the spark of a tight labor market and the fuel of new technology, particularly AI, deliver over the next decade? Of course, we cannot know the size of a future technological disruption in one or many service sectors. Too many unknowns are involved. But past exuberance, such as the pandemic productivity narrative, highlights the prudence of more-conservative predictions, particularly if juxtaposed with the last realized productivity shift. For that reason, we argue that the productivity boom expected from the adoption of generative AI is more likely to deliver 25 to 50 bps than 150 bps of additional trend growth.

Should that be considered a disappointment, or looked forward to as meaningful impact? Some will see this as pessimistic and wonder if we have spent enough time playing with ChatGPT and all its generative-AI siblings. We assure readers that we have and are duly impressed. But we continue to believe in the hurdles of technological maturity (we've all seen the AI hallucinations), of societal resistance (not in my daughter's classroom), of regulatory friction (What will the new rules be?), and of cost. And while the potential to displace labor looks real, it seems more idiosyncratic than systemic. AI will likely be impactful over here (perhaps call centers), and then over there (perhaps graphic designers), and so on. Broader gains will take time to manifest.

Meanwhile others will realize that even 50 bps in extra growth per year is quite a big deal. In plain dollar terms, an extra 50 bps of growth on an economy with a GDP in excess of $26 trillion is more than $130 billion. It's an extra economy roughly the size of New Mexico's (or Morocco's)—every year. Or consider the impact in cumulative terms. If trend growth is 2%, the US economy will expand by 81% over three decades. But if generative AI can durably boost trend growth by 0.5 percentage points, the economy would expand by 110%. Put differently, it would pull forward a decade of growth. And critically, these gains would be occurring on a per capita basis, meaning that individual incomes would be that much bigger. Nothing to sniff at.

A World without Work?

What if we're off—by a lot? What if generative AI and a new wave of technology is simply different because it develops an absolute advantage over human workers? What if this technological wave happens much faster than innovation embodied in physical capital? What if productivity leaps higher—and displaces labor at scale along the way? What if we are entering a world without work?

We engaged in this debate with Daniel Susskind, the author of *A World without Work*, in the fall of 2020.[9] We were surprised that Susskind focused on so-called technological unemployment but didn't acknowledge its corollary: technology's deflationary nature and thus positive impact on real incomes and thus its creation of new demand and new jobs. We believe the world-without-work narrative is a false alarm.[10]

Technological unemployment is not a new fear. Decades ago, the concern was captured well by a possibly apocryphal but nevertheless enlightening conversation between Henry Ford II and the president of the United Auto Workers (UAW). Looking out over new industrial robots, Ford asked, "How are you going to get those robots to pay your union dues?" To which the UAW president replied, "Henry, how are you going to get them to buy your cars?"[11]

The fearful outcomes (no jobs and no demand) are easy to imagine, but both sides miss the point. Higher productivity delivers real wage gains through technology's deflationary impact, allowing dollars to be spent elsewhere, which in turn creates more employment and more income in other sectors. It is not just luck that new jobs have emerged alongside every wave of technological innovation. Rather, job creation has been causally driven by the tech-cost-price-income cascade of productivity growth we outlined in the preceding chapter.[12]

The long history of employment illustrates the dynamic. Consider figure 8.3. A huge proportion of the population once worked on farms. Yet, as agriculture became more productive, fewer and fewer people worked on farms, and only a small fraction of the workforce does today. But we know that the past century hasn't been burdened by structurally elevated unemployment. In our telling, this outcome was not a case of luck but logic. Productivity growth delivered cheaper products and therefore more disposable

FIGURE **8.3**

Technological unemployment? Rather, technology lowers labor costs and prices, boosting real incomes and spending, which creates new employment

Farmworkers and household food expenditure declined

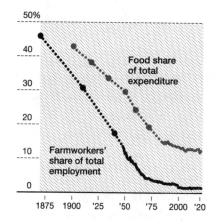

Total number of workers and jobs continued to grow

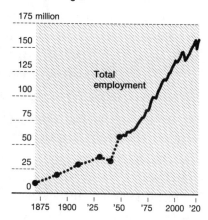

Note: Data through 2021. Dotted lines are extrapolations between available data points.
Source: NBER, Census, BLS, Robert Gordon, analysis by BCG Center for Macroeconomics

income, as can be seen in the declining share of household income spent on food in the left-hand graph in figure 8.3. That increase in disposable income was spent elsewhere, generating new incomes and new employment. As is also shown in figure 8.3 (right side), the US economy added nearly 150 million jobs over a period that spans multiple technological waves (not just the shift away from agriculture). The new incomes were often spent on goods—but typically on services—that were barely known at the time the disruptive technology arrived. Put simply, technological unemployment is a long-standing narrative that has never delivered.

We don't seek to downplay challenges and difficulties. Particularly when disruption occurs quickly it will be painful for many. Adjustment and retraining efforts are warranted, but the fears of overwhelming technological unemployment are not well founded in our view. Just consider the march of automation in production over the last few decades that coexists with generational lows in unemployment since the late 2010s.

A thought experiment can highlight additional problems with the idea of technological unemployment. What if we are wrong and technology's impact is far bigger and faster, ushering in an era of enormous labor slack? If that happened, the deflationary cascade discussed above would be supercharged—costs and prices would fall precipitously, and real incomes and spending would rise. An era of extraordinary deflation driven by a boom of productive capacity would result. Social challenges would emerge, but this would be about *prosperity*, not macroeconomic crisis. We would expect this prosperity to eventually remove labor slack as markets adjust.

Taking this thought experiment to the extreme, if technology truly gained an absolute advantage over humans across all production—something that we find even harder to believe—the cascade of tech-cost-price-income-spending-employment would break down, because new work would always go to a machine. This would be a world of superabundance, rendering the traditional role of economics (that is, the allocation of scarce resources) looking for a new mission. We have never considered how to make an economy work when everything (at least all produced goods) is essentially free. It would be a new challenge but one that is hard to see as bad—a remarkable world indeed.

Putting this thought experiment in a different, less extreme light: If we need a universal basic income (UBI) to address mass unemployment, we will be able to afford it. And if we can't afford UBI, then we don't really need it.

Remember, Small Numbers Mean Big Things in Macro

We've given special attention to the role of productivity both because it is where the growth upside is clearest and because it matters in a unique way. As we argued in chapter 5, the other factors of growth are more costly and more constrained. One can add labor, but that doesn't increase per capita prosperity. One can spend lavishly on the capital stock, but that becomes less and less impactful. Productivity—the true magic of economic growth—is doing more with less. This happens when technology is put into the hands of workers of all stripes, particularly when labor scarcity nudges them toward finding better ways of doing things.

So, what to watch for?

- *Look at the labor market, not just at technology.* Remember that productivity is not merely about technology but about getting technology used in the production process. And that happens most efficaciously when the production process is short on labor. An era of tightness aids the potential for strong productivity growth.

- *"Soon" is years, not quarters.* Productivity growth is a credible prospect as tight labor markets push firms to adopt new technologies, but it is a process that takes years, not quarters, to show meaningful impact. When assessing the timing of productivity gains, don't skip the many hurdles that technology must (and eventually, in aggregate, will) overcome. They may begin modestly, but large gains will accrue over many years if the growth can be sustained.

- *Remain realistic about size.* It's tempting to extrapolate impressive case studies of productivity gains to the macroeconomy. When assessing the size of a growth boost, keep in mind that large and sustained boosts to trend growth are a high bar. An acceleration of 50 bps would be significant.

- *Be skeptical of narratives of technological unemployment.* The idea that technological progress creates mass unemployment has a long history that has failed to play out. Recall that technology's impact is through lower cost and prices and that this boosts real incomes, new spending, and ultimately new employment. That will take time and involve friction, but a world without work is an ahistorical proposition.

In trying to divine the timing and size of technology's next wave of productivity growth, we must stay grounded. In the United States, technology can and will deliver a growth boost in our view. The big promises are too exuberant, but remember that in macroeconomics, small numbers mean big things.

!

PART TWO

FINANCIAL ECONOMY

Good Strains and Systemic Risks

Stimulus

Inflation

Other Financial Risks

CHAPTER 9

The Compulsive Stimulus Machine

Risks of systemic macroeconomic collapse can never, unfortunately, be ruled out. Twice in fewer than 20 years, the US economy came relatively close to the macroeconomic precipice, opening the possibility of an economic depression akin to that of the 1930s. But the awesome power of existential stimulus prevented that from happening, both in the global financial crisis of 2008 and in the pandemic of 2020.

Stimulus is also deployed outside of such crises. In fact, it is used constantly. When recession looms, or recoveries are sluggish, tactical stimulus is pursued. Central bankers cut interest rates, and fiscal authorities lean into deficit spending to de-risk the cycle. What's more, stimulus is even used to opportunistically goose growth when the economy is strong.

Between its existential and tactical use, we have become addicted to stimulus. Without the modern stimulus machine, systemic risks could not be averted, and cyclical risks would be harder to manage—and good macro could not endure. But stimulus also creates its own risks. The tolerance and even stoking of bubbles to foster growth is one example. And if the power of stimulus itself were to fail, the fallout from future exogenous shocks, like Covid, and endogenous crises, like the global financial crisis, could not be backstopped effectively.

Executives and investors must have a thorough understanding of the stimulus regime if they are to navigate systemic risk and cyclical gyrations successfully. This involves grasping how the regime works, how it could sputter, and what it would take to break down. Many macroeconomic risks simply cannot be assessed without considering the role of stimulus.

This chapter is a detailed introduction to the modern stimulus regime (while the following two chapters discuss the specific risks to existential and tactical stimulus, respectively). We believe the best way to analyze the stimulus regime is by tracing its rise over the past roughly 50 years. Tracing its rise brings out the objectives of stimulus—existential redemption, tactical protection, or opportunistic goosing—as well as its constraints. As we will learn, stimulus depends on the willingness, and ability, of politicians and policymakers to deploy it.

We trace the origins of this stimulus regime back to the Reagan deficits of the 1980s. We then follow it through the stoking of the 1990s dot-com bubble, the housing bubble of the 2000s, and the bubble in government debt (fed by quantitative easing) of the 2010s. The story of the compulsive stimulus machine culminates in the turbocharged, all-encompassing stimulus that pushed an astounding $5 trillion into the US economy when Covid hit—and that number only includes the fiscal efforts.

Our story about the stimulus machine concludes with a concise framework for stimulus-regime analysis, urging readers to distinguish between existential and tactical stimulus and to focus on the ability and willingness that each depends on. This is the basis for the next two chapters: What is the risk that existential stimulus might fail? And has the era of effortless tactical stimulus already ended? Understanding the foundations of the stimulus regime will help answer these legitimate, intimidating, and critical questions about macroeconomic risks.

The Rise of Stimulus Willingness and Ability

Stimulus has been so ubiquitous and natural in modern life that it's easy to forget it's more of a historical anomaly than the norm. Between World War II and the early 1980s, stimulus was remarkably modest by modern standards. Though taxes were cut, for example, in the early 1960s, such fiscal efforts came with declining public debt ratios, as seen in figure 9.1B, which summarizes the rise of compulsive stimulus over the past 70 years.[1]

FIGURE **9.1**

How we've become addicted to stimulus

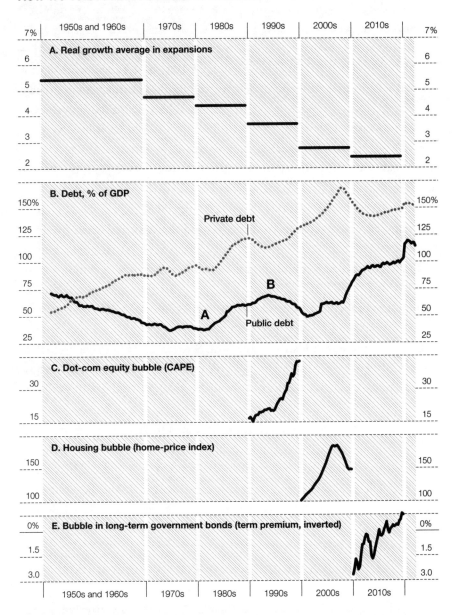

Note: Debt through Q2 2022. Nonfinancial (households, firms, government) debt = debt securities + loans in the domestic nonfinancial sector. Debt, % of GDP is using potential GDP to smooth cyclical gyrations. CAPE (a valuation for equities) = Shiller Cyclically Adjusted S&P Price to Earnings ratio. Home-price index = S&P CoreLogic Case-Shiller Home Price Index: United States. Term premium (a valuation metric for bonds) = 10-year ACM term premium.
Source: Federal Reserve Board, BEA, CBO, Robert Shiller, Standard & Poor's, Federal Reserve Bank of New York, Sanford C. Bernstein, analysis by BCG Center for Macroeconomics

But in this period, two changes unfolded that have shaped stimulus to this day and will do so in the future.

First, the willingness to use debt began to shift. Even after the Great Depression cracked dogmatic opposition to stimulus, there was still a widespread and strong belief that public deficits were for fighting wars only—and then those debts should be paid back.[2] But the Keynesian revolution gradually legitimized the use of deficits to fight downturns, and politicians of both stripes were quick to see the electoral benefits in doling out cash. President Kennedy's tax cut comes to mind; later even President Nixon is said to have reflected "We are all Keynesians now."

Second, the ability to deploy stimulus increased. Until 1971, the United States operated on a fixed exchange-rate regime with foreign currencies tied to the dollar and the dollar tied to gold. While not a classic gold standard, it still imposed constraints on fiscal policy and deficits. But when President Nixon broke the gold peg, he did so in part because of a desire for stimulus.

These changes in the willingness and ability to resort to stimulus coincided with a period of bad macro during the 1970s, which witnessed the highest unemployment since the Great Depression, high inflation, numerous recessions, and poor growth. Stimulus would have been an attractive policy instrument, but it still had to wait. Structurally high inflation effectively replaced the gold standard as a constraint on stimulus ability because bond markets reacted negatively to fiscal efforts. Bond traders, known since as bond vigilantes, sent interest rates higher in the face of fiscal profligacy, offsetting the stimulative effects from extra spending.

The shifting constellation of need, willingness, and ability was epitomized by President Carter's experience when the bond market rejected his budget in 1980.[3] The need was there, the willingness was there, but the ability was lacking, because the bond markets effectively vetoed any fiscal expansion.

Reagan Ushered in the Modern Era of Stimulus

By appointing Paul Volcker as Fed chair in 1979, it was Carter who triggered a path toward aggressive monetary policy that successfully conquered structurally high inflation in the early 1980s.[4] The *Volcker inheritance* is the term we have used in the past to describe the subsequent structural decline in inflation and interest rates. Because of it, stimulus ability grew

FIGURE 9.2

Reagan deficits usher in a new era of debt-focused growth

Federal budget balance by presidency, share of GDP

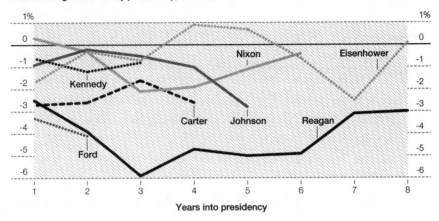

Years into presidency

Note: President tenures: Eisenhower (January 1953–January 1961); Kennedy (January 1961–November 1963); Johnson (November 1963–January 1969); Nixon (January 1969–August 1974); Ford (August 1974–January 1977); Carter (January 1977–January 1981); Reagan (January 1981–January 1989).
Source: OMB, analysis by BCG Center for Macroeconomics

rapidly, and the Reagan administration had the willingness to use debt growth to tactically charge the cycle, thereby ushering in the modern era of stimulus.

Many readers may intuitively doubt that characterization, for fiscal rectitude is commonly associated with the Republican party to this day. But the facts speak for themselves. As President Reagan cut taxes and spent more on the military, the cost of stimulus mounted.[5] Figure 9.2 shows that Reagan's deficits far outstripped those of his post–World War II predecessors. Perhaps his willingness and ability to stimulate played a small role in his becoming the first president since Eisenhower to complete a full eight years.

Reagan eventually practiced more fiscal discipline, with a series of tax hikes that tapered deficits as the decade progressed. Yet none of that changes the fact that public debt as a percent of GDP structurally inflected during the Reagan revolution, bottoming out in the early 1980s, as marked by point A in figure 9.1B. The president took the credit for delivering morning in America, but he had paid for it with leverage.[6]

Though Reagan ushered in the modern stimulus era, his stimulus was tactical and modest compared with both the ability and willingness that would fuel much bigger stimulus in the future.

Not Just Debt—Bubbles Too

With the willingness and ability to use debt stimulus now established, the next engine of the compulsive stimulus machine came from bubbles—a form of stimulus that was embraced by policymakers in their quest to goose the cycle (see also chapter 16 on bubbles).[7]

To be sure, bubble stimulus didn't arise in tandem with debt stimulus. Until the late 1990s, debt was still a politically charged subject and bond markets were still feared. Enjoying the tailwind of a booming economy, the Clinton administration worked to rein in deficits and to stabilize the debt-to-GDP ratio (see point B in figure 9.1B). Politically, this helped woo voters who still saw deficits as a major issue, and it reduced the risk of market rejection that had impacted Carter.[8] Economically, an argument was made that lower deficits would lower interest rates and thereby be stimulative.[9] This paradoxical antidebt stimulus paid off, as rates fell in the 1990s.

But as interest rates fell and money became cheap, asset markets started to run up too far, too fast. The dot-com bubble (see figure 9.1C) became a new form of stimulus, and it was at least tolerated, even stoked, by monetary policymakers who paid only lip service to trying to slow it down.[10] The stimulative quality of the bubble can be seen in the wealth effects of a booming equity market. Figure 9.3 highlights the increase in households' equity wealth from $2 trillion at the start of the decade to nearly $11 trillion at the end. Though nominal and heavily concentrated at the top, this increase fueled household consumption. This was a new source of stimulus for a remarkably strong economy.

As the dot-com bubble popped in 2000–2001, policymakers afraid of a painful downturn pivoted back to debt stimulus. President George W. Bush delivered two major tax cuts, while Vice President Dick Cheney reportedly declared that "deficits don't matter."[11] What's more, the Federal Reserve cut short-term interest rates to 1%, and rock-bottom mortgage costs delivered a housing boom. With long-term interest rates further suppressed by a global savings glut, the boom turned into a bubble.[12] See figure 9.1D.

FIGURE **9.3**

Dot-com bubble stimulates economy by driving up wealth (even for middle income)

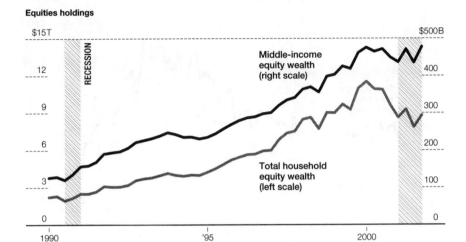

Note: Household sector includes nonprofits. Equities holding based on direct corporate equities and mutual-fund shares. Middle income is 40th to 60th percentile. Data through 2001.
Source: FRB, NBER, analysis by BCG Center for Macroeconomics

This wasn't just a coincidence. Some went so far as to argue a new bubble was necessary to counteract the wealth-effect hangovers from the dot-com crash.[13] While that wasn't an official view, this new bubble was aided by monetary policymakers, who left rates low for a sustained period for fear that significant negative wealth effects would deliver a protracted downturn.[14]

The housing bubble resulted not only from domestic factors. Even when monetary policy tightened, a global savings glut kept US long-term rates very low. When global capital in the 2000s searched for yield and liquidity, it thought it had found them in new financial products spurred by lax regulation of credit creation. Demand for US debt pushed down interest rates. It contributed to a new real-estate bubble only a few years after the technology one had burst.

The stimulative impact on the economy was enormous. Figure 9.4 summarizes the run-up in housing wealth from roughly $4 trillion to roughly $14 trillion (right axis). And as home equity rose rapidly, households could

FIGURE **9.4**

Housing bubble boosts the economy as homes turn into ATMs

Housing wealth and mortgage-equity withdrawal

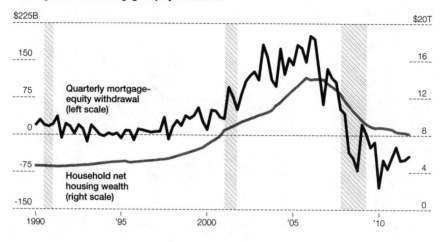

Note: Households include nonprofits. Data through 2011.
Source: FRB, NBER, analysis by BCG Center for Macroeconomics

access that wealth for consumption through home-equity loans. Figure 9.4 also highlights the rise of home-equity withdrawals (left axis)—running at $100 billion a quarter, a remarkable $3 trillion over the six-year period (2002–2007). The housing boom wasn't simply about housing construction. It was about consumption, real-estate transactions, and financial activity facilitated by a bubbly housing market.

When the housing-credit bubble popped, an era of systemic crisis began, which demanded a new era of stimulus.

Systemic Risk Paved the Way for Supercharged Stimulus

The collapse of the housing bubble was a turning point for the US and global economies in many ways. The global financial crisis supercharged both the willingness and ability to enact stimulus, cementing and expanding its use cases, variety, and tool kit.

As the housing bubble collapsed, unprecedented (at the time) existential stimulus was necessary to prevent a total breakdown of the financial system and the economy (see chapters 3 and 4). From conservatorship of housing agencies (Freddie Mac and Fannie Mae), to the backstopping of money-market funds, to rescues of auto manufacturers, to—critically—bank recapitalization, the awesome power of stimulus was on full display, helping arrest the most severe financial crisis ever.[15]

But as the recovery proved persistently sluggish—a consequence of a financial recession that left weakened balance sheets in its wake (see chapters 3 and 4)—policymakers resorted to yet more stimulus, developing new delivery mechanisms in the process. The Fed's instrument of choice—the short-term, or policy, interest rate—had already been slashed to zero, so the central bank embraced quantitative easing (QE) buying up long-term bonds (government and agency) to push down (long-term) interest rates.

It is not a wild exaggeration to say that one goal of QE was to spawn an anything and everything bubble. The structural demand deficiency that afflicted the post-global-financial-crisis economy was to be cured with much lower interest rates that would spur activity. QE succeeded in that the valuation of government bonds (as captured in the inverse of the term premium in figure 9.1E) soared.

FIGURE **9.5**

QE era pushes economy by growing household wealth by more than $35 trillion

Household net worth, change since Q4 2011

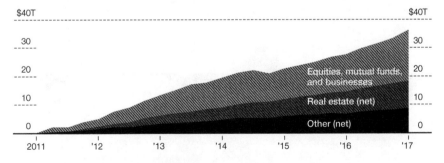

Note: QE = quantitative-easing. Households include nonprofits. Data through 2017.
Source: FRB, analysis by BCG Center for Macroeconomics

If the goal was to generate any form of demand, it had a mixed record. It pushed up wealth by making assets more valuable, which somewhat helped spur demand. But while household wealth grew by $35 trillion, as seen in figure 9.5, the economic recovery plodded along slowly. In response, policymakers added yet more stimulus. The Trump administration delivered a tax cut in 2018, followed by the Fed's decision to cut the policy rate in 2019—never mind that the United States was by now enjoying the best labor market in decades and the longest expansion on record (at the time, recall that the prevailing policy concern was that inflation was too low).

Then Covid struck, and stimulus willingness and ability soared to even greater heights. Back in 2008, $700 billion of taxpayer-funded fiscal stimulus had been controversial, but during the pandemic, more than $5 trillion of fiscal stimulus was pushed into the economy, the monetary balance sheet exploded (again), and policy rates returned to zero. This impulse came under two administrations—President Trump signed the CARES Act delivering

FIGURE 9.6

The pandemic's fiscal stimulus dwarfs all prior efforts

Fiscal-impact measure
Fiscal-policy contribution to real GDP growth (percentage points)

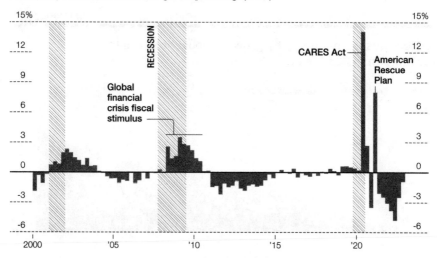

Note: GDP growth is Q/Q seasonally adjusted annual rate. Data through 2022.
Source: Hutchins Center, BEA, NBER, analysis by BCG Center for Macroeconomics

a fiscal stimulus worth $2.2 trillion. President Biden pushed through the American Rescue Plan, adding a further $1.9 trillion in deficit spending.

Fiscal and monetary policy innovation—ranging from student-loan and mortgage deferrals to a variety of special credit facilities—was essential and happened in a flash, as the compulsion to deliver overwhelming stimulus reached its apotheosis. This stimulus was remarkable in size and speed—involving everything from one-off checks to payroll protection to corporate bailouts to childhood-poverty initiatives. The fiscal growth impulse is seen in figure 9.6, but its size came at a cost. The impulse turned sharply negative over the following years, as fiscal stimulus was not renewed.

Remember, Stimulus Is about Willingness and Ability

The rise of the compulsive stimulus machine focuses our attention on two dimensions, schematically summarized in figure 9.7. Together they provide a concise framework with which to analyze all situations of stimulus past, present, or future.

- *Distinguish between stimulus objectives.* Existential stimulus is effectively deployed to backstop systemic and structural risks to the economy—as was done in 2008 and 2020. That is very different from tactical

FIGURE **9.7**

How to analyze economic stimulus: Objectives and enablers

		STIMULUS OBJECTIVE	
		Existential (structural)	Tactical (opportunistic)
STIMULUS ENABLER	Willingness (political, cultural)	Do policymakers believe it's their role to backstop the economic system?	Do policymakers believe it's advantageous to push the economy?
	Ability (financial)	Will markets allow policymakers to backstop the economic system?	How do financial constraints affect the net impact of stimulus?

Source: BCG Center for Macroeconomics

stimulus, which is used opportunistically to defend or goose the cycle—aiding expansion longevity, accelerating recoveries, and pushing up growth rates (and sometimes risk). Tax cuts and interest-rate cuts that are delivered midcycle are two common forms.

- *Be aware of the stimulus enablers.* All stimulus policies of the future will depend on the willingness of policymakers and politicians to enact them, and that willingness can change. Likewise, all stimulus policies of the future will depend on government's ability to deliver them, which in turn depends on acceptance by financial markets. This too can change in significant and subtle ways.

Our swing through stimulus history has traced the indispensable role of stimulus in managing existential risks and cyclical threats, along with its more frivolous use to push cyclical growth at will—which itself can be a source of risk. This raises two critical questions: Could government lose the ability to deliver existential stimulus, depriving us of a safety net we have come to take for granted? And, has tactical stimulus ability already been diminished, thereby undermining the ability to manage the cycle? The next chapters explore these two questions, respectively.

CHAPTER 10

Could Existential Stimulus Fail?

C onsider the drama that played out in the fall of 2008. With the US economy in freefall and the banking system on the brink of collapse, the Bush administration put the Troubled Asset Relief Program (TARP), a $700 billion stimulus package, before Congress. It was voted down, and markets plummeted (see figure 10.1), with the broad stock index dropping 3% within 10 minutes and 9% on the day. The US economy had come to its most perilous moment since the Great Depression, a dramatic demonstration of systemic risk to politicians.

Having been punished by the markets, Congress soon changed its mind and passed TARP, and in the prior chapter we presented those measures as a qualified success in the history of stimulus. But the episode epitomizes important and legitimate questions on the minds of many leaders. Will future crises be addressable by stimulus? Can we rely on it?

Executives and investors need solid analytical tools to assess such risks effectively, not least because public discourse reliably veers into doomsaying. Building on our prior discussion of stimulus willingness and ability, this chapter discusses the risks to existential stimulus. We consider the three scenarios that can lead to stimulus failure and economic collapse and explain why all three dangers are highly unlikely to materialize in the United States.

FIGURE **10.1**

Voting down TARP: Political error risked economic depression

S&P 500 Index performance on September 29, 2008
Indexed to 4 p.m. on September 26, 2008

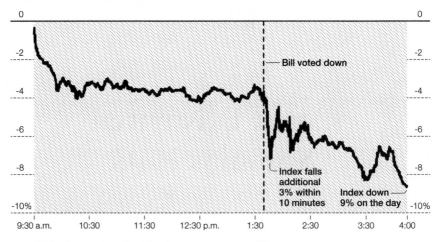

Note: TARP = Troubled Asset Relief Program.
Source: Bloomberg, analysis by BCG Center for Macroeconomics

We separate this discussion of risks to existential stimulus from our analysis, in the next chapter, of risks to tactical stimulus.

Three Ways Existential Stimulus Can Fail

The specter of systemic collapse is a popular staple of macroeconomic discourse—despite the modern history of successfully backstopping the economy. Fears reach a fever pitch during crises, but they generate a steady hum even in healthy times. Though we argue here that risks are routinely overstated, we acknowledge that the fears are natural and the risks are real. It is the asymmetry of the risk—low probability but existentially impactful for business, investors, workers, and governments—that makes the anxiety understandable.

When we experienced this negative bias during the Covid crisis, we did our best to offer reassurance as commentators. At the start of the pandemic, when fears about a depression proliferated, we argued that swift policy inter-

FIGURE **10.2**

Three pathways to existential-stimulus failure

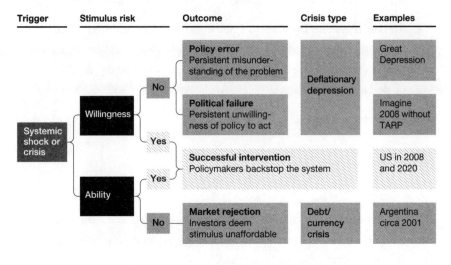

Source: BCG Center for Macroeconomics

ventions would save the economy from structural damage (see chapter 4).[1] But even after stimulus was on the way in the weeks that followed, the doomsaying did not abate. We followed up with a systematic discussion of the scenarios that can lead policymakers to fail to deliver existential stimulus, highlighting how high a bar this is. Early in the crisis we argued that the United States was not heading toward a new Great Depression.[2]

The pathways to stimulus failure, schematically summarized in figure 10.2, draw on the building blocks we identified in the previous chapter. Faced with macroeconomic collapse, if willingness and ability align, policymakers can control risk and prevent calamity. It is only when either willingness or ability is lacking that a collapse awaits. The advantage of this framework is that it is broadly applicable, not specific to the pandemic crisis.

Seen this way, we can think about three paths to failure for existential stimulus:

- *Policy error:* A first problem of willingness is when policymakers fail to act because they mistakenly believe the right policies are already in place or they don't have the tools they need.

- *Political failure:* A second problem of willingness is when politicians stand in the way. They know what needs to be done but are unable to agree to it even as the economy slides deeper into depression.

- *Market rejection:* Problems of ability arise when markets are unwilling to finance stimulus. Depending on whether a country is a monetary sovereign, a financial-market backlash may lead to an inflationary or deflationary collapse.

We review each path in some detail.

Risk of Policy Error

As our recounting of the TARP debacle highlighted, the idea that policymakers—fiscal and monetary—would prove persistently unwilling to address a major crisis sounds farfetched.

Farfetched, yet it has happened. The Great Depression was a case in point. After the financial bust of 1929, fiscal timidness and restrictive monetary policy allowed the economy to bleed out.[3] In the early 1930s, the appropriateness of stimulus was still controversial, which helps to clarify why policymakers watched so passively as a financial bust spread into a deflationary depression. It is this type of conceptual error that is most plausible when considering the risk of sustained policy failure. When policymakers think they are doing right but are not, they might persist in error and help bring about calamity.

Could that happen today, or have policymakers learned from past mistakes? They have come a long way since then—monetary policymakers have admitted that their forebears erred grievously in the early 1930s and have promised not to do the same thing again.[4] Indeed, policymakers have walked the walk, acting to avoid deflationary depressions in 2008 and 2020, as we saw in prior chapters.[5] But economics is not a science, and policy is never settled, so we cannot simply assume that these errors have been consigned to history. The policy debate of the 2010s was consumed with pro-austerity narratives, and the eurozone crisis was aggravated by such narratives being put into practice. Just think of Greece, where per capita GDP fell by a quarter, nearly matching the depth of the Great Depression in the United States in the 1930s. Worse still, Greece has experienced a far slower recovery.[6]

The best argument for a policy's (eventual) success is a persistent willingness to experiment. A do-whatever-it-takes attitude has kept policymakers from paving the pathway to depression.[7] Faced with existential crises, when the need for action and response is overwhelmingly clear, governments are willing to rise above nuance. As a result, moments of hesitation are generally brief. In 2008, the US government failed to stop the disorderly collapse of Lehman Brothers but then acted forcefully to backstop all manner of other financial institutions. Likewise, as we saw, Congress initially refused to pass the TARP stimulus but soon relented.

The disaster in Greece was an exception that followed the incomplete nature of European integration. The rich northern economies of Europe had the power to determine whether Greece received assistance, but their leaders did not answer to Greek voters, so those leaders were content to let the Greek economy fall off a cliff. For European leaders, it was a matter of willingness. For Greek leaders, it was a matter of ability. Such can be the price of joining a currency union and giving up monetary sovereignty.

In countries that do have monetary sovereignty, misjudgment of which policy to pursue is a greater risk than an unwillingness to act. In difficult circumstances monetary policy can misjudge what it means to be accommodative, since central banks have to set interest rates in a way that anticipates unknown conditions.[8] Meanwhile, fiscal policy is just as susceptible to error. Budget authorities must navigate between imposing harmful austerity and delivering excess stimulus. Yet while policy will never be perfect, policymakers are unlikely to be persistently negligent in the face of an existential crisis. The damaging dogma of the so-called healthy downturn, all too prevalent in the Great Depression, has been more or less buried. Policy might get it wrong, but it won't sit idly by as the economy falls apart.

It's easy to forget that the recession that kicked off the Great Depression started in 1929. Economic activity declined until March 1933, the same month President Franklin D. Roosevelt took office. It's hard to imagine a 21st-century US administration persisting with a tepid response for so long, as President Herbert Hoover's had.

Risk of Political Failure

As seen in the introduction to this chapter, and in the second branch of figure 10.2, the second failure of willingness comes from politicians. To readers who have lived through recent years of political gridlock, government shutdowns, and debt-ceiling debacles, predicting that politicians will cause damage may sound like a safe bet. But it's one thing to lament the exhausting inelegance of democracy. It's quite another to predict that these conditions will extend so far as to prevent a response to an economic collapse underway.

A comparison of the pandemic crisis and the earlier TARP crisis underscores this point. The pandemic elicited immediate political willingness to come to the rescue of the economy. Why? Companies, financial firms, and consumers could hardly be blamed for the exogenous disaster that had struck in the form of a virus. In contrast, the mortgage meltdown of 2008 involved plenty of reckless behavior by Wall Street and Main Street, causing a reluctance on the part of politicians to bail out bad actors. As a result, politicians and policymakers in 2008 divided into two camps: those who pointed to the imminent failures in the financial system and the risk of a deflationary depression, and those who were more preoccupied by the dangers of rewarding irresponsibility and thereby fueling moral hazard. When TARP was initially put to a vote in Congress, the anti-moral-hazard camp won. But then financial markets collapsed, as seen in figure 10.1. On the second attempt, TARP passed.

The moral of the story is that the political willingness to rescue an economy in existential crisis runs deep. The politics of bailing out bankers will always be awful. Yet even in this case, the hesitancy to deliver assistance was brief. As the economic damage became clear, the political calculus changed. Faced with systemic collapse, partisan political games tend to be replaced by collective action. Crises align interests. Crises lubricate dealmaking. Existential brinkmanship is different from tactical brinkmanship.

The redeeming fact is not that politicians will act optimally, but that they don't need to—they just need to act eventually and sufficiently. And because a looming disaster raises the political risk of being blamed for inaction, partisan considerations are pushed to the side and significant stimulus is ultimately delivered.

Risk of Market Rejection

Beyond the question of willingness to deliver stimulus, there is the question of the ability to do so (see the lower branch in figure 10.2). The good news is that here, too, the United States and most other advanced economies are highly unlikely to lose the capacity to intervene at times of an existential economic threat.

Consider that at one point during the global financial crisis, when the insurer AIG was teetering, Federal Reserve Board Chair Ben Bernanke proposed to inject $85 billion of public funds to stop it from imploding. A skeptical member of Congress asked Bernanke whether the Fed had that much—$85 billion was more than the federal government spent annually on transportation. The central-bank chairman responded that he had $800 billion.[9] He was saying that in a fiat currency system, the central bank can conjure up as much money as it chooses.

Even though technically Bernanke was correct, there are nevertheless two pathways to stimulus failure. Both are by-products of markets rejecting policy plans.

The first path to failure involves markets reacting negatively to stimulus and thereby offsetting it. If investors flee the country, causing the stock market, bond market, or currency to collapse, no amount of government spending can offset the flight of private capital. This disaster occurred in several emerging economies during the 1990s, when policymakers were especially reckless about testing market patience. Mexico's currency crisis of 1995 was followed by collapses in Thailand, Indonesia, and South Korea in 1997, in Russia in 1998, and in Argentina in 2001, to name a few.

The second path to failure involves a more specialized case, when a nation doesn't control its own currency (and therefore monetary policy) and thus may lack the policy tools to respond to a downturn. We encountered this sort of case in Greece during the 2010s.

The United States is exceedingly unlikely to travel down either of these two paths. The second is categorically impossible since the United States has its own currency and its own central bank. The first is merely wildly improbable. Indeed, when a shock threatens the economic system, the US government's capacity to deliver stimulus is typically enhanced as investors flee to safe havens. And the safest of all havens is US government bonds. With the onset of Covid, and despite growing deficits to finance the stimulus response, for example, investors clamored for US government bonds rather than fleeing them. Far from offsetting the government's stimulus policy, private capital reinforced it. And not only in the United States. Consider figure 10.3, which shows that across the G7, the Covid crisis enhanced stimulative power as rates broadly fell—even in the heart of crisis.

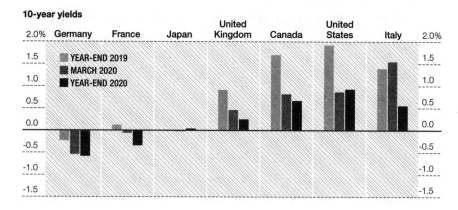

FIGURE **10.3**

Rates fell in the heart of the Covid crisis, not just for the United States

Source: Bloomberg, analysis by BCG Center for Macroeconomics

Fears of temperamental markets in an age of higher rates and large debt are reasonable. But it will remain important to distinguish between tactical abilities—which are constrained by higher rates, inflation, and correlations (see next chapter)—and existential-crisis abilities. Even President Carter, whose modest deficits were rejected by markets in the context of structurally high inflation, would very likely have been able to provide existential stimulus if faced with a systemic crisis. Rejection during an existential crisis would be consistent only in a world where the dollar was not only not the reserve currency but barely an international currency at all. This is theoretically possible—but neither plausible nor imminent—and would require an extraordinary shift in the macro landscape (see chapter 20).

Remember, Don't Cry Wolf

Many executives, investors, policymakers, and consumers (meaning, frankly, all of us) are prone to batten down the hatches when systemic threats arise. Recall the automakers who canceled their orders of semiconductors in the early days of Covid (see chapter 4). This survival instinct is nothing but natural.

But we need to remain rational and recall that economic collapse remains an exceedingly high bar—and it doesn't help if we cry wolf at every stage of a crisis. Instead, we should focus on the dimensions of willingness and ability and how they could shape the pathway to failed existential stimulus:

- *Name the path to failure.* If you fear systemic collapse in times of crisis, you should be able to ascribe that failure to a lack of ability (and to market rejection) or to unwillingness by policymakers or politicians. Once we replace top-down fear and sentiment with causal narratives, systemic collapse begins to look like the high bar it truly is.

- *Don't underestimate policymakers.* Modern central bankers have grown to embrace a philosophy of trying until something works—particularly with economic stimulus. To believe they persist in error, a prerequisite for a systemic failure, we would need to believe their independence is compromised, or that a grave conceptual misunderstanding dominates their thinking.

- *Know the politics of stimulus—crises help.* No political party wants to be blamed for letting the economy burn while they stand by. An existential crisis will align interests and grease dealmaking to deliver even politically unpalatable stimulus. For tactical stimulus, the political calculus is very different, as we will see.

- *Be realistic about the odds of market rejection.* Markets may reject stimulus, but in times of crisis, debt markets in the United States and other advanced economies often rally rather than sell off. (See also the discussion about structural inflation in chapter 12 and about US dollar reserve-currency status in chapter 20.) This could change under extreme circumstances, but it is exceedingly unlikely.

The capacity for existential stimulus won't fail easily, and leaders should be skeptical of ubiquitous narratives of systemic collapse. It is a different story for the *tactical* stimulus that is used to manage the cycle. We turn to those risks in the next chapter.

CHAPTER 11

Why Tactical Stimulus Sputters

As we argued in the preceding chapter, though the risk of failure is low in the case of existential stimulus, the outlook for tactical stimulus is decidedly less robust. In the 2010s, tactical stimulus was deployed with the reliability of a well-oiled machine, delivering a steady stream of tax cuts and accommodative policy rates (including reactive and preemptive rate cuts with hair-trigger sensitivity), as well as enlarged central bank balance sheets courtesy of quantitative easing. In the future, this tendency to opportunistically goose the cycle will be more constrained by risk. Though the tactical stimulus machine is not broken, it is sputtering.[1]

Consider the crisis that played out in the United Kingdom in the fall of 2022, when market reaction to a misguided stimulus package forced the British chancellor to resign and, eventually, the prime minister as well.[2] The offense was not their use of standard policy instruments (a mix of tax breaks and additional government spending) to lean against a looming recession. Rather, it was their policy mindset, which was still stuck in the 2010s, a time when such tactical stimulus knew no constraints. The politicians displayed classic willingness to push stimulus, but their ability to do so was vetoed by the financial markets in which they had proposed to borrow.

Though we think the bar is higher for this to happen in the United States, the British experience demonstrated that the era of riskless tactical stimulus may be over. In the future, the risk of a binding constraint on tactical stimulus will be higher than it was in the 2010s. Moreover, as we will see in this chapter, a market veto is only one of four risks to tactical stimulus. Each will likely be more binding than in the past.

Business leaders and investors seeking to understand the ups and downs of the economic cycle must have an active understanding of the shifting nature of tactical stimulus. This need for understanding is urgent, as supercharged tactical stimulus of the past has created a false sense of comfort. The risks to stimulus that we discuss here always existed, but a confluence of favorable conditions kept them in check. This is changing.

Four Ways the Tactical Stimulus Machine Can Sputter

Figure 11.1 illustrates the four drivers of tactical stimulus, making use of the willingness and ability constraints we developed in chapter 9 and applied to existential stimulus in chapter 10. There are two risks to willingness:

- *Monetary objection:* Independent and well-run central banks may be unwilling to goose the economy tactically with rate cuts when inflation is too high.

- *Political objection:* Political support is always harder to align for tactical stimulus than it is for crisis-driven existential rescue efforts.

Even if stimulus clears the hurdles of monetary or political willingness, its ability to boost growth can still be at risk of being offset by two forces:

- *Market offset:* Markets may reject fiscal stimulus by driving up rates and neutralizing the impact of any new spending.

- *Policy offset:* Monetary policymakers may offset the impact of fiscal stimulus by tightening (that is, by raising short-term rates), if the stimulus is seen as inflationary.

We think the four constraints on tactical stimulus apply to all economies and all situations. What differs is the context that determines how serious and binding the constraints are. Awareness of these constraints may be modest in

FIGURE **11.1**

Risks to tactical stimulus

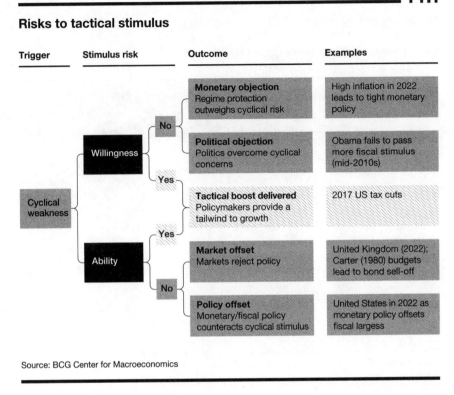

Trigger	Stimulus risk	Outcome	Examples
		Monetary objection Regime protection outweighs cyclical risk	High inflation in 2022 leads to tight monetary policy
	Willingness — No	**Political objection** Politics overcome cyclical concerns	Obama fails to pass more fiscal stimulus (mid-2010s)
Cyclical weakness	— Yes	**Tactical boost delivered** Policymakers provide a tailwind to growth	2017 US tax cuts
	Ability — Yes	**Market offset** Markets reject policy	United Kingdom (2022); Carter (1980) budgets lead to bond sell-off
	— No	**Policy offset** Monetary/fiscal policy counteracts cyclical stimulus	United States in 2022 as monetary policy offsets fiscal largess

Source: BCG Center for Macroeconomics

the minds of many, because rarely has tactical stimulus been constrained in recent history.

Monetary Objection: The End of the Free Fed Put?

When inflation is low, or too low, a tactical lowering of the policy rate to goose or protect growth—a so-called Fed put—carries little risk.[3] The penalty for cutting interest rates—more inflation—would actually be welcome. That is why the Fed put became a reliable engine of the stimulus machine in the 2010s. With low growth and inflation biased to the downside— inflation struggled to reach its 2% target—the cost of the put was arguably negative.

In 2019, for example, the Fed responded to an economic slowdown and an equity sell-off with a series of rate cuts—a controversial but defensible

FIGURE **11.2**

Monetary policy defends inflation regime, not cycle, in 2022

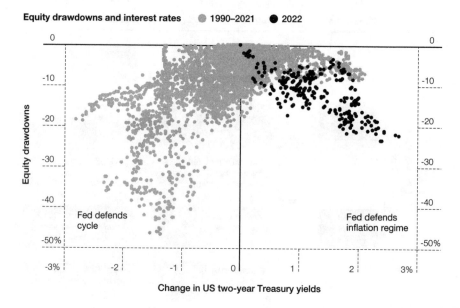

Equity drawdowns and interest rates   ● 1990–2021   ● 2022

Note: Drawdown measured as negative deviation from six-month rolling max of the S&P 500. Change in US Treasury yields is the difference between the measured period and date of prior equity max. Data from 1990 through 2022.
Source: S&P, Federal Reserve, analysis by BCG Center for Macroeconomics

decision given that inflation was below its 2% target even though the expansion was in its ninth year and unemployment was very low. Tactical stimulus was essentially a free form of insurance.

Fast-forward to 2022, and the United States found itself in a different position. As in 2019, the economic expansion was perceived as wobbly. But this time, with inflation above its target, the Fed did not rush to defend growth. Instead, it raised the policy rate to keep a lid on prices, turning monetary policy into a key economic headwind. The willingness to help flagging growth had evaporated because inflation concerns now outweighed growth concerns.

Figure 11.2 illustrates how the prioritization of inflation over growth in 2022 stood in sharp contrast to anything seen in the prior three decades. Historically, when the equity market fell significantly (*y* axis), short-term Treasury yields (a proxy for monetary policy, *x* axis) nearly always declined—

that is, the Fed moved to defend the cycle by slashing rates. But in 2022, yields continued to move higher even as the equity market sold off materially—the Fed was prioritizing the defense of the inflation regime over the defense of the cycle (see the dark dots representing 2022 in figure 11.2). The authorities preferred the risk of a near-term recession to the risk of sustained inflation.

In other words, when inflation returned in 2022, the Fed put was replaced by Fed pain, as the central bank looked to use falling asset prices as a means of slowing the economy and reining in inflation. That is not because the postpandemic inflation spike represented a shift to a broken inflation regime (see chapter 12) or a likelihood of this occurring in the years ahead. But it did represent a shift in inflation risk that needed a response. And inflation is likely to retain its upside bias—the opposite of the 2010s environment—requiring more-frequent policy tightness (see chapter 13). This is one reason to think that the tactical stimulus machine will not work as smoothly as we'd grown accustomed to in the 2010s.

Political Objection: Risks to Tactical Stimulus Will Remain

In the previous chapter we saw that when systemic crises threaten, political interests align quickly, and forceful existential stimulus is likely to be delivered. But opportunistic, tactical goosing lacks such forcing mechanism. It can be held back by differences in the parties' views on how to stimulate—for example, tax cuts versus spending increases—and by partisan political calculus. Divided government can limit tactical stimulus.

Consider the years 2011–2013. The structural overhang of the financial crisis (see chapter 4) translated into a sluggish recovery—a classic context for fiscal stimulus. But political willingness to enact stimulus was not there. The Democrats had lost the House of Representatives in 2010, which put an end to more expansionary fiscal policy. Republicans objected in the name of preventing greater deficits.

In 2017, as if to provide a textbook demonstration of the overtly political nature of stimulus, unified Republican control of the executive and legislative branches created the conditions for a tax cut aimed at boosting growth. Commenting on his party's earlier rejection of an Obama stimulus,

Republican Representative Mark Walker said of the deficit, "It's a great talking point when you have an administration that's Democrat-led . . . it's a little different now that Republicans have both houses and the administration."[4] Of course, this partisan opportunism describes both sides of the political divide.

As mentioned, unified control of the executive and legislative branches must be reinforced by party discipline. Consider the obstacles encountered by the Biden administration—even when it had unified control of government after the 2020 election. Its initial ambitions for a new New Deal were thwarted because of resistance within the Democratic party.[5] More-conservative members of the party rejected supersize stimulus, even if a significant boost eventually came in the form of the Inflation Reduction Act (which predominantly finances investments in infrastructure and the energy transition). Should we expect the future of political constraints on stimulus to change? There is less certainty here than with the other three risks discussed in this chapter. Political interests and power have always been, and always will be, in flux. How these interact with the politics of stimulus will depend on the idiosyncratic circumstances in Washington at any given time.

Market Offset: Return of the Bond Vigilantes?

Even if the hurdles of willingness are cleared, stimulus still faces the constraints of ability. As already mentioned, markets can offset fiscal stimulus that is perceived as misguided, with higher interest rates and tighter financial conditions.

The veto power of bond markets over fiscal stimulus has a long and proud history—so much so that it has inspired the respect of generations of politicians and policymakers. Bond traders skeptical of fiscal profligacy—sometimes referred to as bond vigilantes—can sell government debt and push up interest rates when they perceive spending plans to be stoking inflation and eroding the value of long-term bonds they hold.[6] By pushing up interest rates, bond vigilantes essentially neutralize the impact that stimulus has on the economy.[7]

Prominent in the 1970s and 1980s, the bond vigilantes—gradually—became a shrinking threat to politicians as structurally high inflation was conquered and reset to low levels. James Carville, President Bill Clinton's strategist, still paid respect to the bond vigilantes in the early 1990s, famously stating he would want to be reincarnated as the bond market, because "you can intimidate everybody."[8] But as inflation waned, so did the intimidation. By the early 2000s, inflation was so low and inflation expectations so thoroughly anchored that Vice President Dick Cheney reportedly felt unencumbered enough by bond vigilantes to declared that "deficits don't matter."[9]

Has the return of the bond vigilantes already happened? Many commentators thought so in the fall of 2023, when jumping bond yields were readily ascribed to high debt levels, bloated deficits, and dysfunctional politics. Some even claimed that postpandemic inflation had destroyed the attractiveness of US Treasuries, and that global reserve holders were causing the rate spike by selling their US securities. In our view, that was a misguided interpretation. Higher rates were driven by the cyclical and structural strength of the US economy and idiosyncratic financial drivers.[10]

To be clear, the veto power of bond vigilantes is a matter of degree, not kind. The context matters. For softer versions of bond-vigilante power, we don't need to return to an era of a broken inflation regime like the 1970s and early 1980s. But the power of a market veto will still be strongly influenced by the strength of the inflation regime. Thus, the rejection of President Carter's budget by the markets in 1980 occurred in the context of a regime of high and structural inflation. When the inflation regime is weak, the power of bond vigilantes will be strong. This points to the growing risk of markets offsetting stimulus in the future. Though we argue later that a broken inflation regime is an unlikely outcome (chapter 12), upwardly biased *cyclical* inflation is not (chapter 13), making market vetoes more likely than in the 2010s.

Policy Offset: Central Bankers versus Politicians

Finally, tactical fiscal stimulus can be nullified if central banks offset its impact. Just as central banks may refrain from their own (monetary) stimulus when price stability is in danger (what we identify as monetary objection above), so they may also offset politicians' fiscal stimulus if they see it driving inflation.

A recent illustration of central bankers offsetting the efforts of politicians is the Biden administration's stimulus of early 2021. This fiscal effort, spurred by the Democrats' unified control of Washington, was a brazen bet on super-charging an already strong Covid recovery—and it did spur growth.[11] While that part of the bet paid off, it did not pay out fully, as the stimulus contributed to the postpandemic inflation surge that resulted mostly from supply constraints. Because inflation rose and proved stickier than hoped, the Fed aggressively moved to slow the economy in 2022, undoing some of the effect of Biden's stimulus.

This constraint on fiscal stimulus is likely to persist as long as the economy is pushing its potential and inflation risk remains biased to the upside. Fiscal policy may be more beneficial when it is less ambitious—when the spending mix is optimized, but the deficit is held in check.

UBI, MMT: The Stimulus Dreams of Yesterday

One way to see the constrained future of tactical stimulus is to analyze the risks above and how they have already asserted themselves. Another way is to look at former ideas and dreams for even greater stimulus—ideas and dreams that are no more.

During the 2010s, chronically slow growth, ascribed to structural demand insufficiencies, triggered calls to expand the already turbocharged tactical-stimulus machine.[12] Specifically, proposals for a universal basic income (UBI) and advocacy for modern monetary theory (MMT) illustrate how far this debate went.[13] During the Democratic presidential primaries in 2020, both concepts moved from the fringes of the policy debate to the main stage.

Both policy proposals are, in retrospect, an illustration of how unencumbered policy discourse had become from the stimulus constraints we outlined above. Both UBI and MMT seek to permanently entrench procyclical stimulus—not as a tactical choice, but as a constant and automatic force. In the case of UBI, stimulus would flow permanently via transfer payments (incomes) to individuals irrespective of labor-market participation.

In the case of MMT, the argument is that governments need not tax to spend—they can rely instead on central banks simply to create money. This money creation should be pushed to the point where all resources in the economy are fully utilized, and workers are fully employed. Taxes should only be used to moderate inflation. Such thinking requires a dramatic—and, in our view, unworkable—organization of fiscal and monetary operations.

While these policy ideas will not disappear, their appeal has fallen in a world with less labor-market slack, more cyclical inflation, and diminished tactical-stimulus capacity. We no longer discuss the need for a new set of stimulus tools. Yet, should an era of slack and sluggish inflation remove the risks and constraints from tactical stimulus, such ideas may very well return.

Remember, Tactical Stimulus Will Be Harder to Come By

Throughout the cycle, tactical stimulus often dominates the debate. Understanding its dynamics, chances of success, and risks of failure matters when assessing tactical growth prospects and cyclical risks. As with existential stimulus, the concepts of ability and willingness provide the analytical approach. Unlike in the case of existential stimulus, these foundations have shifted materially. The automaticity of stimulus is likely gone. Whereas in the decade prior to Covid, tactical stimulus, particularly monetary stimulus, was nearly unconstrained, the present decade has already seen more constraint, and that is likely to remain.

- *Upside inflation bias delivers constraints.* The free Fed put has been put away. Monetary policymakers are unwilling to stimulate at the first sign of trouble as long as inflation remains elevated.

- *Political calculus remains.* Political partisanship and differing visions of how to use fiscal stimulus have always existed—and will continue to lower the willingness to use tactical stimulus when political power is not unified.

- *Bond vigilantes are making a comeback.* Though their power isn't fully restored—and will not be unless the inflation regime breaks—there is a more credible prospect of bond markets reacting negatively to egregious fiscal stimulus, except in crisis situations.

- *Monetary policy offsets fiscal policy.* When fiscal policy drives upside inflation, it will be at risk of being offset by monetary policymakers as they look to rein in price growth—leaving little net impact. Such political independence is required to allow the Fed to protect the inflation regime.

Postpandemic inflation has already constrained tactical stimulus. If inflation were to become durably entrenched, stimulus policies would be even more constrained. What it would take for the structurally anchored inflation regime to end is where we turn next.

CHAPTER 12

Breaking the Inflation Regime Is (Very) Hard

Low and stable inflation is the cornerstone regime of the good-macro world. We've already seen how it enables stimulus ability and cycle longevity. In later chapters we'll see its role in debt sustainability and modest interest rates (which contribute to high valuations).

We have called this anchored inflation regime the Volcker inheritance, a reference both to Paul Volcker, who reanchored broken inflation expectations in the early 1980s, and to the enormous structural benefit this has conferred on generations since. As shown in figure 12.1, the low inflation regime also powerfully anchored interest rates. Let this one regime break and a cascade of structural downgrades will follow. All recessions are bad, and financial ones particularly ugly as we've seen, but a break in the inflation regime is worse than simply a recession. A persistent shift to high and volatile inflation would bring an era of stagnation and an entirely altered business environment—much like the bad macro of the 1970s to which Volcker put an end.[1] It must not happen.

When inflation soars, as it did postpandemic and as seen in figure 12.1, it commands the attention of leaders. Above all, executives and investors must focus on the right question: Is this a structural regime break or a cyclical spike in inflation? A structural inflation regime break is very different from

FIGURE **12.1**

The Volcker inheritance

US inflation and interest rates

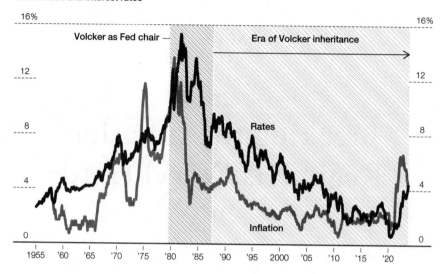

Note: Inflation is core CPI and through August 2023; rates are 10-year Treasury yields and through September 2023.
Source: BLS, Federal Reserve, analysis by BCG Center for Macroeconomics

an episode of cyclical inflation, which can be sharp and painful but is not entrenched and does not have the same macroeconomic consequences.

We must not conflate the two—they deliver fundamentally different challenges for firms and investors. Distinguishing effectively between them is what this chapter is about—before we turn to cyclical inflation more comprehensively in chapter 13.

Conflation of a structural inflation break and a cyclical surge was exactly what happened in public discourse as inflation lurched higher after the pandemic. Having seen no significant inflation in over a generation, commentators feverishly embraced the "return to the 1970s" narrative—a reference to a bad-macro world where elevated inflation was expected to persist in the long run. But equating high inflation with structural inflation made for a false alarm that generated misguided fears and actions and spurred calls for policy to preemptively trigger a recession to bring inflation down. The key argument here is that, fortunately, a regime break remains a high bar. Such a break would require persistent mistakes from policymakers and neglect over time—an unlikely prospect.

Unlike forecasting cyclical inflation with accuracy, which is not possible (see next chapter), making the structural-versus–cyclical call is. Here we describe what to look for in identifying structural risk. The scare of the early 2020s was a false alarm, and one that was possible to diagnose at the time—despite the many twists and turns in the story.

Distinguishing Structural from Cyclical Inflation

How can one tell if inflation is structural? Perhaps surprisingly, whether price growth is running at 5%, 10%, or even 20% will not answer that question. To derive a set of meaningful criteria, we juxtapose two inflation episodes in figure 12.2: that of the 1940s, a cyclical inflation squeeze, and that of the 1970s, a structural inflation regime break. These offer durable insight about what differentiates cyclical from structural inflation.

FIGURE 12.2

Cyclical or structural? The level of inflation doesn't tell

1940s: Up and down (bottlenecks)
Inflation squeezes higher, then resets . . . bond yields never respond

1960s/1970s:: Up and up (structural break)
Inflation higher and higher . . . bond yields reflect sustained upward pressure

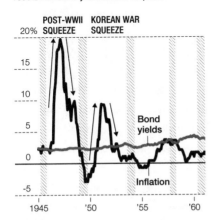

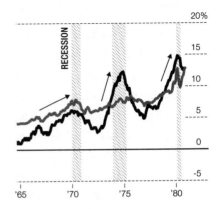

Note: Inflation is Y/Y percent change in CPI; bonds yields on long-term government bonds.
Source: FRB, BLS, NBER, analysis by BCG Center for Macroeconomics

First, let's recognize that inflation in the late 1940s was far higher than it ever was in the 1970s—hitting nearly 20%, when a year prior it had been under 3%. Second, since 1940s inflation was not entrenched, it was ultimately transitory, even if it lasted several years. Third, it didn't require an overwhelming monetary shock to be brought down and didn't come with an era of slack and stagflation, as did the bad-macro inflation of the 1970s. It's fair to say that even though 1940s inflation was much higher and emerged much faster, it was nowhere near as problematic as the inflation of the 1970s.

Of course, much of the above cannot be known in real time. But we can ask three questions to help decide whether inflation is likely to become structural:

> *Demand/supply mismatch.* Are supply and demand disrupted in unusual ways? Such mismatches are significant differentiators of cyclical and structural inflation. In the late 1940s, the inflation surge was driven by an abrupt shift to peacetime consumer demand, but supply was unable to pivot as quickly from its wartime footing.[2] The demand surge and resulting bottlenecks squeezed price growth to 20%. As the bottlenecks eased, so did inflation. In contrast, 1970s inflation did not begin with a sudden mismatch of supply and demand. Instead, the inflation regime cracked and crumbled gradually as fiscal stimulus pressed on an already tight economy, and monetary policy kept accommodating it. Paradoxically, a particularly sharp inflation spike is more likely to be indicative of a cyclical problem, not a structural shift.

> *Inflation expectations.* Have long-term inflation expectations unanchored? Expectations are indicators of whether inflation is structural. When inflation is expected to durably persist, those expectations establish a baseline for wage and price negotiations, ensuring that inflation endures. Despite high inflation, long-term expectations did not seem to move higher in the 1940s. While today we have more direct measures of expectations, in the past, stable expectations were suggested by flat yields on long-term government bonds (bond yields embed the compensation for inflation that investors demand; see gray lines in figure 12.2). While the Treasury market was held down by monetary policy for years after World War II, it is reasonable to conclude from flat bond yields that investors expected inflation to mod-

erate in the medium run—and it did.[3] But starting in the late 1960s and throughout the 1970s, bond yields rose in near lockstep with realized inflation as expectations unanchored. Upward moves in inflation were expected to be sticky, indicating a broken regime.

Monetary-policy signals. Will monetary policy push back against price growth? As economies evolve and absorb shocks, central banks are the ultimate guardians of price stability. They do make mistakes, including grave ones, but the key is their persistence in pushing back against inflation. Any prioritization of other policy objectives above price stability when inflation is uncomfortably high would be a serious warning sign—particularly if central bankers' political independence appears compromised.[4] The early 1950s saw monetary policymakers fight to free themselves from the control of the Treasury Department so that they could raise the yield cap and push back against inflation.[5] Conversely, in the late 1960s—the key window to what delivered the inflation of the 1970s—monetary policymakers *coordinated with* fiscal policymakers and failed to push back against rising inflation. Persistently (too) easy monetary policy led to a crack, crumble, and collapse of the inflation regime, as political pressure was combined with conceptual error—a belief in a long-run trade-off between inflation and unemployment. This unholy brew allowed policymakers to persist with too-easy policy for a sustained period of time.[6] Policy will never be just right—errors will always occur—but if policy is committed to price stability above all else and willing to keep at it, such commitment will serve as a powerful guardrail against regime breaks.[7] Inflation, particularly structural inflation, is a monetary *policy* phenomenon.[8]

Postpandemic Inflation Spike Never Looked Like a Regime Break

The 1940s and 1970s are not simply historically intriguing.[9] They offer a sound (if fallible) lens through which to assess the structural risks of inflation. In 2021 and 2022, when fears of a regime break moved to the top of the agenda for many, the problem could be boiled down to one question:

Was the post–Covid inflation surge more like that of the 1940s (cyclical) or more like that of the 1970s (structural)?[10] We return to the three analytical angles above:

First, the Covid recovery delivered an epic mismatch of demand and supply, similar to distortions seen both after World War II and as the Korean War commenced, upon which consumers, fearing rationing, rushed out to buy goods. Figure 12.3 highlights overshooting demand for goods during the pandemic (left panel), stoked by excessive fiscal stimulus and pent-up demand, which coincided with a supply crunch, as seen in depressed and falling inventories (middle panel). This unusual situation conferred atypical pricing power on firms, who normally risk losing market share with any rise in price. But when strong demand met constrained supply, all firms could raise prices without losing market share. Collectively, this delivered an infla-

FIGURE 12.3

Mismatch of demand (surge) and supply (crunch) opened a window of pricing power, then went into reverse

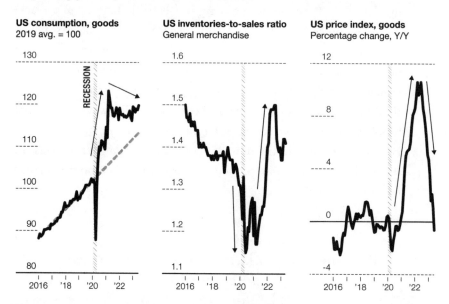

Note: Consumption is real personal consumption expenditures in US$(2012), and price index is PCE goods. Trendline based on 2015–2019 linear regression. Consumption and price data through June 2023. Inventory data through May 2023.
Source: BEA, Census Bureau, NBER, analysis by BCG Center for Macroeconomics

tion spike. Yet, as the demand overshoot wore off and inventories rebuilt (and overbuilt), pricing power waned—as did inflation.

Second, long-term inflation expectations never materially moved—something visible in real time. Figure 12.4 shows realized inflation versus market-implied expectations between six and 10 years in the future (the introduction of inflation-protected bonds, so-called TIPS, in the late 1990s, allows inflation compensation to be measured directly). Even as inflation climbed to over 9%, a stunning 40-year high, investors never believed that we had entered a new era akin to the 1970s. It is worth noting that consumers' expectations were aligned, as seen in survey data (right panel of figure 12.4). Consumers' five-years-ahead expectations gave little indication of anticipated unanchoring.

Third, monetary policy. Here public discourse strongly felt that the Fed was asleep at the wheel and was delivering a regime break. Yes, against a series of exogenous shocks, including the Ukraine war and its energy impact,

FIGURE **12.4**

Covid inflation surge did not move long-term inflation expectations meaningfully, neither for markets nor for consumers

Market expectations and CPI

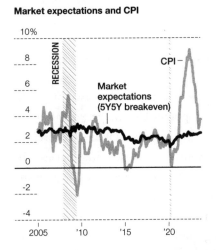

Consumer expectations and CPI

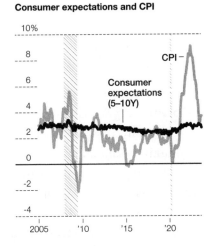

Note: CPI is Y/Y. 5Y5Y = expectation for five years of inflation starting five years into the future.
University of Michigan survey medians (right). Data through September 2023.
Source: BLS, Bloomberg, University of Michigan, NBER, analysis by BCG Center for Macroeconomics

the Fed's rate-hike campaign started too late. But was its sluggishness a credible driver of a regime break? The Fed was not slow to hike because it had deprioritized price stability or because it had been politically undermined. The idea that the Fed would sit idly by as the inflation regime cracked was never credible in our view.[11]

Despite not presiding over an inflation regime break, the Fed faced the biggest challenge to the anchored inflation regime in a generation. This may say more about how deeply anchored the regime is than the severity of the crisis, but it is never comfortable or wise to dismiss structural risks lightly—not least because structural inflation will always start out as cyclical inflation. Moreover, the path of inflation is never linear and is subject to shocks—the risks and drivers will shift over time. After the initial price surge of 2021, additional challenges—externally, the energy-price shock delivered by the Ukraine war, and internally, wage growth driven by labor shortages—meant inflation's peak was higher than it would have been and came later than it otherwise would have. And the longer inflation persisted, the greater the possibility that a crack in the regime would emerge.

Of the three angles discussed above, policymakers' role is the most controversial, most debated, most difficult to judge, and ultimately the most important. Let's look at the role of policymakers in more detail, and the choices they face.

Regime Insurance Is Available but Costly

Though a regime break is much less likely than public discourse suggests, the asymmetry of that risk (low) versus its potential damage (very high) is striking. Why allow any chance of a break if the downside is so severe?

Intuitively appealing, this type of reasoning is challenging, because its logical policy prescription is to trigger a preemptive recession to unwind inflation—rather than trying to gradually cool an overheated economy (a so-called soft landing). Indeed, in 2021 and 2022, some argued for such draconian measures to reduce risk of a regime break, fearing that monetary policy wasn't taking inflation seriously.[12] But policymakers' sluggish response reflected a belief that inflation was driven completely by one-off factors; it did not reflect any doubt at the Fed about prioritizing price stability. And policymakers' aggressive and sustained response when inflation broadened clearly showed their commitment to price stability and their seriousness about protecting the inflation regime.

In an economy with well-anchored long-term inflation expectations, we find a preemptive strike hard to justify. The problem is its cost. An inflation-busting recession exacts a steep price in terms of human welfare. If inflation is well-anchored and a structural break in the regime is a distant possibility, why pay that price?[13]

Paul Volcker, who repaired America's broken inflation regime in the early 1980s, is often invoked to argue for preemptive strikes. But his draconian measures were not preventive; they were curative. The disease was evident: it had been metastasizing in the economy since the late 1960s. What Volcker did was to *reanchor* a broken regime—not defend a healthy one. It's a different calculation if a regime break is only a possibility, not an accomplished fact.

The cost of forcing inflation down is high—not just in terms of a recession, but also in terms of the expansion that could have been. If the cycle had been cut short in March 2022, when the Fed began its belated rate-hiking cycle, the economy would have missed out on an exceptionally strong labor market that benefited the bottom of the income distribution most.[14] By the fourth quarter of 2023, the US economy still had experienced no recession, while inflation had fallen from 9.1% to near 3%, with unemployment still near decade lows.

The US economy's performance in 2023 clearly fell within the definition of a soft landing and contradicted the claims of naysayers who argued that a meaningful recession was necessary to get inflation lower. In June 2022, the economist Larry Summers said, "We need five years of unemployment above 5% to contain inflation—in other words, we need two years of 7.5% unemployment or five years of 6% unemployment or one year of 10% unemployment."[15] While another recession will inevitably come, 2023 demonstrated that the chance of achieving a successful soft landing is worth the risk—provided one has gone through the exercise of gauging whether the inflation regime can hold. In the case of the post-Covid economy, the risks of structural inflation were overstated and the Fed was right to attempt a soft landing.

We think Paul Volcker's legacy matters in a different way here. Today, policymakers don't have to be so draconian precisely because they enjoy that Volcker inheritance. His actions set the US economy on a path of secular disinflation, with deeply anchored inflation expectations—the cornerstone of the good-macro world we highlighted at the start of this chapter. Undoubtedly, the Fed dipped into that inheritance in 2021 and 2022. Its response to the inflation surge was late in hindsight, but the Volcker inheritance meant expectations were anchored enough to absorb such a misstep. The important thing is that the Fed looks like a good steward of the inheritance, having run monetary policy tight enough to guide inflation back down. The Fed chose to reinvest in price stability, not squander it. That, we believe, was predictable to any thoughtful observer of the central bank.

So, What Breaks the Inflation Regime?

Future regime risk ultimately rests in the hands of monetary policymakers. Will they squander or reinforce the Volcker inheritance? A return to structurally unanchored inflation cannot be ruled out, but such a shift would not be the result of a single shock or policy misstep.

To move from elevated cyclical inflation to embedded structural inflation will require a persistent failure of monetary policy to push back against entrenching price growth. This does not occur overnight.[16] It is a process of years, not months or quarters, during which policy sticks to the wrong course. Recall that the 1970s inflation was not just a product of the oil spikes and the shock of Nixon taking the United States off the gold standard. That characterization is too simplistic. Its roots went back to a policy that wanted both guns (Vietnam War) and butter (Great Society social programs), and to a monetary policy that lacked the courage to fight inflation as it set in. As early as 1966, the Fed *eased* monetary policy even though inflation was uncomfortably high.[17]

What lies at the root of this sort of persistent error? In assessing structural risks, the deprioritization of price stability in favor of employment (or anything else) is the key to watch. If such a deprioritization occurs while long-term inflation expectations are too high and rising, the tracks have been laid for disaster. Another key to the disaster of the 1970s was that, once inflation had entrenched itself, the Fed's leaders viewed the price of reestablishing a healthy regime as too high.[18]

Today policymakers are vulnerable to error as well, but two realities make a persistent policy failure less likely than in the past. First, the Fed today is more independent. It's not that politicians wouldn't like to lean on central bankers to accommodate their fiscal urges, but that such leaning is discouraged, particularly by monetary policymakers.[19] In the past, a closer fiscal-monetary relationship was seen as not only reasonable but appropriate. Second, the fact that monetary policymakers see it as their job to deliver economic pain, if needed, to protect the regime also makes the risk of sustained error smaller. While policymakers are far from infallible, their awareness of their own fallibility and their prioritization of price stability help keep regime risk contained.

Remember, a Regime Break Is a Process, Not an Event

Though an inflation regime break is possible and is a risk that needs to be taken seriously, we should recognize that public discourse overstates the risk too readily. During the postpandemic inflation squeeze, a regime break was routinely portrayed as an accomplished fact. Leaders need to approach such claims with skepticism. As cyclical inflation is likely to be upwardly biased in the years ahead (see next chapter), the question of regime break will reappear. Leaders will be forced to make the cyclical-versus-structural call more frequently.

Above all, they should understand that an inflation regime break is a process, not an event. Here are some of the key takeaways:

- *High inflation says little about regime break.* The height of the spike or the speed with which it is reached can be disconcerting, but those tell us little about whether the spike is the beginning of structural inflection. An enormous squeeze (like that which produced the 1940s spike) can reset entirely, whereas much lower inflation could signal the onset of structural decay (as was the case in the late 1960s).

- *Trust the signals, not the headlines.* Though not fail-safe, the underlying drivers of demand-supply mismatches, inflation expectations, and policy actions reveal a lot about structural risks. Signals, not headlines, are where focus should remain.

- *Have a little faith in monetary policy.* An inflation regime break requires one or more of the following: persistent misjudging of appropriate policy; prioritization of objectives other than price stability; a loss of independence. All these are worth watching—but we should not begin by assuming they have happened. And remember that preemptive strikes against regime risk are costly: they may be warranted to avoid a rise in unemployment and are not a failure to appreciate the Volcker inheritance.

- *Be clear on the business implications.* Inflation reflects the collective pricing power of firms. Leaders who believe in the false alarm of a structural inflation crisis in 2021 and 2022 made a miscalculation as pricing power waned. That said, greater upside bias and volatility of cyclical inflation make managing price movements more important than it has been in many years.

While the structural inflation regime remains intact—and we see it as likely to stay that way—inflation has changed in important ways relative to the 2010s. A new upward bias in cyclical inflation is what we address next.

CHAPTER 13

Living with Upside Inflation Bias

T hough there has been no postpandemic inflation regime break, and though we think the risk of one remains low (as argued in the preceding chapter), that doesn't mean cyclical inflation will return to a pre-2020 pattern. That pattern, decidedly tilted to the downside, is likely a thing of the past.

For much of the 2010s, inflation struggled to reach the Fed's 2% target and at times was uncomfortably low. But there is a strong likelihood that this downward bias of cyclical inflation has reversed into an upward bias as an era of tightness in the real economy frequently pushes inflation above the 2% policy target. We see this upside bias as persisting for years, even as price growth will continue to fluctuate with cyclical conditions (including to the downside and below the target). Though nowhere near as damaging as an inflation regime break, the reemergence of cyclical inflation, requiring monetary-policy vigilance and intervention, represents a material shift in the business environment.

How can cyclical inflation risks be assessed? Unlike making the call about structural versus cyclical inflation, discussed in the preceding chapter, accurately predicting the path of near-term inflation is not feasible. Rather than

relying on forecasts, which fail regularly, leaders should frame cyclical inflation in terms of biases and tendencies. Ultimately, those hoping to effectively
gauge and appreciate the consequences of inflation must also factor in the
reactions of monetary policymakers. As a result, this chapter also discusses
two instruments of "Fed watching."

Why Cyclical Inflation Can't Be Reliably Predicted

Why not just rely on forecasts when looking at near-term inflation? Cyclical inflation is hard—or, more accurately, impossible—to predict consistently. We don't just say that because we ourselves underestimated the
post-Covid inflation surge. Nor is it merely that shocks, including wars and
supply-chain disruptions, can upset prices unpredictably. Even without
shocks, there is no framework that provides reliable forecasts of inflation's
path. Figure 13.1 demonstrates this by comparing the one-year-ahead forecast

FIGURE **13.1**

Inflation forecasts failed before, during, and after the pandemic

Consumer Price Index and consensus forecast
Change, Y/Y

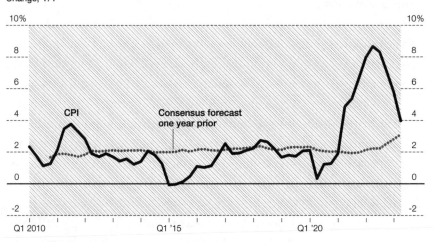

Note: Data through Q2 2023.
Source: Bloomberg consensus (median forecast), BLS, analysis by BCG Center for Macroeconomics

since 2010 with realized inflation. The forecast is wrong most of the time, and significantly so—even before the postpandemic inflation surge, when price growth was a relatively quiet affair. And when it was right, it was because realized inflation coincided with the 2% inflation target—even a broken clock is right twice a day.

The postpandemic inflation surge fits this pattern of unpredictable change. Yes, the fiscal policy–induced demand overshoot was visible and led some to warn against coming inflation in early 2021.[1] But was that warning for the right reasons? The supply constraints that unfolded simultaneously were less predictable—both the sustained hiccups in physical supply chains and the convoluted recovery in labor participation that gradually came to light later that year. Certainly, the war in Ukraine and the resulting energy shock were unpredictable and caused inflation to peak later and higher than it would have. The forecasters who congratulated themselves for ascribing inflation to fiscal stimulus were simultaneously taking credit for a range of supply shocks that they did not anticipate.

Rather than looking for forecasters who get it right or looking for a model that works, one should understand that no model captures the path of cyclical inflation well. Throughout this book we strive to give the reader frameworks, models, regimes, and drivers (see chapter 2) that capture macroeconomic dynamics. While we often argue that these tools can't provide final answers, here we go further and argue that the drivers are too unreliable and the mechanics too opaque to go beyond pointing toward directional biases. Let's see why common approaches have failed to predict inflation accurately.

First, monetarism. Milton Friedman's famous quote that "*inflation is always and everywhere a monetary phenomenon* in the sense that it is and can be produced only by a more rapid increase in the quantity of money than in output*" (emphasis in original) seems to have been burned into the minds of many, including those in the business community.[2] Yet, despite its logic, the dictum has been internalized in too simplified a form. Money will play a role in inflation. But knowing what has happened to money (which is harder than one might think, given the multiple measures of money and the complexity of the financial system) tells you almost nothing (with any confidence) about what has happened or will happen to inflation. The linkages are simply too complex. It remains true that easy money risks nudging inflation higher and tight money nudging it lower. But as figure 13.2 demonstrates,

FIGURE **13.2**

Monetarism suggested positive correlation of money supply and price growth, but that is not visible empirically

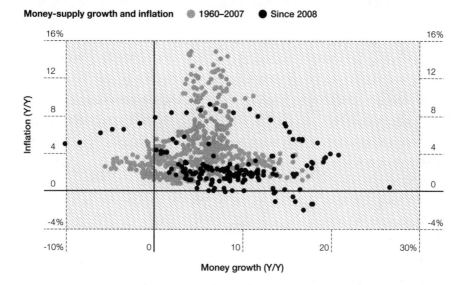

Money-supply growth and inflation   ● 1960–2007   ● Since 2008

Note: Inflation as measured by the Consumer Price Index. Money growth is represented by the change in M1.
X axis truncated at 30% for scale. Data through June 2023.
Source: Historical Statistics of the United States, Federal Reserve Board, BLS, analysis by BCG Center for Macroeconomics

there is no precision to this link that would allow us to predict inflation reliably: the correlation of money growth and inflation simply isn't visible. Inflation may be always and everywhere a monetary phenomenon, but money is also always and everywhere a weak and unreliable predictor of inflation.[3]

Second, consider the variety of quantitative prediction models—most often used at banks to build near-term forecasts. (We discussed the topic of physics envy in chapter 2, of which this is a good example.) What is most noteworthy about such models is that inertia is often the most powerful variable. Put simply, the forecast's foundation comes from saying that tomorrow's inflation will be what it was today. That works well when inflation is stable (and in part explains why one-year-ahead forecasts hug so closely to 2%; see figure 13.1), but probably says more about the weakness of models than anything else. While there is value in these models, particularly in understanding details about the composition of inflation, they don't offer reliable precision about the path ahead.

Third, consider the famous Phillips curve. This model is based on a belief that inflation and labor-market tightness are linked. A lower unemployment rate means higher inflation. Here too there is valid logic—if low unemployment rates embolden workers to demand higher wages, and if wage gains outstrip productivity gains, then higher inflation is a likely outcome. However, as unemployment soared and then fell after the global financial crisis, there was only a weak impact on inflation in either direction. And in the postpandemic inflation scare, prices soared well before labor markets would have suggested they should—and inflation began to moderate even as the unemployment rate continued to fall. This is not to say the Phillips curve has no value—it does. Wages matter, particularly for services inflation. But the Phillips curve offers no predictive precision.[4]

There are additional approaches to understanding inflation, ranging from the more academic, such as the fiscal theory of the price level (that the credibility of fiscal policy underpins inflation); to the more political, such as greedflation (that corporate profits drive prices higher); to the more microeconomic, such as market concentration (that monopoly power is driving inflation).[5] None will reveal with any precision the path of cyclical inflation. Their commonality is some degree of logic and a lack of accuracy. They simply won't tell you what will happen next.

From Downward to Upward Bias

Does the lack of precision mean leaders are powerless in the face of cyclical inflation risks? Not quite. In the absence of precision, being smart about inflation's tendency and bias is possible—and necessary—even if inflation's precise path is unknowable.

We think a reversal of inflation's underlying bias is likely playing out. Only a few years ago the corridors of central banking were filled with worry about inflation persistently undershooting the policy target, and even about Japan-style deflation. So worried was the Fed that it conducted a monetary-policy review to think through how to operate in this world of downside risk.[6] But the findings looked obsolete almost by the time of publication in August 2020.

There is strong and growing indication—but no certainty—that the drivers that delivered downside bias in the past are reversing, likely delivering upside bias:

From labor-market slack to an era of tightness. A key driver of downward inflation bias in the 2010s was sustained slack in the labor market. The global financial crisis delivered a high unemployment rate that took the better part of a decade to come down. The labor market turned tight by 2017 (see also figure 13.3) and a continuation of such tightness would have eventually pushed up prices. This trajectory was interrupted by Covid, an exogenous shock, that drove unemployment even higher than it had been during the global financial crisis. Yet, in little over a year, the recovery returned an even tighter labor market than in 2019. There is no certainty that such tightness will be sustained over the coming years and cycles. AI may ease labor-market pressures, whereas an aging population may add to them.[7] Yet we are skeptical either would unfold fast enough to shape the 2020s (see also discussion in chapter 21). We believe that—barring a new structural shock such as a severe financial recession or an inflation regime break—the era of tightness will endure.

From disinflationary to inflationary global value chains. In the past few decades, the thrust of global production was to prioritize cost and efficiency over all else. The emerging web of global value chains delivered many years of deflation in durable goods markets (see chapter 19). As global value chains begin to lean toward security and resilience, the prospect that the disinflationary impulse will be more modest—or maybe even inflationary—is real. This will add to the upward bias in cyclical inflation risks.

From subdued to confident investment imperatives. A structural shift is occurring from a global economy that saw a period of tepid investment toward one that needs (and wants) to invest more. Such desire has emerged not only because of the need for additional capacity as the economy pushes its potential but also because of strategic reasons, ranging from decarbonization to national security to technological leadership. This suggests that capex demand may be higher for some time. Elevated investment spending adds to upside inflation risk, even if (in the long term) the resulting additional output capacity will be disinflationary.

We stress that upward inflationary bias need not be permanent and a return to a downward bias in inflation remains possible. In fact, we believe that over a long enough time—say 15 years—a return to downward inflation bias is even likely. Yet for the 2020s, the odds point toward upward inflationary pressures (see also chapter 21).

Fed Watching

Accepting the unpredictability of inflation and focusing on (upside) biases is an important foundation for those who want to gauge cyclical inflation. But that is only half the story. The other half is how monetary policy reacts to it. Policymakers' understanding of inflation is imperfect too, and their tools are blunt. But watching and understanding their view of inflation risks and their likely reaction are critical.

How can we gauge monetary policymakers' actions? Fed watching is a complex cottage industry in and of itself, which dissects every word uttered by central-bank governors and relies on elaborate models—none of which is of use to executives. But executives should know two concepts that inform much of central-bank thinking.

First, how do central bankers determine if the economy is too tight, meaning at risk of inflation? Central bankers tend to look at the unemployment rate relative to a benchmark that is considered neutral (or natural)—that is, neither tight (inflationary) nor slack (disinflationary). But this neutral rate, referred to as $u^\star$ ("u-star"), changes over time.[8] Thus, there cannot be an absolute level of unemployment that is considered problematic. Rather, it's the gap between the unemployment rate (u) and the neutral rate ($u^\star$) that matters. Figure 13.3 shows the history of labor-market tightness and slack within this framework—as well as the emergence of what we see as an era of tightness, as already mentioned (labor-market tightness set in several years before the pandemic, which was an interruption of that trajectory).[9] It is important to recognize that $u^\star$ is unobservable—nobody knows it for sure. But knowing what the Fed believes $u^\star$ to be, and therefore whether it views the economy as tight or not (and driving inflation risk or not), is critical when following the Fed's actions.

FIGURE **13.3**

Labor-market slack (u > u*) and tightness (u < u*) since 1950

Unemployment rate (u) and neutral rate (u*)

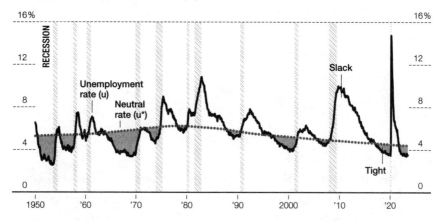

Note: Data through July 2023.
Source: CBO, BLS, NBER, analysis by BCG Center for Macroeconomics

Second, once the Fed has a view on risks, how does it determine how high interest rates should be? Again, there is no absolute answer—only a relative one that takes into account another neutral benchmark. The so-called neutral rate of interest, r★ ("r-star"), is also an estimate and changes over time. When the Fed sets the short-term interest rate at r★, it neither accelerates nor slows the economy. As before, r★ cannot be directly observed, but knowing what the Fed views r★ to be will provide some insight into where and how high interest rates will go. Figure 13.4 shows the history of r and r★. When the cycle has run too hot (with upside inflation risk), we tend to see r > r★.

The backdrop of cyclical inflation, inflationary risk bias, the state of tightness, and the state of r★ will feed into how monetary policy is made. Understanding those factors also provides a better footing for business leaders watching the Fed than attempting to decipher the utterings of Fed officials.

All of this imprecision may make it seem like the Fed's job is hopeless. And in the sense that policy will never be precisely right, it is. But the good news is that it doesn't need to be perfect. What is needed is a persistence to keep trying, to treat monetary policymaking as a search in the dark. Policymakers'

FIGURE 13.4

Tight (r > r*) and easy (r < r*) monetary policy since 1985

Policy rate (r) and neutral rate (r*)

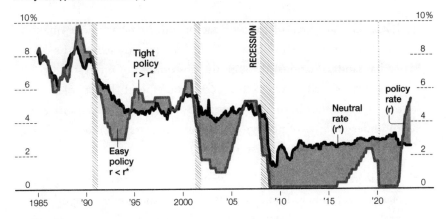

Note: Data through July 2023. r* based on Holston-Laubach-Williams natural rate + core PCE inflation before
2% inflation target formalized, + 2% after target formalized.
Source: Federal Reserve, BEA, NBER, analysis by BCG Center for Macroeconomics

awareness of the limitations of their own knowledge enhances the odds
that, by dint of trial and error, they will eventually get policy right.

Remember, the Too-Low 2010s Are Over

Investors and leaders care about cyclical inflation because—even when it is
not structurally threatening—it shapes cyclical risk. They especially care
when policy is pushing back hard (see chapter 3).

- *Upside bias isn't a law but is likely to persist.* Several cyclical and
  structural factors have delivered what is likely to be a durable upward
  inflation bias—most significantly, the continuation of an era of tightness. That is not the same as an inflation regime break, nor does it
  make a regime break likely, but it does make cyclical bouts of uncomfortably high inflation more likely.

- *Watch biases, not forecasts.* When gauging inflation's near-term prospects, forecasts may be a reasonable place to start. But remember that

the specific path of inflation is essentially unforecastable—it's more important to understand inflation's durable biases and how to distinguish cyclical inflation from the risk of structural inflation (see chapter 12).

- *Watch the stars.* All of this will factor into monetary policymaking, which will play a key role in cyclical risk and determining the cost of capital (and valuations) through the positioning of interest rates. The tendency of Fed watchers to deconstruct speech has a role on the trading desk, not in the boardroom. But for executives and investors, an understanding of policymakers' guiding stars ($u^\star$ and $r^\star$) is essential for following the monetary policy debate.

- *Pay more attention to pricing strategy.* When inflation is upwardly biased and prone to bouts of cyclical speed, the importance of pricing strategy for firms—particularly compared with a decade when prices were extraordinarily sluggish—will matter even more.

As we have seen, a shift in cyclical inflation matters for monetary policymakers, and that in turn influences cyclical risk. Interest rates are the main channel through which it happens. That makes a discussion of interest-rate regimes a natural continuation in the next chapter.

CHAPTER 14

Higher but Healthy Interest Rates

I n January 2020, a well-circulated paper argued that real interest rates were on a 700-year downtrend and destined for negative territory, as shown in figure 14.1.[1] To be sure, shards of data from Renaissance money lenders would seem a doubtful basis for predicting rates in the 21st century. But after a decade of ultralow, sometimes even negative real rates, the analysis resonated with many—even more so when Covid hit and falling rates appeared to confirm the trend. The 700-year destiny offered a compelling lower-forever narrative for that most critical of markets: money, and its price (the interest rate).

Only, interest rates have not followed that script since. Accompanying the Fed's inflation-fighting campaign that started in March 2022, 10-year real rates went from negative 1.0% to positive 1.5%, a massive 250 bps swing in just seven months. They then surged another 100 bps higher, to 2.5% in the fall of 2023. Even as real rates did not sustain those lofty levels the reality of higher rates was sinking in.

Though interest rates will continue to fluctuate cyclically, including materially to the downside as policymakers respond to changing conditions, we are not likely to return to the regime of ultralow interest rates that executives and investors had grown accustomed to in the 2010s. Tight policy represents

FIGURE **14.1**

Are 700 years of falling interest rates destiny?

Real interest rates over time

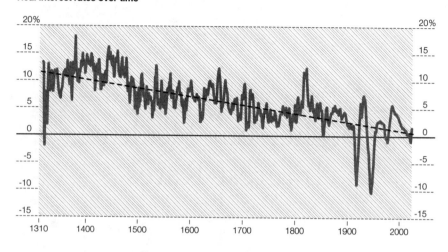

Note: Seven-year moving average of GDP-weighted real interest rate across select advanced economies (1317–2018); yearly average of daily US real 10-year yield (2019–September 2023).
Source: Bank of England, Bloomberg, analysis by BCG Center for Macroeconomics

a material shift in the economic environment for firms, households, and governments. It will force them to think twice about borrowing in order to spend. A world of higher rates also implies valuation headwinds for all manner of assets, from stocks to bonds to real estate. Higher rates reflect a shift in how policymakers encourage investment, and they will alter how the economy allocates capital: away from spurring *any* demand and toward more-disciplined allocation of capital to more-productive uses.

This chapter offers a framework for thinking about what shapes different interest-rate environments (that is, beyond cyclical fluctuations) and why.[2] We then use this framework to show why we expect a world of *higher but healthy* interest rates for the rest of the 2020s. An economy biased toward cyclical tightness will translate into higher interest rates than those of modern memory (that is, those of the late 2010s). We call this *healthy* because rates can rise for good and for bad reasons—when a strong economy is the primary driver, that is a good rise. We also entertain the possibility of a return to a low-rate environment.

As interest rates rose postpandemic, the sense of loss many executives felt stood out to us. So accustomed had many become to ultralow rates that the rise triggered withdrawal symptoms, as cheap credit for everything from funding buybacks to mergers and acquisitions to capital expenditures vanished. To be sure, executives will have to adjust, but the financial strains that come with higher rates are not generically bad—they can be *good strains* if they reflect better utilization of capital and labor in a strong economy. A higher but healthy regime is an environment more reminiscent of the good 1990s than of the bad 1970s. It will deliver rates higher than in the 2010s, but the good news is that these higher rates will largely be a by-product of a strong economy—a different macro world, but still a good-macro world.

Sketching a Map of Interest-Rate Regimes

The idea of a 700-year downward destiny for interest rates is seductive—and who is to say that over the next 100 years this will not play out? But the limitations are also clear. Though visually compelling, it offers no causal explanation other than time, the variable shown on the x axis in figure 14.1. Nor does it help us anticipate the next five years, a strategic horizon relevant to many executives.

We offer a driver-based framework in figure 14.2. By decomposing the drivers behind interest rates, it allows us to build coherent scenarios of the future. We think the map is durable, if not precise to level or timing. The main drivers, which we covered earlier in the book can—and eventually will—change. Nonetheless, we expect this map will continue to be helpful.

First, we must determine the structural inflation environment: Are long-term inflation expectations anchored or not (see chapter 12 for a detailed discussion)? The answer splits our map in half—with broadly favorable outcomes in an anchored world and unfavorable ones in an unanchored world.

In the second step, the analysis focuses on the prevailing (cyclical) inflation bias (see chapter 13 for a detailed discussion). Is it high and upward or low and downward? When inflation expectations are anchored, cyclical inflation bias is significantly influenced by economic tightness—is the economy, especially the labor market, overutilized (tight) or underutilized (slack)? Are there excess resources, or is there broad scarcity? In contrast, when

FIGURE **14.2**

Derivation of interest-rate regimes

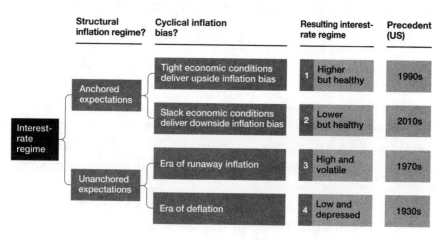

Source: BCG Center for Macroeconomics

inflation expectations are unanchored, the second step clarifies the direction of broken expectations—structural inflation or deflation.

This framing results in the four regimes shown in figure 14.2, illustrated with historical precedents.[3] Consider the first two regimes, both happening in the context of anchored inflation:

1. *Higher but healthy.* A strong economy with tight labor markets delivers upside inflation bias that demands tight monetary policy (that is, higher rates).[4] The 1990s are a powerful example of a strong and tight economy and a higher but healthy rate environment. (Yes, it is true that in the 1990s, interest rates were lower than in the 1980s, but they should be seen relative to those of the 2010s, when inflation expectations were also anchored.)

2. *Lower but healthy.* A tepid economy with too much slack in labor markets (underutilization) delivers too little inflation, and this motivates a low interest-rate regime that is attempting to spur demand and reduce slack. The 2010s are the prime example.

In the context of a broken (unanchored) inflation regime, two different interest-rate regimes would need to be considered:

3. *High and volatile.* An economy in which rates are driven by unanchored long-term inflation expectations rather than by the economy's tightness or slack. This leads to high (and volatile) short rates, high (and volatile) long rates, high-term and high-risk premia, low valuations, and likely stagflation, where unemployment is also elevated. The 1970s are a powerful (and frightening) illustration.

4. *Low and depressed.* A structurally broken economy in which rates are driven by deflation also likely comes with depression. This leads to low short and long rates in nominal terms, but due to falling price levels, potentially very high real interest rates and disastrous economic outcomes. The 1930s are a depressingly potent illustration.

Though we ordered the scenarios according to our perceived likelihood, we emphasize that the probability drops off sharply as we move to regimes 3 and 4. As we argued in chapter 12, a broken inflation regime, their precondition, is unlikely.

The Case for Higher but Healthy

We believe higher but healthy is likely to be the prevailing interest-rate regime for the remainder of the 2020s, as an era of tightness persists.[5] To be sure, interest rates will fluctuate with cyclical conditions, including to low levels in downturns, but across cycles they will tend to be higher than they were in the recent memory of the 2010s. Though higher, this environment implies a healthy economy as the key drivers of higher rates are fully utilized resources and businesses wanting to borrow and invest because they feel confident about the future.[6]

Against the backdrop of the 2010s, an era of too-low inflation and ultralow rates, higher rates may appear intimidating and they are not without risk. Policymakers may find themselves engaged in a sustained balancing act between restraining the economy and (often unexpected) challenges—from losses on bank balance sheets to credit problems to income burdens—that higher rates may bring. But we should not forget that such challenges are the result of managing a strong economy, not a weak one. And while living with tight monetary policy (r > r★) will prove dangerous for some, it need not be so for the macroeconomy. Certainly, the late 1990s

FIGURE **14.3**

Precedents of higher but healthy and lower but healthy

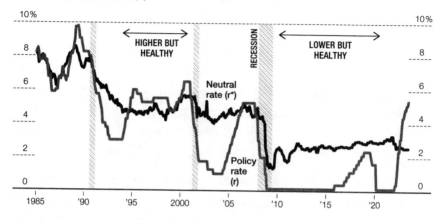

Policy rate (r) and neutral rate (r*)

Note: Data through July 2023. r* based on Holston-Laubach-Williams natural rate + core PCE inflation before 2% inflation target formalized, + 2% after target formalized.
Source: Federal Reserve, BEA, NBER, analysis by BCG Center for Macroeconomics

was a very healthy—if sometimes bumpy—economic period. Figure 14.3, which we have shown previously in a different context, shows this precedent for higher but healthy (as well as the period of lower but healthy).

So, why is higher but healthy likely in the years ahead? Leveraging our framework in figure 14.2, and prior chapters, we point to the following:

- A conviction that the anchored inflation regime will remain in place (see chapter 12).

- Within the anchored regime, we expect inflation bias to the upside because of tight labor markets, retreating global value chains, and higher investment demand (see chapter 13).

- A recession will happen sooner or later, but we have no predisposition to thinking that contemporary risks point toward a structurally damaging one. Recessions with structural overhang can inject slack into the economy that takes time to overcome—think 2008. But that should not be our base case. Remember that Covid was a more intense macro shock, as seen in much higher unemployment in 2020 than in 2008, but the economy rebounded quickly as structural damage was avoided (see chapter 4).

What level of interest rates might this point to? The analogy with the 1990s might point to rates that prevailed then—the 10-year (nominal) yield was near 6%.[7] However, such a conclusion would miss a critical shift. What will be required for central bankers to deliver tight monetary policy in the 2020s will not be the same as it was in the 1990s—because the underlying neutral rate of interest has declined since then (as seen in figure 14.3).[8] Estimates show it may have declined by as much as 200 basis points, so the equivalent tightness at 6% in the late 1990s may require only a rate of 4% in the 2020s.[9] That would be higher than in the 2010s, but lower than in the 1990s.

How Likely Are the Other Rate Regimes?

We cannot rule out other regimes. In fact, a shift to another regime is certain over a long enough horizon—and thus understanding the whole map of rate regimes is worthwhile, even if the likelihood of the respective regimes is quite unequal.

First, *lower but healthy*. To get back to 2010s-style easy monetary policy would require persistently too-low inflation. In the 2010s, policy often needed to stretch beyond interest rates to asset purchases (quantitative easing) to try to provide stimulus, because policy rates were at zero. We would have to believe in the opposite of the drivers discussed above, that is to say, too much slack in the economy. Though that is possible in the near term and plausible in the long term, it is not our expectation for the 2020s.

Near-term, a serious macro shock with structural overhangs could deliver that outcome. But even as rates would drop in response to cyclical weakness, we would expect them to bounce back more often to a higher but healthy stance.

Longer term, there is another and more positive path to lower but healthy. Technology could deliver slack in the economy if innovation delivers enough productivity growth to create the necessary slack in labor markets or generates a significant enough disinflationary force. While we think technology has that potential over the long run, we don't think it can be deployed fast enough to shape the next few years in this way (see chapters 7 and 8).

Finally, there is a less healthy variant of this regime—so-called Japanification. In this scenario, inflation becomes anchored below policy targets or near zero and is unresponsive to economic strength or policy stimulus. This delivers low nominal rates but potentially too-high real rates. In that case, monetary policy may be tight even as central banks attempt to make it easy. Japan's experience since the early 1990s until recently illustrates this.

Next, *high and volatile.* We view this scenario as less plausible, because high and volatile rates require unanchored long-term inflation expectations facilitated by a sustained policy error (see chapter 12 on structural inflation). If this were to happen, rates would be driven by shifting inflation expectations and policy rates would matter less. The late 1960s deanchoring of inflation expectations started such an era, which then persisted through the 1970s. As seen in figure 14.4, inflation moved higher, then higher, then higher still. As a result, both short- and long-term rates moved higher, too.

Last, *low and depressed.* The fourth regime we find to be the least plausible, because the requirements to avoid a deflationary depression are known and the motivation and capacity to act are strong (see chapter 10 on existential stimulus). But if policy blunders were extraordinary enough to deliver the sharp deflation required to enter this regime, a period of very low nominal but high real rates would begin. This is reminiscent of the 1930s, as seen in figure 14.5, when prices fell significantly for years, leaving price levels sharply lower and nominal policy rates hugging zero for the rest of the decade.

FIGURE 14.4

The high and volatile rate regime of the 1970s

Source: Federal Reserve, BLS, Shiller/Yale, analysis by BCG Center for Macroeconomics

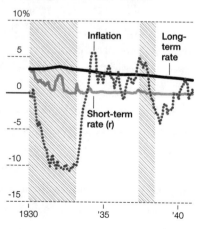

FIGURE 14.5

The low and depressed rate regime of the 1930s

Source: Federal Reserve, NBER, BLS, Shiller/Yale, analysis by BCG Center for Macroeconomics

Remember, Capital Allocation Will Have to Be More Disciplined

Higher but healthy implies a material shift away from an interest-rate regime and policy efforts that hoped to spur any form of demand to one that encourages the efficient allocation of resources. As we saw, this is not a negative story for the economy: tight economies come with more jobs, more investment, more productivity growth, and more real and broad-based wage gains. Though we should generally embrace, not lament, higher rates from a macroeconomic perspective, they bring challenges for firms and executives:

- *The economy is not your firm.* Higher but healthy refers to the macro-economy, but some firms will suffer. Higher rates will require adjust-ment from them, and the weakest ones will fail. Overleveraged firms and those operating at the edge will fold, and resources will flow elsewhere. But don't confuse idiosyncratic pain with the economy's pain: higher rates are likely to signal a good-macro environment.

- *Investing will be harder.* The era of tightness will deliver good strains that demand tight interest rates ($r > r^\star$) more often. Policymakers, by raising the cost of capital, are looking to move resources from less to more productive businesses—one way this happens is through busi-ness bankruptcy. A degree (but not a cascade) of bankruptcies can be good for the economy.

- *Higher doesn't mean very high.* Remember, the interest rate environ-ment is about the relative level of r and $r^\star$. As $r^\star$ has trended down since the 1990s, equivalently tight policy in the 2020s doesn't require rates as high as the 1990s.

- *Rates will still be lowered at times.* Policy rates will continue to respond to cyclical pressures in the higher but healthy regime. When policy rates fall, that doesn't mean the end of the regime—cyclical interruptions will happen.

- *More rate volatility.* In contrast to when policy rates were pinned near zero, elevated policy rates leave more room for policy adjustments—

and surprises—as policymakers attempt to balance inflationary pressures and policy restraint. This means more interest-rate volatility.

One common belief in the late 2010s was that the economy would not be able to handle interest rates moving sharply higher. This played into the stark predictions of recession in 2022 and was based on a view that elevated debt levels across the economy would result in too much pain as rates rose. But by the end of 2023 it was clear that the economy was more resilient. The dynamics were and are more complex than that.

Though higher rates speak to economic health, as we argued in this chapter, the prospect of higher rates also drives fears that elevated debt levels are a macroeconomic Achilles' heel. We explore debt risks in the next chapter.

CHAPTER 15

The Threat of Debt, Imagined and Real

I n Lionel Shriver's dystopian novel *The Mandibles: A Family, 2029–2047*, readers are immersed in a macroeconomic dystopia.[1] Crushed by its mountain of debt, the United States has defaulted, the greenback is worthless, and hyperinflation rages. The crisis stretches beyond macroeconomics and leads to a societal breakdown. Gold, guns, and a farm offer the best chance of hanging on. The Mandibles, a family of wealth, are fighting for survival.

Though this novel is entirely fictional, it speaks to real—and surprisingly common—fears about the macroeconomy.[2] When we discussed the novel with Shriver in 2021, she told us that her plot, which begins in 2029, could turn into reality before a potential movie hits the screen. In fact, fears about a debt-driven economic meltdown are commonplace, particularly among the wealthy, who have the most to lose.[3] The topic also features in boardrooms unexpectedly often.

Yet these worries have been around for a long time, and so far, they have never been substantiated. As far back as 1986, Peter F. Drucker wrote in *Foreign Affairs*: "With every deficit year the indebtedness of the U.S. government goes up, and with it the interest charges on the U.S. budget, which in turn raises the deficit even further. Sooner or later . . . confidence in

America and the American dollar will be undermined—some observers consider this practically imminent."[4]

Over the subsequent nearly 40 years, the US national debt has grown dramatically. And while macroeconomic crises have come and gone, the catastrophe foreseen by Drucker has failed to materialize—despite frequent warnings of its being "practically imminent." Were debt doomsayers wrong (for a discussion of dollar risks, see chapter 20), or are they simply early? Have we inexorably inched closer to an even higher debt precipice?

Concerns about public debt are not unfounded, and it's wrong to say that deficits don't matter. Unease is warranted if for no other reason than that crises—the big and the small—are exceptionally difficult to predict and can have tremendous impact. But the common existential fear is misguided and often rooted in an undue focus on debt *levels*. To better assess the macroeconomic risks that the public debt poses, we instead need to focus on a framework that captures the interplay of nominal growth (g) and the nominal interest rate (r), what we call the g-versus-r framework.[5] We also discuss how risks from private debt differ.

Focus on g-versus-r Dynamics, Not Debt Quantity

In debates about public debt, quantity always takes center stage. The level is easy to measure and looks menacing—as it does in figure 15.1. However, when assessing risk, a focus on the quantity of debt is either outright deceptive (if quoted in nominal terms, as in our chart, the debt is not meaningfully compared over time) or not particularly helpful (showing debt as a share of income still says little about the sustainability of that debt).

The focus on levels harbors an assumption that there is a tipping point. This levels focus became academic dictum in the early 2010s when economists Carmen Reinhart and Kenneth Rogoff concluded that the data said external debts in excess of 90% of GDP would drastically reduce growth rates.[6] This added a counterproductive urgency to austerity and gave credence to the feeling that at some level, an extra billion dollars in debt will deliver a Shriverian dystopia.

But that's not how it works—at all. Growth doesn't fall off a cliff at some threshold. Neither are sovereign-debt crises easily linked to levels. They can happen at surprisingly low levels of debt. They can also fail to materialize

FIGURE **15.1**

Whether in nominal dollars or as a percentage of GDP, debt levels look menacing but say little about risk

Federal government debt

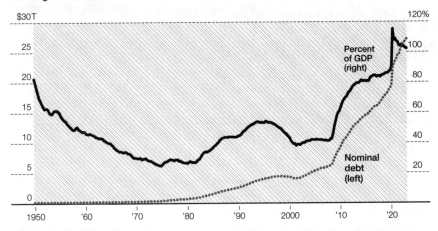

Note: Data through Q1 2023.
Source: Federal Reserve Board, BEA, analysis by BCG Center for Macroeconomics

at very elevated levels. Consider Ukraine's 1998 debt default, with a debt-to-GDP ratio below 30%. Then contrast that with Japan's debt ratio of well over 200% in the 2010s, which sparked little to no concern. The modern history of sovereign defaults shows little correlation between levels and default.

For a better framework for debt risks, we must look at the relationship between nominal growth (g) and nominal interest rates (r). If growth is higher than rates, the debt-to-GDP ratio can be maintained even without using revenue to make any debt-service payments. If, for example, the interest rate is 4%, and a government borrows new money to make that 4% payment, the resulting 4% growth in the debt stock will lead to an unchanged debt-to-GDP ratio if GDP has also grown by 4%. And if the nominal growth rate is greater than nominal interest rates (g > r), we can think of debt dynamics like an airport's moving sidewalk, which helps you get ahead while making minimal effort.

In contrast, if growth is lower than rates (g < r), current revenue—potentially a substantial amount of it—is required to keep debt ratios stable.

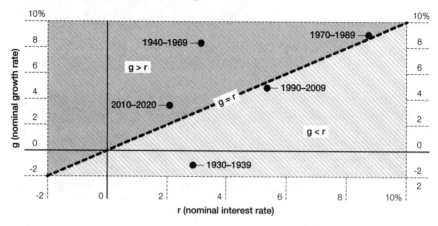

FIGURE **15.2**

**100 years of g-versus-r debt dynamics:
Range of sustainable US configurations**

Source: BEA, Shiller/Yale, analysis by BCG Center for Macroeconomics

Think of it as a treadmill, forcing us to exert effort just to stand still. These unattractive dynamics can be difficult for an economy to sustain and a polity to bear and are less attractive for investors to finance. The tougher the g-versus-r dynamics become, the greater the risk of a crisis.

Figure 15.2 visualizes nearly the last 100 years of the g-versus-r regime in the United States, with various configurations shown by era. The diagonal line (g=r) shows a configuration where the debt ratio can be stable without using any revenue to service it. Points above the line have attractive g-versus-r configurations (that is, the debt ratio can fall without having to use revenue). Points below the line are unattractive (that is, the debt ratio rises unless revenue is used). As the graphic shows, the last decade has been particularly favorable, with nominal growth comfortably outstripping very low interest rates. What is likely in the 2020s and beyond?

Will the United States Face a Hostile g < r Regime?

The overwhelmingly comfortable g-versus-r configuration of the 2010s is already gone. Even though structural inflation remains anchored (see chapter 12), cyclical inflation is biased up (see chapter 13)—and with it, policy rates (see chapter 14). Higher cyclical inflation will shift up both nominal growth and interest rates, and higher real growth may shift real rates in tandem, but the shift in policy rates to address the new inflation bias (see chapter 14) only moves up rates, not growth (in fact, it is trying to restrain growth). This means g-versus-r debt dynamics are very likely to deteriorate compared with those of the remarkably favorable 2010s—making g-versus-r harder, but not necessarily bad.

Is this merely a case of the moving sidewalk slowing to a crawl (or stopping), or will it fully reverse and become a treadmill? The baseline projection for US trend growth approaches 2% in real terms. In nominal terms—that is, adding in future inflation of 2% to 3%—growth can be expected to come in at 4% to 5%. Will interest rates—averaged across maturities—persist well above that level?

In the longer run, neutral rates still seem likely to be lower than in the last few decades (chapter 14), meaning r need not be particularly high. And the prospects for some upside to growth from productivity (see chapters 7 and 8) are real, meaning that g can see a noninflationary boost (even if that may also push up neutral rates). Overall, we think g-versus-r will look far less favorable in the future, much closer to $g = r$. This will represent a significant departure from the 2010s, when g far exceeded r.

Yet when monetary policy needs to be exceptionally tight (such as in 2023), r plausibly exceeds g—swapping out the moving sidewalk for the treadmill, as debt dynamics must digest a higher but healthy interest-rate regime that is forcefully pushing back against growth.

Does that spell a Shriverian debt collapse of the sort that is anchored so thoroughly in the public perspective? History offers some clues as to why it's not a cliff edge—and why the context matters greatly.

Living on the line ($g = r$). In the period 1970–1989 the US economy lived on the $g = r$ line. That is, the moving sidewalk of debt sustainability was standing still. The surging inflation of the 1970s helped to erode debt, but it also drove up interest rates, with the result that r and g remained close. While at no point in this era was sovereign default a risk, what did change was how markets perceived deficits. With r and g in balance, there was no helpful moving-sidewalk effect, so any primary budget deficit (that is, deficit excluding interest costs) would feed directly through into a higher debt-to-GDP ratio. It was only much later, when structural inflation was reined in and interest rates declined, that r fell below g and it became possible to run primary deficits without pushing up debt levels.

Living below the line (g < r). Even below the line—when the moving sidewalk becomes a treadmill—a crisis isn't necessarily around the corner. Consider the 1990s, when nominal growth slowed sharply with the steep fall in inflation, but rates did not fall as quickly.[7] The political system drew the rational conclusion from this g < r world. Both Democrats and Republicans rallied to the cause of smaller deficits, believing that these would bring borrowing costs down. A Democratic-led administration saw an opportunity to push for smaller deficits and stimulate at the same time by driving down the risk premia of long-term rates. Paradoxically, in the 1990s, budget discipline was actually stimulative.

The other below-the-line era—the 1930s—was also paradoxical. Remarkably unattractive dynamics were driven by nominal rates unable to fall much below zero and nominal growth falling dramatically into negative territory. Yet no debt crisis was near—why? Deflationary dynamics made nominal investments (for instance, bonds) very attractive as real returns were large. Indeed, much more debt could have been issued, and eventually was during World War II. Big spending, as is often the case (see chapter 10), was the solution to deflation and depression.

The contrast between the 1990s and 1930s points to a larger lesson. Because the United States issues the world's reserve currency, its debt dynamics can be attractive or unattractive, but they will not portend a crisis (see also chapter 20 on dollar risks). The framework of g-versus-r gives us a measure of debt stress, but debt crises are ultimately about context. Crises tend to occur when rates move sharply higher as growth moves lower (think of Greece in the eurozone crisis). But the United States has the advantage that periods of low growth are almost always accompanied by low interest rates.

Deficits Do Matter

Readers should not conclude from the above that "deficits don't matter," as US Vice President Dick Cheney once unhelpfully put it.[8] Though we've de-emphasized the mountain of debt and emphasized the interplay of g-versus-r, that should not be taken as encouragement for fiscal profligacy—as many who have absorbed the lessons of the 2010s seem to believe.

On the contrary, deficits matter precisely because they can undermine both rates and growth in our framework. As outlined in chapters 9, 10, and 11, stimulus—often via deficits and debt—is a staple of modern economic management. There are good reasons to use debt to prop up growth, particularly in moments of systemic risk, such as 2008 and 2020.

But sustained deficits and elevated debt levels do push up rates, all other things being equal—making debt dynamics less attractive.[9] Additionally, if markets perceive deficits as profligate or policymakers as uncredible, particularly when there is no weak economic backdrop to warrant deficits, rates can move quickly to push back against profligacy—particularly when long-term inflation expectations are unanchored.

While g-versus-r dynamics over the past decade have been part of the reason fiscal capacity was so strong, they will not eliminate the need for tough choices in the future. These choices must account for long-term investment needs—ranging from decarbonization and the energy transition, to an aging population, and to increased military spending—as well as for short-term political realities.

It remains certain that these choices are better made when debt dynamics are favorable than it is to wait until markets force those difficult and painful choices over a short time horizon. And difficult choices can't be avoided indefinitely by keeping interest rates suppressed. The effect of low rates, from poor capital allocation to inflation, will pop up elsewhere.[10]

Healthy debt dynamics should not be used as an excuse for poor fiscal management. Rather, favorable dynamics should be seen as an opportunity to build strength, not squander it.

Private Debt Is Different

Government borrowing is not the only debt threat to the macroeconomy. Private debt can also be a menace. And while g-versus-r has some relevance to assessing private-sector debt sustainability, the main threat from private debt is its systemic potential.

Consider first that private defaults are happening perpetually—and are indeed expected to do so. Defaults normally happen in fragmented and isolated ways across the firm and household sectors—a very different dynamic than the wholesale nature of a sovereign default. This allows defaults to occur, most often, in amounts that are digestible by a credit system built around these events. After all, private lending occurs at a spread because the lenders know they won't always be repaid.

Indeed, private defaults can even be seen as having positive macroeconomic consequences. Business bankruptcies, particularly when the economy's resources are fully utilized, allow resources to be redeployed into more-productive uses. Defaults are a means of accelerating creative destruction—not a painless process, but one of capital reallocation that is essential to move the economic frontier forward.

The relevance of g-versus-r for private debts is that households and firms, too, can offset the burden of interest with fast growth. Capital markets will give fast-growing companies a pass on high leverage, and loan officers may allocate greater leverage to a mortgage applicant with credible career prospects.

Ultimately, however, the real risk arising from private debt is its ability to destabilize the financial system. Banks will take a handful of defaults in stride. But if private debtors default en masse, the resulting depletion of banks' capital can put a stop to lending (see also chapter 4). The more leverage (that is, less capital) the financial system has, the higher the risk it can't absorb losses safely. This is why the banking sector, which is built with significant leverage, warrants special attention. Contrast this with the situation where private debtors stop repaying credit funds outside of the banking system. This will hit nonbank creditors who are in a better position to absorb losses (better capitalized than banks) and even their failure would be far less likely to have serious knock-on effects for the economy.

The threat from borrowers to banks is particularly acute because a blow to a single bank can undermine the stability of other banks. The contagion is partly real and partly psychological. On the real side, the damaged bank will need to liquidate assets, driving down their value and thus harming other banks that own similar positions. On the psychological side, distress at one bank (or even a nonbank financial intermediary) will cause customers of other banks to fear for the safety of their deposits. A bank-run mentality can set in, and funding flight can topple banks like dominoes.

Deleveraging, the process of selling assets to reduce liabilities, can be particularly damaging because the pain of falling asset prices can spread to

FIGURE **15.3**

The 2008 debt pivot:
Government leveraged as households deleveraged

Change in debt-to-GDP ratio in percentage points by sector

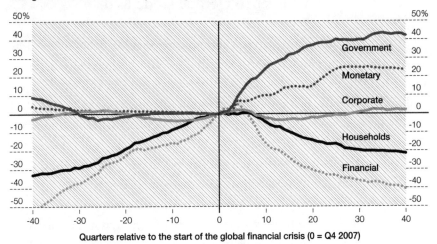

Quarters relative to the start of the global financial crisis (0 = Q4 2007)

Note: Data through 2017.
Source: Federal Reserve Board, BEA, Sanford C. Bernstein, analysis by BCG Center for Macroeconomics

healthy banks, firms, and households—and is difficult to stop once started. As seen in figure 15.3, both US households and the financial sector began to deleverage in 2008. Fortunately, policy, both fiscal and monetary, stepped up to ensure the economy didn't collapse into depression as this deleveraging took place.[11] The private-debt crisis of 2008 had to be arrested with additional public debt. Of particular importance was filling in the financial system's capital holes to stop deleveraging from spiraling out of control.

If more debt is the solution to a debt crisis, what happens when more debt is not possible? What if the sovereign balance sheet is unable to respond? Won't *that* lead to a systemic and societal collapse? What needs to be understood is that, for a monetary sovereign with an international reserve currency, the possibility of being unable to respond is remarkably unlikely. It requires a sovereign default, which—while not impossible—is remarkably rare for sovereigns blessed with reserve status in a world of fiat currency (see chapter 20).[12] Not to mention that the darkest outcomes, which spark so much worry, are about not just debt but institutional collapse, which does not necessarily come with sovereign default.

Remember to Decode Code Red

In 2019, we published a research report arguing that US debt—depending on what is counted and how it is counted—could be anywhere between 100%, 1,000%, or even 2,000% of GDP.[13] The purpose of this exercise was to illustrate, vividly, that too much attention is focused on the level of debt and too little attention on the interplay of g and r. Shortly after, as if to prove the point, a CNBC headline read "Real US Debt Levels Could Be 2,000% of Economy, a Wall Street Report Suggests," seizing reflexively on the headline-worthy 2,000%. Headlines are where nuance goes to die.

It's the economic equivalent of *if it bleeds, it leads*: debt headlines will always telegraph code red, but one must learn to decode them anyway. Perhaps what is warranted is not optimism, but a foundation for pushing back on extreme pessimism. Other than to be distrustful of the headlines, here are a few more lessons:

- *Don't be misled by levels; they are an empty signal.* Much attention will continue to be given to debt levels. They are easy to measure, easy to communicate, and seem to make sense—yet they will continue to either explicitly mislead (in nominal terms) or provide very little information about the profile of risk (in percentage-of-income terms).

- *Always return to g-versus-r.* Though debt can be technical, a sanity check on debt sustainability is always obtainable with a g-versus-r perspective. Growth must drop below rates (or rates rise above growth) to present a problem—and even that does not automatically spell disaster.

- *Think of risk as a rising burden, not a cliff edge.* The g-versus-r dynamics show that debt risk is more about shifts in burdens, constraints, and costs than about sudden and dramatic collapse. Additionally, while debt crises do occur, the collapse that is often feared is about more than just economics—even sovereign defaults do not need to be accompanied by institutional breakdown.

- *Ask who holds private debt.* Not all debt risks are the same. Private-debt risk flows at least as much from those who hold it, and their capacity to withstand losses, as it does from any default itself. Defaults that impact the banking system—where capital bases are small compared with balance sheets—are the epicenter of debt crises that matter for the macroeconomy.

Expect many more debt headlines telegraphing code red—but also expect true risk to be much more nuanced.

CHAPTER 16

Learning to Love and Live with Bubbles

B etween 1989 and 1993 the price of a breeding pair of emus, large birds heralded as the "new red meat," went from a few hundred dollars to $28,000. In the mid-2010s, the fracking rig count went from a few hundred to well over a thousand amid talk of a new energy market. In the late 1990s, against the backdrop of a so-called new economy, the tech-heavy Nasdaq equity index shot up nearly 90% in fewer than five months.[1] And toward the end of the 1920s, equity valuations reached a multiple of over 30 times earnings.[2]

These are all examples of bubbles: unsustainable trends that build over time and typically deflate rapidly. They also have very different macroeconomic consequences—which is what makes them relevant to us and why we devote an entire chapter to them. Above, the macroeconomic fallout ranged from negligible (emu bubble), to threatening the cycle (fracking), to delivering a recession (dot-com), and finally to a severe structural break (late 1920s).

Bubbles pose dual challenges for policymakers, executives, and investors. Their amorphous nature makes them hard to spot and stop, and their potential for macroeconomic destruction makes them difficult to ignore. But why are bubbles so common? Why can't they be identified—or, better yet, prevented? How should their risks be managed? Do they have any redeeming features? And what are investors and executives supposed to do in a bubbly world?

This chapter addresses these questions. We introduce a simple bubble framework to argue three things: spotting and stopping them is exceedingly hard and typically not possible or wise; preventative efforts should focus only on macroeconomically threatening bubbles, particularly those with systemic relevance—otherwise, policymakers are better off on cleanup duty; and despite their reputation, bubbles can have positive legacies, as they mobilize action and resources.

The reality is that executives and investors must accept bubbles—because they can't just sit them out. Perhaps we won't learn to love bubbles, but we need to learn to live with them, as the structural environment is tilted toward bubble ubiquity.

Why Bubbles Are Ubiquitous

Bubbles are hardly new. In addition to the examples cited above, there were bubbles in tulips in the 17th century, Mississippi stock in the 18th century, and railroads in the 19th century.[3]

But have bubbles become more prevalent? Beginning in the shadow of the dot-com bubble, the 21st century has already run up an astonishing number of bubbles. We discussed the housing and credit bubble that imploded in 2008 in chapters 4 and 10. We also saw how the policy response to the global financial crisis spawned a bubble in long-term government bonds engineered by ultra-easy monetary policy including large-scale asset purchases (quantitative easing) that bid up bond prices (and lowered interest rates). And since supposedly risk-free government rates are a reference value for many other asset classes, the bubble in long-term government bond valuations spawned an "everything bubble." By 2021, everything from equity valuations to soaring cryptocurrency and NFT prices signaled froth.[4]

We believe a bubbly backdrop is a feature, not a fluke, of the modern economy for several structural reasons.

First, greater cycle longevity (a theme we covered in chapter 3) allows excesses to build. When recessions came along every few years, the runway for exuberance was limited. The cycle's tendency to longevity is aided by lower volatility of output and by stimulus looking to extend the cycle whenever possible.

Second, the shift toward a more deregulated and financialized economy encourages bubbles. Financial innovations can even *become* the bubble (see cryptocurrencies) or they can help inflate them (see the complex mortgage securitization during the housing bubble). And even if the forces of deregulation weaken, ample room for financial innovation remains.

Third, lower interest rates push investors and speculators to stretch for returns, while lowering opportunity costs and increasing the present value of distant profits. The argument that low rates deliver bubbles is old but gained new persuasiveness as the interest-rate environment was lower structurally (due to a lower neutral rate of interest; see chapter 14) and lowered cyclically through aggressive policy, including quantitative easing.[5] Some even suggested that too low inflation of the early 21st century meant that the interest rate that delivers full employment may be too low to be consistent with financial stability.

Though the interest-rate environment is set to be higher but healthy (again see chapter 14), a consequence in part of upside inflation bias (chapter 13), we think that it may restrain but not stop the emergence of bubbles. Recall, the 1990s dot-com bubble occurred in the context of higher rates also.

A Taxonomy of Bubbles

As we saw above, bubbles are not homogenous. To bring some structure to their diversity, we like to think about them in two dimensions—their *characteristics* (any bubble may take on more than one) and the magnitude of their *damage* (bubbles have a spectrum of macroeconomic consequence). The taxonomy in figure 16.1 illustrates both characteristics and consequences.

On the vertical axis, we highlight three common characteristics, recognizing that in many cases a bubble will comprise multiple characteristics. First, valuation is a feature when asset prices are far outside historical norms (most bubbles have an element of such excesses). Various episodes of equity bubbles come to mind, but valuation bubbles are also found in government bonds (which we discuss in detail later), property, and art markets. Second, velocity can be a feature—the speed at which prices, valuation, or economic

FIGURE **16.1**

A bubble taxonomy

		MACROECONOMIC RISK OR DAMAGE			
		Idiosyncratic "Bad for those exposed"	Broad "Amplified by linkages but contained"	Cycle-ending "Expansion cannot survive"	Structural break "Put the economy on a different course"
Valuation "Stretching historical range"		Contemporary art market (2010s/2020s) "New masterpiece"	Government bonds (late 2010s/ early 2020s) "Negative term premium"	Swedish housing (early 1990s) "New financial liberalization"	US equities (late 1920s) "Great Depression"
and/or					
Velocity "Exponential growth"		NFTs (2021) "Digital assets"	Cryptocurrency (2021) "New currency"	US equities (late 1990s) "New economy"	Japanese assets (1989) "Lost decade"
and/or					
Quantity or quality "Too much" or "bad"		Texas emu bubble (mid-1990s) "New red meat"	Fracking investment (mid-2010s) "America as oil exporter"	US subprime (2000s) "Home prices only go up"	Mississippi (early 1770s) "Pathway to French Revolution"

BUBBLE CHARACTERISTIC(S)

Source: BCG Center for Macroeconomics

activity moves matters as well. Cryptocurrency's rapid rise in the early 2020s illustrates this feature. Third, quality and quantity features highlight unsustainable assumptions. The assumptions about the demand for emu meat, about the profitable quantity of fracking rigs, the quality of securitized mortgages, or the quality of French paper money did not hold up.[6]

Yet, we're interested most in the macroeconomic damage that bubbles are capable of inflicting, shown on the horizontal axis. We differentiate between four escalations, broadly correlated to how many macroeconomic linkages the bubbles have:

> *Idiosyncratic bubbles* are confined to a single asset class or activity, with little to no linkages with the rest of the economy. The collapse of the emu bubble did not affect other sectors. A reset of the art market

would hurt some ultrawealthy folks but would not provoke a recession. For now at least, cryptocurrencies exist in a largely self-contained environment with few significant linkages to the traditional financial sector or to the real economy.

Broad bubbles have macroeconomic relevance because of forward and backward linkages. Fracking drove a boom in investment in both the real form (rigs) and the financial form (high-yield bonds). It also created a surge in demand for certain specialized workers. When the fracking boom stopped, the drawdown in investment and the tightening of credit raised a more credible concern about recession. Crypto and digital assets may one day reach such relevance but have yet to do so. And we'll return to the idea of a bubble in government bonds via a negative-term premium bubble below.

Cycle-ending bubbles are large and broad enough to end the cycle decisively, but their severity varies. The dot-com bubble and the housing bubble were both cycle-ending but of clearly different severity.

Structural breaks occur when a bubble permanently puts the economy on a different path. While the global financial crisis may seem to qualify as having caused a structural break, its consequences—across social, political, and economic dimensions—were not nearly as significant as those of the Great Depression of the 1930s, which redefined the role of government in the economy. That shift better illustrates the spectrum of bubbly consequences.[7]

Spotting, Stopping, Stoking

Pressed to define obscenity in films, a Supreme Court justice once famously quipped "I know it when I see it."[8] Bubbles are similarly difficult to define, but in contrast, spotting bubbles is even harder. Their amorphous nature, as seen above, is part of the challenge. They can emerge anywhere in the economy and have multiple characteristics. And it is hard to distinguish between harmless froth and a dangerous price level about to reset. Indeed, some bubbles may be impossible to spot because it is only their popping that makes them visible. Consider again the fracking bubble of the 2010s. Oil prices around $100 per barrel spurred an investment boom, but when oil prices fell in 2014, such investment looked less wise. OPEC deliberately pushed down prices to break the fracking business model; consequently, with hindsight, a reasonable investment boom looked like a bubble. Yet by 2022, Russia's war in Ukraine and the reordering of global energy flows raised the possibility of a further change in that assessment.

Stopping bubbles isn't much easier than spotting them. Even if our collective ability to spot bubbles were better, monetary policymakers would need surgically precise policy instruments to deflate them without causing significant collateral damage. To contain a bubbly area of the economy, is it worth ending a cycle by rapidly raising interest rates? In the 1990s, much higher interest rates would likely have been needed to contain the dot-com bubble—prematurely ending a cycle that delivered strong wage gains and low unemployment. A similar argument can be made for 2008. The magnitude of the policy-rate increase needed to stop easy credit standards would likely have inflicted widespread pain across the economy—if it had worked at all.[9]

Beyond spotting and stopping, there is also the reality of stoking bubbles. As we saw in chapter 9 on the compulsive stimulus model, bubbles have become part of the policy tool kit to goose the economy. But is stoking irresponsible or can it be economically justifiable? In fact, bubbles are less controversial than it may appear. Policymakers can use bubbles as an instrument to drive activity. But bubbles do invite risks, and choices must be made in how to manage them.

When does the macroeconomic benefit (reward) outstrip the cost (risk) from a bubble, and vice versa? To illustrate, consider the case of high unemployment. When the economy is suffering under a large amount of slack, stoking some bubbles can be an appropriate instrument to increase economic utilization.[10] The use of quantitative easing in the context of deflationary fears in the years after the global financial crisis is a (controversial) case in point.

One problem is that bubbles are hard to reverse. Using a bubble opportunistically to achieve recovery is a seductive option—but taking away stimulus is much harder and more disorderly than deploying it. The 2010s offer at least two stark reminders. In 2013, when the Fed tried to taper its quantitative-easing program, it prompted market convulsions known as the taper tantrum. Similarly, at the end of 2018, the Fed planned to continue to raise rates—but a bout of intense market volatility ensued and the Fed reversed course.

But these episodes of financial-market volatility are poor arguments against easy policy—financial volatility (in stock markets) is strictly preferable to real volatility (in employment).[11] And if bubbles emerge as a consequence of having stimulated a weak economy, policymakers are better suited to cleaning them up, given a weak ability and a limited toolbox to fight them.

Cleanup Duty versus Financial Stability

As noted, bubbles occur naturally and can also be a policy tool in a weak economy. Yet, no one knows what shifts in activity are real and which are bubbles—spotting them is hard. And no one is equipped with the tools to easily stop them. In this light, policymakers should focus on minimizing the damage when bubbles pop.[12]

The best approach is to improve the financial system's ability to absorb shocks and to perfect ways of backstopping the system with official interventions if the private sector's buffers are not enough. Realistically, the role of policymakers is more like that of the fire department than of the diagnostics lab. There is plenty of fire prevention and inspection, but fires can't be entirely avoided—and so we expect the fire department to be the best it can be.[13]

That said, not all fires are the same—some threaten the system. When a deflating bubble would pose a risk to financial stability, cleanup might be very costly or might not be possible. While the 2008 crisis was eventually contained, its cost was high and its legacy severe. The impacts of the 1920s bubble in the United States, and the 1980s bubble in Japan, were even more destructive.

This places our discussion on the right side of the bubble taxonomy in figure 16.1, where macroeconomic damage is systemic. The key is to focus on containing bubbles where they have potential to threaten the stability of the financial system, particularly the leveraged financial system (banks). Would an unwinding leave a capital hole that freezes credit and forces a cycle of deleveraging? If so, aggressive action is warranted to preemptively fill the hole or stop one from occurring. But if a bubble can burst without such dire consequences, it is typically wise to let it do so.

A juxtaposition of the 1920s and the 1990s equity bubbles illustrates this. In our bubble taxonomy, both were comparable valuation and velocity bubbles (with some quality and quantity characteristics as well). And while the 1990s bubble may have been even larger, the 1920s bubble left macro-economic carnage, because it played a role in crippling the banking system. More than 9,000 banks failed during the 1930s, whereas in the early 2000s just 22 did.[14] The 1930s brought the Great Depression. The early 2000s featured only a shallow recession.

But monitoring and managing risk in the banking system through regulation is easier said than done. Let's not forget that leverage and risk are design features of banks—not bugs. Policymakers face a trade-off between the availability of stable, expensive credit that poses little systemic risk and cheaper but risky credit that fuels growth. Banks can always be better capitalized, but that comes with a price. Policymakers could force a bank to hold enough cash and capital to cover all its liabilities—but then it would be a vault, not a bank.

Stress tests can be employed to evaluate risk in the system. The goal of these tests is to ask hard questions: What if a particular activity stopped, or a particular valuation reverted? Would these shocks create a capital hole? Stress tests are only as good as those designing and conducting them, as was illustrated by the surprising, years-long failure to test the impact of a jump in interest rates, before precisely such a jump caused the collapse of Silicon Valley Bank. But while stress tests will never be perfect, they hold merit in our view if skillfully designed. Policymakers should strive to look for where a bursting bubble could impair the banking system and attempt to stop that impairment from happening.

Bubbles Can Even Be Good

Though the reputation of bubbles is universally bad, it is not entirely deserved. We already saw that bubbles can be employed as a stimulus tool. Beyond that, bubbles can have positive macroeconomic legacies, precisely because their exuberance mobilizes action and resources in ways that would not otherwise occur.

This argument may seem surprising. Bubbles are, by definition, wasteful, since their implosion is evidence of inefficient capital allocation. Yet that view is too theoretical and too narrow. In the real world, some economic activity likely wouldn't happen at all without some form of irrational exuberance. In fact, bubbles can help address collective-action problems: few are going to risk betting on a new technology unless suddenly everyone is doing it. Entrepreneurial exuberance is a key ingredient of capitalism—and bubbles can spur entrepreneurial fervor.

To see a bubble's positive potential, we should ask if the bubble has enhanced the economy's capacity. In macroeconomic terms this comes down to a larger capital stock, more productivity growth, or greater mobilization of labor and talent. The most persuasive case can be made about the capital stock. The railroad bubbles of the 19th century imploded painfully— but the tracks remained on the ground. The same is true of fiber that was laid below ground and on the seabed in the 1990s—even if investors in Global Crossing lost their capital, their investments helped fuel the digital economy. It's not hard to imagine how a bubble in green energy technologies could leave a positive legacy and accelerate the energy transition. In an ideal world disciplined capital allocation would unfailingly propel economic capacity, but it doesn't always happen—so while the undisciplined capital formation of bubbles is not ideal, it still leaves a legacy that can be positive. One might say a little irrational exuberance is needed from time to time.

Bubbles may also boost productivity—even if with lags. The dot-com bubble left wild stories of wasteful projects and frivolous spending (think Pets.com commercials), but the hype also led to a shift in the way the world consumed. WebVan—a failed dot-com darling—became part of Amazon, where executives took what the startup had learned to build Amazon Fresh, a grocery-delivery service. Again, while a bubble may look bad to investors, the learning that occurred along the way can accelerate innovation, development, and implementation of new technologies and processes.

Finally, an argument can be made for the positive impact on labor. Consider the bubbly valuation of tech startups in 2021—this helped recruit and pay talent. Even if most of those startups go on to fail, a few may do well enough to transform an industry. Meanwhile, a large cohort of workers will have been inducted into the culture of startups: think of the bubble as a huge scholarship program for hands-on learning about entrepreneurship.

All three macroeconomic upsides are underpinned by the microeconomic impact of bubbles. Frothy finance inspires confidence and perceptions of opportunity, which emboldens risk-taking and attracts entrepreneurs, while providing the funds to invest and hire.[15] Bubbles have the power to help economies overcome collective-action problems, as an irrational exuberance in capital, ideas, and labor can spur something that would have seemed impossible in more sober times. Of course, these potential silver linings must be seen in context of bubbles' destructive capacity.

Remember, Bubbles Won't Go Away

Like it or not, the modern era is prone to bubbles, a structural predisposition that will hold even in a higher-interest-rate regime (don't forget that the dot-com bubble came in an era of higher but healthy rates and a tight economy). Where does this leave private-sector leaders—executives and investors alike?

They do not have the luxury of standing aloof from bubbles. Consider the (in)famous case of Citigroup, the bank that suffered enormous losses during the global financial crisis. Charles "Chuck" Prince, the then chief executive of Citi, was widely derided for saying, in reference to the sub-prime mortgage bubble, that you have to keep dancing while the music is playing.[16] But it's hard to say that he was wrong. An investment bank that had stayed away from the securitization boom in 2005 and 2006 would have struggled to retain both investors and employees. So much money was being made in securitization that Prince could not pull out: he would have forgone immediate and certain profits in order to protect himself from future losses whose size could not be forecast.

The same logic applies in the nonfinancial sector. When an industry is caught up in a bubble, the deluge of cheap finance delivers new capacity that can redefine the marketplace, pricing, and competition. It is often far too risky to stay out of the game, even if there is a danger that the game will yield few winners. If the frothy activity generates the next big thing, those who thought they were staying out of a bubble may find they have been surpassed.

Our key insights in this chapter are:

- *Learn to live with bubbles.* Bubbles are a natural part of the fabric of capitalism—fed by the same enthusiasm that fuels entrepreneurship, inventions, and transformation.

- *Spotting and stopping bubbles remains an illusion.* The belief that all bubbles can be prevented is a byproduct of hindsight bias. It's implausible to consistently know which are false promises and which have true rewards. And even if one could, the tools to stop them are not typically available. Instead, policymakers must focus on the potential for systemic problems after bubbles burst—the most important aspect is to keep them from infecting the financial system.

- *Bubbles are better than their reputation.* Bubbles are not all bad. They may not be textbook efficient, but in the real world they can accelerate investment and innovation and bring together talent that can deliver on promises that otherwise may not have a chance. As we saw, the long-term legacy of bubbles can be positive.

- *Remember, firms don't have a choice.* Watching from the sidelines is not a neutral act for firms—not participating in a bubble is an active bet. If the bubble changes the industry, firms that abstained may be left behind. They must participate in a way that keeps them competitive. At the same time, they must keep an eye on their ability to survive if the music stops. An eye toward strategic optionality—where the upside is available but the downside protected—is key.

!

CHAPTER 17

After the Convergence Bubble

I n recent years, leaders have experienced enormous geopolitical whiplash. Following an era of rapid global integration across multiple dimensions—what we call the convergence bubble—the geopolitical narrative has inflected. After the convergence bubble, divergence overshadows global security, political and economic systems, and the financial realm. Where geopolitics used to be a benign backdrop to global business and investors—a pillar of good macro—it now looks to be an ever-present challenge.

The financial analogy of a convergence bubble is appropriate for the extraordinary exuberance that underpinned the narrative's ascent. Expectations were linearly extrapolated from a unipolar moment that followed the end of the Cold War. The term is also appropriate because when bubbles pop, exuberant boom flips to defeatist doom. But while some of the pain is an *absolute* downgrade to the good-macro world, some is only *relative* to formerly exalted expectations of convergence.

This is not to belittle the real flux and risks in the geopolitical realm. But here, too, executives need to carefully decode often exaggerated narratives. In this chapter, we seek to anchor readers by analyzing the bubble's four dimensions—security, political, economic, and financial—tracing the original expectations, the extrapolation of evidence, the inflections in each, and the downgrades that followed. In other words, we're taking stock of the convergence bubble and the subsequent divergence. This will provide context for the chapters that follow.

In terms of analytical instruments, when assessing geopolitics, decision-makers need a sound grasp of history and an awareness of how to use it to reveal the underpinnings of geopolitics. Without a doubt, using history comes with traps. The ascent of the convergence bubble in the 1990s was underpinned by a history-is-history mindset, dispensing with deep-rooted forces and context. Since the 2010s, a history-is-destiny mindset has emerged, a defeatist and gloomy narrative of old great-power rivalry and of conflict that inevitably repeats. A corollary is that exuberance about US hegemony has turned into doomsaying about US declinism. Both uses of history pull us toward extremes, and to read geopolitical risk effectively, executives will need to resist and decode that pull.

Using History

Why care about history? For those analyzing geopolitics—or macroeconomics—history matters because today's arrangements are the accumulation of past processes, norms, events, and decisions. There are many famous quips about history, including "History repeats itself, first as tragedy, second as farce"; "History doesn't repeat itself, but it often rhymes"; and "What is history but a fable agreed upon."[1] One that truly resonates with us is William Faulkner's: "The past is never dead. It's not even past."[2] We'd ask skeptics of history's value how they would understand *any* system's performance under pressure, if not by studying its construction?

But historical narrative is treacherous, as the discussion of the convergence bubble demonstrates throughout this chapter. There are two competing mindsets, and both are traps.

The *history-is-history* mindset analytically ignores the past's relevance. The mindset can be willful and conscious—even leading professional historians occasionally to see the past as over—or it can be the result of ignorance or agnosticism.[3] The outcome is similar: the past has been superseded by new sets of beliefs, rules, drivers, and dynamics. The *history-is-history* mindset lends itself to imagining new futures, often with unbridled optimism. Frequently, extrapolations are made by those enmeshed in the technological frontier, who argue that innovation will change the rules of the game entirely. Recall that the internet was once touted as a major force of global institutional convergence and freedom. This mindset can be turbo-charged with confirmation bias—the tendency to focus on evidence that confirms prior assumptions, while disregarding evidence that doesn't. Yet history shapes the present, and history's path dependencies, influences, and dynamics will continue to matter. As Faulkner said, it is not even past.

The *history-is-destiny* mindset, by contrast, is a deterministic reading that ascribes to history the role of a predictive machine. Inputs deliver outputs—we are destined to repeat the many grim episodes of the past. This gloomy view holds that doom is predestined and often imminent. And if it hasn't happened yet, it is only because we are holding on to the edge of a histori-cal cliff.

The popular narrative of Thucydides's trap—the idea that the rise of an emerging power will inevitably lead to a conflict with the prevailing power—is an illustration of the template-like use of history.[4] The concept has made a stunning jump from being a thoughtful if reductive framework (as if all conflicts were the same) to being received wisdom about the inevitability of great-power conflict despite abundant contradictions. Most obviously and simply, the United States and the United Kingdom did not come into con-flict as the former colony superseded the former global power in the early 20th century. And let's not forget that the Soviet Union too was a rising power that sought to displace the United States. But conflict did not happen the way Thucydides's trap darkly suggested it would. The narrative is still often employed to predict inevitable military conflict between the United States and China—skipping over the fact that the most relevant episodes do not fit the template well.

History is a necessary and powerful instrument for geopolitical analysis. To reject it, or to embrace it too tightly, is risky. Neither a precise map nor a useless artifact, history can provide insight about drivers and context, their relevance reverberating over the long term. But history always risks leading us astray. And that is key to understanding the convergence bubble.

The Rise of the Convergence Bubble

The early 1990s embodied a perfect moment for the history-is-history mind-set to take hold of the collective narrative. The end of the Cold War was a unipolar moment set to replace great-power rivalry. It coincided with technological renewal, economic growth, and unbridled optimism about having reached a final form of political and economic governance.

With the system competition of the Cold War over, the history-is-history narrative fastened onto the prospect of global systems convergence. Democracy and liberal market economies were cast as two sides of the same coin, mutually reinforcing their benign, global impacts; individual liberty was seen to underpin both sides of that coin. All societies appeared to be converging toward this democracy-markets-liberty trifecta. Hence the extrapolation toward the convergence bubble.

The convergence bubble comprised four elements.

> *Security convergence.* In August 1990, less than a year after the fall of the Berlin Wall, the world witnessed the Gulf War, a successful, surgical, and multilateral effort to expel Iraq from Kuwait. The sharp contrast with the Cold War's specter of mutually assured destruction underlined the unipolar moment and fueled bubbly extrapolation toward a future without major military conflict, stabilized by a benign hegemon.[5] This relaxation fed through to a decline in US military spending, as seen in figure 17.1A.

> *Political convergence.* The end of the Cold War also suggested the end of (political) systems rivalry, and the impending and final victory of democracy. A rise in democratization did follow, as seen in figure 17.1B. These shifts in sovereign governance were underpinned by a loose set of rules for democracy, including political pluralism, freedom of expression, rule of law, and fair elections. And while successes varied locally, global sentiment was bending toward liberal democracy. The advancing and receding tides of political history appeared to have been replaced by a river flowing in one direction.

> *Economic convergence.* The rivalry of competing economic systems was also seen as settled, paving the way for convergence toward a neoliberal version of capitalism.[6] A polished set of principles emerged to shape new market economies across the globe. Often disseminated through institutions like the IMF and the World Bank, the so-called Washington Consensus offered a playbook for how to get economics right.[7] Figure 17.1C shows the degree of global trade liberalization as

FIGURE 17.1

The rise and fall of the convergence bubble

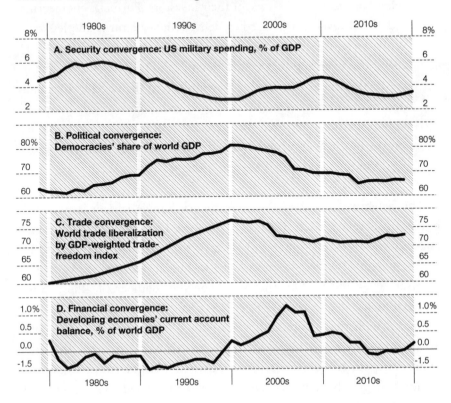

Note: Data through 2020 (panels A and D) and through 2019 (panels B and C). Developing economies' current account balance is the sum of individual developing countries' current account balances. Trade freedom index 100 = full trade freedom.
Source: OMB, Varieties of Democracy, Fraser Institute, IMF, analysis by BCG Center for Macroeconomics

a proxy for the playbook's success. This also represented a bubble in economics, the discipline. Not short of hubris, the profession believed it could fix the macroeconomies of the emerging world the way a surgeon would fix a broken body (or, to paraphrase Keynes, the way a dentist fills a cavity).[8]

Financial convergence. The convergence bubble also reached into the financial realm, where a belief that open and flexible capital markets, including currencies, would facilitate investment flows that could generate returns and adjust economic imbalances in the process—if only the world would fully adopt capital openness. Risk-return-optimizing financiers would seek out the most-attractive opportunities, helping accelerate growth, particularly in less developed economies, while delivering attractive returns for their investors. Financial engineering and global markets promised to deliver higher returns and less risk. While no single metric can capture this complex space, figure 17.1D does show, in an apparent vindication of this optimistic vision, that in the 1990s, capital was flowing downhill from the developed economies to the emerging world. Developing countries' negative current account balance suggested that global investors were seeking higher returns in catch-up economies and simultaneously spreading prosperity to the nations that needed it the most.

The seductive appeal of the convergence bubble lays in its seeming internal coherence. Each dimension reinforced the other. For example, not only was free trade going to help growth, but growth would also be an instrument of political convergence to liberal democracy. As former adversaries became wealthy, they would become democratic allies, a rosy narrative that helped the WTO's enlargement in 2001. The bubble also coincided with the economic boom of the 1990s, when a technology-driven surge in productivity growth promised a new economy. And each dimension pointed away from history, toward a brighter future. Confirmation bias took hold: every data point that confirmed convergence was celebrated, and those that confounded the narrative were seen as anomalous. History was history.

But the convergence bubble, and the rejection of history that helped fuel it, also provided a catalyst for the "arrogance of power."[9] Limited strategic competition caused the United States to mistake a unipolar moment for unfettered and enduring control. Indeed, inside the convergence bubble festered a *hegemony* bubble. The history–is–history mentality allowed an extrapolation of geopolitical developments well beyond what a view anchored by history would have.

It is easy to forget that even in the 1990s, warning signs flashed across the system but were dismissed as aberrations from the new trend. On the security side, terrorist attacks on the World Trade Center (1993) and the US embassy in Kenya (1998) foreshadowed the testing of the power of military hegemony to come. On the political side, newly minted democracies lacked the institutional strength to avoid corruption, which augured subsequent disappointments. On the trade side, the Seattle WTO riots of 1999 portended the crumbling consensus around the supposed overwhelming benefits of trade. And on the financial side, the 1997–1998 Asian financial crisis demonstrated the risks of contagion and brittleness in a world of ever-greater capital-market integration. The writing was on the wall—history was not even past.

Convergence Bubble Peaks

Despite accumulating evidence that history was, in fact, not history, by the early 2000s the mindset of the convergence bubble was not going to be easily turned off. Rather, it comfortably outlasted the actual path of convergence. The belief in history as history underpinned the decisions of political and policy classes whose interests and ideals made it difficult to give up on the narrative of benign convergence. Yet by holding on to the unrealistic assumptions of the bubble mentality, they hastened the end of the convergence bubble, in each of the four dimensions.

On the security front, the response to the attacks of September 11, 2001, illustrates the point. The hegemon's response assumed a unipolar world in which the United States could achieve its objectives, through force, with the ease it had in the Gulf War of 1990. But "mission accomplished" came only on a banner, never on the ground.[10] As the war in Afghanistan dragged on—and the war in Iraq commenced without UN support—the false facade of an omnipotent global policeman cracked and ultimately crumbled. The inflection can also be seen in figure 17.1A, as military spending began to rise again.

On the political front, the dream of political convergence delivered via economic development became harder and harder to defend, as nondemocratic countries achieved strong growth without concomitant political reforms. Evidence mounted that liberal democracy was not a prerequisite for growth, nor did it seem that growth necessarily led to the demand for individual freedoms. As global growth occurred without political convergence, democratic countries' share in global output, as seen in figure 17.1B, peaked around 2000 and began to fall.

On the economic front, the dot-com bust and recession of 2001 had already deflated the high-growth narrative, as the late 1990s productivity boom began to fade. But it was the 2000s housing bubble, which US policymakers allowed to fester, that indelibly tarnished the idea of a final economic model on which all countries would converge. As the Western financial system came dangerously close to systemic collapse, the global financial crisis of 2008 severely undermined the narrative of a natural order based on liberal market democracy. It also stripped away the scientific veneer of macroeconomics—engineering, let alone physics, it is not and never will be. Meanwhile, as the global economy slumped, China propped up global demand and elevated growth—a demonstration of the viability of alternative economic models. The high-water mark for the "Washington consensus" came around the middle of the 2000s, as shown in figure 17.1C.

On the financial front, the convergence narrative was also found faulty. The hope of finance as a risk reducer was arguably always too Pollyannish (as with the idea of the omnipotent economist, belief in the financial engineer as a positive force lost credibility). But even the intuitive idea that financial capital would flow to where new physical capital would be the most productive came up short. While capital appeared to flow downhill from advanced to emerging economies before the late 1990s, afterward it flowed uphill from emerging to advanced economies, particularly from Asia to the United States. Emerging economies ran huge export surpluses and saved their proceeds (often in US assets), wishing to avoid a repeat of the emerging market crisis of the late 1990s (see figure 17.1D). In a final irony, though booming trade had helped accelerate development, the accompanying emerging-economy savings glut held down interest rates in the United States, contributing to the housing bubble that came to define 2008's inflection point.[11]

Taking Stock of Divergence

The four dimensions of benign convergence peaked at various times in the early or mid-2000s, but we think of 2008 as *the* inflection. As the geopolitical whiplash unfolded, the role of historical narrative once again proved a powerful driver—only in reverse. Since 2008, the history-is-history mindset has been in full retreat, replaced by the now-dominant belief that history is destiny. History, under this belief, is destined to repeat itself. The return of great-power rivalry, inevitably resulting in conflict, has become the new received wisdom. US declinism has replaced the narrative of US hegemony. And the fact that the zeitgeist has taken a dark turn is often seen as a sophisticated rejection of the Pollyannish convergence narrative of before—never mind the (we think likely) possibility of merely replacing Pollyanna with Cassandra.[12]

Where do we stand? How much has the convergence narrative unraveled? We revisit the four dimensions once more:

> *Security divergence.* Disappointment in war's ability to deliver hegemonic ends has grown, while military buildups and tensions have too. Wars in Iraq and Afghanistan dragged on, cementing downgraded expectations for what the West could accomplish militarily—with a botched exit from Afghanistan closing a chapter after nearly 20 years of war with little to show for it. China's continued military buildup pointed toward its dissatisfaction with the status quo. Russia's annexation of Crimea in 2014 (foreshadowed by incursion into Georgia) showed military might still mattered and would be used as a force for changing borders, foreshadowing the larger invasion of Ukraine that began in 2022. The history-is-destiny mindset pointed toward ever greater conflict, as emerging powers seek to remake the existing global order. In the eyes of many, Thucydides' trap has been set.

> *Political divergence.* Instead of convergence to liberal democracy, democratic drift and decay have taken hold. A return of strongman leaders has fueled the degradation of liberal democratic aspirations, and autocratic economies have grown—taken together, democracies' share of output has fallen (see figure 17.1B). The appeal of strongman leaders who siphoned powers away from legislatures grew globally. Even in the United States, democratic slippage occurred as an orderly transition of power was called into question following the election of 2020. With the stalling of democracy's proliferation, the history-is-history mindset—feeding on the notion of US declinism and a return of system competition—gained currency.[13]

Economic divergence. The global financial crisis of 2008 and the slow recoveries that followed tarnished the Western economic model. The same happened again when the sovereign-debt crisis unfolded in Europe. Policy paralysis didn't stand up well to state-led development that was willing to aggressively backstop challenges and bull-doze blockages to growth. State-planned industrial strategy was back in vogue, as "Socialism with Chinese characteristics" continued to run ahead. (See also our discussion of the limitations of factor-led growth, particularly capital, in chapter 6.) Rather than the East adopting the West's "final" economic model, the East has sought to export its model through significant investments like the Belt and Road Initiative and institutions like the Asian Infrastructure Investment Bank.[14] But when the Covid crisis tested the resilience of competing systems, each system's response left something to be desired. There were no clear winners. In the United States, the response revealed that fiscal efforts would increasingly prioritize domestic demand and production (for instance, domestic input requirements and renewed industrial policy)—something that would have been looked down upon in prior years but has become normal in the time of trade wars.

Financial divergence. Global financial imbalances have persisted even as their composition has shifted. China's vast trade surpluses fell as a share of GDP during the 2010s, but that of the Northern European economies remained large, not least because fiscal austerity policies left them with inadequate domestic demand. No longer was there any hope that global financial flows would create stable and healthy markets, or that finance itself could be a source of stability. Rather than letting capital flow freely, policymakers turned to the question of how to control finance and keep it from destabilizing the rest of the economy. There would be no benign rebalancing. The history-is-destiny camp concluded that countries deeply in debt would inevitably fall into crises.[15] Then, after Covid struck, inflation roared higher, particularly in the West, curtailing tactical stimulus (see chapter 11), while remaining more contained in the East. This sparked questions about dollar hegemony, as history-is-destiny saw the dollar's demise. Yet here, too, dark determinism is being taken too far (see chapter 20).

Remember, History Is Something, Not Nothing or Everything

Our helicopter tour of the past 30 years leaves little doubt that the convergence bubble has popped. But readers should resist the dark and defeatist narratives that have supplanted the exuberant ones. Instead, they can consider geopolitical doom through the following takeaways.

- *Beware history's role in geopolitics.* Linear extrapolations are seductive frameworks for analyzing geopolitics. But the belief that history is history failed to forecast the geopolitical trajectory of the last 30 years. And though we can't know for sure that the belief that history is destiny will fail, it's reasonable to expect that it will overshoot as well. The dangers are real, but they don't follow templates. Geopolitics remains about risks, not rigid trajectories. In addition, as we will see in the next chapter, the translation from geopolitical flux to macro-economic damage is far from linear.

- *Be conscious of the role of expectations.* The collective experience of geopolitical discomfort is shaped by the expectations we measure against. There is no doubt that *absolute* downgrades of divergence have replaced the dreams of benign convergence, yet much of the fraying we have experienced has been *relative* to the unrealistic dreams. What matters more is the actual damage and changed realities.

- *Don't forget to de-layer geopolitical risk.* There are multiple interrelated dimensions. Geopolitical narratives weave these together into persuasive trajectories. Disaggregating security, political, economic, and financial themes will improve risk assessment by isolating the drivers without ignoring their intersections.

- *Frame risks, not outcomes.* Rather than seize upon a seductive narrative, stay focused on multiple futures and what would be required for each to occur. The challenge is to frame the risk associated with each of them.

Executives are growing into the reality of geopolitical flux, with little background. You would have to be over age 60 to have firsthand (professional) experience of geopolitics before the convergence bubble. But readers can think about the transmission of geopolitical risk to economic impact in the next chapter and dive into the details of trade risk and dollar hegemony in chapters 19 and 20 respectively.

CHAPTER 18

From Geopolitics to Economic Impact

When World War I broke out on July 28, 1914, the US stock market dropped 10% in three days and was subsequently shut, as shown in figure 18.1. When it was reopened 136 days later, it was down another 20%. The stock market reaction captured an enormous geopolitical shock to the economic landscape and the world order: a seemingly straightforward pass-through from geopolitics to macroeconomic impact.[1]

Yet, when World War II broke out on September 1, 1939, the US stock market popped 13%, also shown in figure 18.1.[2] This time, another geopolitical calamity had materially improved the economic landscape. World War II delivered an enormous demand boost to the US economy, effectively ending the Great Depression.

Our juxtaposition highlights that markets aren't moral gauges but narrowly reflect expected profits, cash flows, and other financial considerations. While geopolitical shocks can be bad for the economy, in the cold calculus of markets, there isn't a linear connection. The translation from geopolitics to macroeconomic impact is more complex and treacherous.

That geopolitical prediction is hard is hardly a new idea. George Kennan, the influential mid-20th-century US diplomat, once said of geopolitical

FIGURE **18.1**

War is bad, but the direction of economic impact can be surprising

US stock market performance at onset of war
Dow Jones Industrial Average (WWI) and S&P 500 (WWII), indexed

Note: DJIA indexed to July 27, 1914; S&P 500 indexed to August 31, 1939.
Source: Bloomberg, analysis by BCG Center for Macroeconomics

analysis and prediction: "In no field of endeavor is it easier than in the field of foreign affairs to be honestly wrong; in no field is it harder for contemporaries to be certain they can distinguish between wisdom and folly."[3] What Kennan didn't consider is that in addition, many must gauge the economic impact of geopolitics, a compounding of complexity and uncertainty.

Given the difficulty of distinguishing wisdom and folly, what are executives and investors to do—or avoid doing? Powerlessness can chafe boardroom mentalities and tempt leaders to outsource geopolitical assessment to expert opinion or to sophisticated data models. Both have limitations, as we will see. That makes scenario analysis—in effect supplanting a single plan or point forecast with multiple futures—a valuable and necessary alternative. But as we argue in this chapter, leaders should not approach geopolitical analysis like the corporate-strategy function: there is no such thing as a meaningful five-year geopolitical plan. Rather than following the approach used in preparing corporate strategies, we see geopolitical risk assessment as being closer in style to the role played by the CFO. It requires the ability to react, quickly assess impacts, and disseminate directional guidance to organizations. For that, leaders must enable their organizations to build the skill and muscle memory necessary to execute bite-size macro impact analyses ongoingly—rather than invest in an assessment of grand geopolitical strategy.

But how? The focus is far too often on the gun firing, rather than how the bullet will ricochet in a complex maze of real, financial, and institutional transmission channels. But if geopolitics is to shift the business environment, it must do so through those same linkages—and that's where the focus needs to be.

(Dis)Trusting Experts and Models

Executives are used to commanding vast budgets. They often have access to political power, and some even have the ability to nudge public discourse. But in geopolitics their influence is typically de minimis. Against the benign backdrop of the inflating convergence bubble that did not matter much. But as the tailwind of unipolarity has turned into a headwind of system competition, a sense of powerlessness has become palpable in the boardroom.

As leaders try to correct for that and get ahead of geopolitics, they are often offered two shortcuts to reading the future. On the qualitative side, great trust is often placed in experts, frequently past practitioners of statecraft who were in the room. On the quantitative side, a growing number of approaches for measuring and modeling geopolitics are on offer. We think leaders want to be careful with each.

When considering the last 100 years or so, we find enough examples to illustrate George Kennan's warning about wisdom and folly; expert predictions of big geopolitical turning points have had a poor track record. With the 1909 bestseller *The Great Illusion*, Nobel Peace Prize–winner Norman Angell helped shape the then-conventional wisdom that a great-power war was impossible.[4] Too intricate were the interdependencies and trade relations of the modern world, went the argument. Angell's book contributed to World War I coming as a relative surprise.[5]

Fast-forward to 2020 and assessing the risk of war hasn't gotten easier. In *Geopolitical Alpha*, a book promising investors a "framework for predicting the future," the author, a geopolitical analyst in an advisory firm, offered up an analytical framework of "constraints." Illustrating the constraints on geopolitical ambitions and conflict, he called the idea that Vladimir Putin would attempt to recreate the Russian empire by force "flawed." Specifically, Russia's "symbiotic relationship with Europe is a major constraint . . . it is actually Berlin that has Russia by the . . . pipelines." Thus, invading Ukraine could never happen because it "would be economic suicide to turn off the tap to Europe." Sadly, none of that analysis and resulting prediction have held up.[6]

Of course, geopolitical experts also make prescient calls. But even then, the limitations are striking. Consider Kennan himself, who penned one of the most prescient geopolitical predictions on record. In his famous essay "The Sources of Soviet Conduct," published in *Foreign Affairs* under the pseudonym "X," Kennan wrote that "Soviet power . . . bears within it the seeds of its own decay, and that the sprouting of these seeds is well advanced."[7] But he published the article in 1947. If the seeds were "well advanced," placing the Soviet Union perhaps in the second half of its life cycle, why then did it take over 40 years for his prediction to come true?

As Kennan's accurate, if not timely, analysis reminds us, forecasts have a time component that pulls analysts to shakier ground. By focusing on the foundational weakness of the Soviet Union rather than on strict time horizons, Kennan was able to produce valuable insight. Yet experts are often rewarded for boldness and precision. These rewards encourage confirmation bias and the ability to rationalize former misses—each feeding into overconfidence. In 1988, academic Philip Tetlock asked an august panel, including Nobel laureates, to forecast five years into the future. Questions included whether they thought the Soviet Communist Party would remain in power. The experts who assigned confidence of 80% or higher to their answers were correct only 45% of the time.[8]

We do not wish to argue that there is no value in leveraging geopolitical experts. On the contrary, real insight often comes from those who professionally analyze geopolitics and from former practitioners who provide perspective and historical context. The problem comes when executives expect the impossible and try to buy the future. Experts cannot consistently make accurate geopolitical calls, much as economists cannot get it right consistently. Their genuine insight must be used with that in mind.

. . .

Geopolitical quantification, the other tempting tool for taming geopolitical risk, stems from the allure of models, indexes, and dashboards. These have the scientific veneer of command and control. As management scholar Peter F. Drucker argued, "What gets measured gets managed—even when it's pointless to measure and manage it, and even if it harms the purpose of the organization to do so."[9] This pertains to internal corporate dynamics, but it can also pertain to external risks.

The desire to quantify has led in recent years to the emergence of indexes that purport to measure geopolitical stress and risk. Perhaps in keeping with a general societal thrust toward quantification, the numerical expression of risk should, in theory, allow decision-makers to compress complexity into inputs that can be used in decision-making. And because these indexes measure and weigh linguistic signals in public discourse in near real time, they are both timely and avoid anchoring on any specific expert.

But such indexes suffer from significant shortcomings. Consider figure 18.2 (left panel), which charts levels of risk via a geopolitical risk index

FIGURE 18.2

Geopolitical risk is hard, probably impossible, to quantify

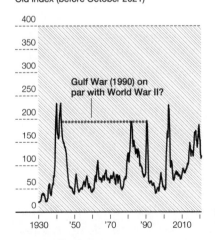

Geopolitical risk index
Old index (before October 2021)

Gulf War (1990) on par with World War II?

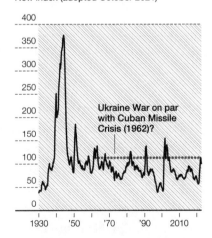

Geopolitical risk index
New index (adopted October 2021)

Ukraine War on par with Cuban Missile Crisis (1962)?

Note: 12-month midpoint average. Data through March 2021 (old) and December 2022 (new).
Source: Dario Caldara and Matteo Iacoviello, "Measuring Geopolitical Risk,"
Board of Governors of the Federal Reserve Board; analysis by BCG Center for Macroeconomics

that was created by researchers at the Federal Reserve and that was in use until late 2021.[10] While the time series seems to capture moments of known stress—World War II, 9/11, and others show up as spikes—these prints are not realistic on a relative basis. Would anyone believe that the geopolitical stress of the Gulf War, 1990–1991, was anywhere near that of the Second World War?

Yet quants are always looking to improve their methodology, as seen on the right-hand side of figure 18.2. The Fed's new-and-improved index has shifted into something more superficially sensible—World War II now towers over everything else. But can one meaningfully say that the Ukraine War that began in 2022 prompted the same uncertainty as the Cuban Missile Crisis of 1962, when the United States and the Soviet Union came close to nuclear annihilation? Sure, comparing the two could result in prolonged debate—but that only proves the point. It is unsatisfying to equate the complexity of these two episodes with the flatness of a single number. The false equivalence exposes the weakness of quantitative approaches to geopolitical risk management.

As with expert opinion, it is not that quantification itself is fatally flawed; the hazard lies in how the quantification is used. With experts, the danger is overconfidence; with quantification, it's oversimplification. It is worth remembering the adage that what counts can't always be counted—and what can be counted doesn't always count.

From Geopolitical Scenarios to Macroeconomic Impact

Faced with the severe limitations of geopolitical prediction, many organizations will find themselves contending with scenario analysis, a much-used but little-loved variant of prediction.

Of course, scenario analysis is a sensible approach. A single-point forecast gives way to a range of outcomes. However, as with expert opinions and data, scenarios are at risk of being misused if they give a sense of comfort that the problem has been answered. The fact that these are often thoughtfully arranged on a spectrum, or in a matrix, can appear to suggest that all possible versions of the future are covered. But if a false facade of comprehensiveness hides a subtle mix of possibilities, it has undermined the value of scenario exercises. The value is less to foster confidence than to help the organization build the skills and muscles needed to respond when geopolitical shocks materialize.

So, what to do? Rather than focus on events, timelines, and probabilities, the effort should focus on gauging consequential economic impact. If a geopolitical shock is to impact the macroeconomy, it must work through real, financial, and/or institutional linkages to alter the business environment:

- *Real linkages* transmit geopolitical shocks to incomes and economic activity directly. This will be visible in consumption, investment, or trade, all directly linked to GDP.

- *Financial linkages* transmit geopolitical shocks to balance sheets or credit flows. This can happen quickly through asset markets and/or painfully if the banking system's capital or liquidity is undermined.

- *Institutional linkages* transmit geopolitical shocks to the written or unwritten rules and arrangements that underpin the global macroeconomic and business environment. These changes can be slower moving than real or financial shifts, but they can have durable impact.

As we saw in the introduction, the translation from geopolitics to macroeconomic impact cannot be assumed to be linear. World War II is no outlier here. In the postwar period, even material crises didn't always shift the global business environment. The war in Afghanistan, America's longest, didn't materially alter the three transmission channels outlined above; neither did the Iraq War, nor many other conflicts that are clear geopolitical crises and human tragedies. In fact, the economic impact of geopolitical crises is often overstated, particularly early on.

In contrast, the war in Ukraine has impacted all three dimensions in a way that mattered for cyclical risk and has also imposed structural risks—with regional variation.

The real economy (households, firms) got hit because of the war's impact on commodities—most notably gas and wheat. Commodity inflation slashed real incomes of consumers, particularly in Europe, and damaged the competitiveness of firms—hurting confidence and, thus, consumption and investment. The details of this cascade could not have been predicted—even if one had predicted the invasion itself. But the contours of the impact were foreseeable. It was feasible to analyze the real linkages between the West and Russia (and Ukraine). Understanding such dynamics allowed analysts to draw sharp distinctions among regions: the United States, Europe, and Asia all have different vulnerabilities. Likewise, there were distinctions among industries: the experience of chemical producers, manufacturers, shipping firms, and so forth would all be different.

Next consider financial linkages in the Ukraine War. Again, the full or precise impact could not be foreseen or analyzed—but the contours could. A valuable starting point was to analyze which banks had exposure to Russia, on both the asset and liability side of the ledger. Who might have booked losses, been stuck with illiquid assets, or experienced a funding run? And did any of those possible shifts point toward a systemic threat? Again, the details were impossible to foresee: the rapid, often by choice, exodus of Western firms; the excluding of Russian banks from the global payment system SWIFT; the resilience of Russia's financial markets aided by a deft central bank. But the contours could be sketched out.

Though far from perfect, financial markets can lend a helping hand. Price signals provide a first pass at assessing geopolitical risk and can typically be observed across many markets, geographies, and sectors. The signals are volatile and are more directionally revealing than precise, but they do offer a continuously updated, crowdsourced view of risk and impact. For example, as the Ukraine War became an imminent possibility, and then a fact, relative price movements between US and European banks captured the varying degrees of exposure to Russian assets and liabilities. And even among European banks, relative price movements suggested where exposure and vulnerability were greatest.

Finally, the Ukraine War can illustrate the institutional linkages—both formal and informal. Formally, alliances shifted: Finland joined NATO, and Sweden is expected to. Sanctions were imposed and collaborations curtailed. Informally, norms shifted: Germany committed to increased military spending and businesses moved away from unreliable partners. The range and specifics could not have been anticipated; the best one could strive for is discerning the directional effects of facing a common enemy.

The Shock Is Only Half the Story

When assessing the economic impact of geopolitics, we must not forget that the shock itself is only half of the story—if that. An economy's ability to absorb a shock also matters, as does the reaction of policymakers. This reaction can end up being more important than the initial shock itself, particularly with respect to the biggest shocks.

Consider again how equity markets responded at the start of World War I and World War II, as seen at the start of this chapter. The drivers of this disparity harbor lessons about the role of policy response. World War I saw a collapse in US equity prices because of the enormous supply and demand disruption that the war would bring; because of specific worries about a credit squeeze and bank stress in the United States as Europeans would pull out money to fund the war; and because of the war's surprise.[11] Theretofore misplaced faith in Norman Angell's argument that great-power war was impossible only intensified the surprise.

World War II, in contrast, started against a backdrop of slack—a persistent legacy of the Great Depression. In the eyes of markets, the war promised to end a decade-long slump of huge unemployment, deflation, and slow growth. After all, a war is a positive demand shock, filling slack with demand for military matériel. Meanwhile the financial implications were less important at the onset of World War II because the banking system wasn't as reliant on foreign funding. Besides, the war was less of a surprise than World War I had been.[12]

The uncomfortable reality is that war can create macroeconomic positives, and this is true not only of past centuries. Though the Ukraine War was a genuine and real economic shock to Europe (less so to the United States), almost delivering a recession in 2022, it also likely changed the narrative about Europe's structural outlook. Recall that depressed investment demand has long been identified as a structural European ailment, but the war's impact has driven a strategic increase in military spending and accelerated investment in energy infrastructure, pulling forward the energy transition. These developments have improved Europe's chances of a stronger investment backdrop.

Beyond absorption, we must also consider the reaction, as it is policymakers and political actors who often define the second-order impact of shocks. As the old adage suggests, policymakers should never let a good crisis go to waste: big policy interventions tend to come from crises, particularly existential crises, as the need to act grows and the willingness to act is discovered.[13] Recall that in chapters 9 through 11 we discussed stimulus, and existential stimulus in particular. It is easy to see how external threats provide a common enemy aligning incentives and creating a compelling narrative to act on.

The mobilizing effect of geopolitical threats may appear to be a negative for the business climate, but paradoxically those threats can galvanize governments and spur actions that, under the right circumstances, leave the economy stronger than it otherwise would have been. This is particularly true if the economy is operating below potential or if the capital investment that the conflict spurs delivers innovation, encourages the adoption of new technologies, or leads to an embrace of new methods of production. To be very clear, wars are tragic and should never be viewed as economically desirable, or even close to optimal. But the reality of their catalyzing effect remains.

FIGURE **18.3**

A positive shock: World War II returns the US economy to its pre–Great Depression trend

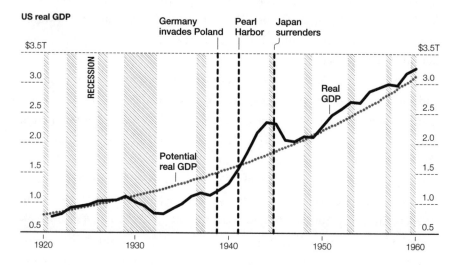

Note: US real GDP in constant US$(2012).
Source: Historical Statistics of the United States, BEA, NBER, analysis by BCG Center for Macroeconomics

Consider once more the example of World War II—this time with respect to economic output. As seen in figure 18.3, at the time the war began, output was well below trend (creating an output gap) as the economy remained in the shadow of the Great Depression. Even after the conflict began, the output gap only modestly narrowed. But when the United States entered the conflict (after Pearl Harbor), the output gap closed rapidly, as an overwhelming fiscal impulse resulted from the war effort. GDP surged past its potential.

And while fears persisted that the economy would slump sharply after the war ended, GDP fell only so far as to return to that stronger trend line. Sadly, the fiscal innovations of the New Deal in the 1930s did less to shift the economy out of its depressive state than did the war effort.

Remember, Skills Matter More Than Plans

The economic impact of geopolitical risks is often absent, rarely linear, and occasionally the opposite of what could reasonably be expected. Due to its labyrinthine nature, it can be tempting to try to outsource the geopolitical puzzle, check off the box, and leave a prepackaged plan on the shelf. But our discussion in this chapter leaves us with the following recommendations:

- *Build skills, not plans.* Big forecasts, calls, scenarios, or plans will offer solace, the feeling that efforts are being made, but they will not deliver any certainty that challenges will be met when they arise. What organizations need is skill and muscle to meet challenges quickly and adroitly—not a grand master plan, a brilliant strategy that graces a shelf. Value lies in many small, granular insights. It lies in building up skill—a process that requires regular investment rather than the commissioning of an elegant five-scenario exercise. As Eisenhower and others before him said, "Plans are worthless, but planning is everything."[14]

- *Use experts wisely.* Neither qualitative assessments, perhaps by former statesmen, nor quantitative wizardry offer firm answers to figuring out an organization's vulnerability to geopolitical crises. Experts will not consistently predict correctly, and even if they make the right call, the risks facing a particular business are idiosyncratic. Rather, the value of experts lies in their ability to build the reactive analytical skills we emphasized.

- *Focus on linkages.* Strained geopolitics seems to be a source of persistent and obvious damage, but it need not always play out like that. Unless we can clearly articulate the linkages to macroeconomic damage, we should shy away from conclusions. Remember, a shock must alter the economy's real, financial, and/or institutional dimensions. Surprisingly often, geopolitical shocks come and go without changing the realities of the business environment.

- *The shock is only half the story.* There remains a temptation to understand every detail and every development of the shock. But more value may lie in understanding the system's absorption (or amplification) of and policy reactions to the shock. Surprising outcomes, sometimes the opposite of what we intuitively expect, can be the case when the policy reaction overwhelms the shock's initial impact.

The discussion above has focused on the tools we can employ to translate geopolitical risk and stress to macroeconomic realities. In the following two chapters we do exactly that—with reference to trade and the dollar.

CHAPTER 19

Trade, Not as Bad as It Sounds

Global trade may be the most tangible exposure to geopolitics that many executives and investors experience. The era of global convergence spawned an integrated trade architecture that firms spun into an intricate web of global value chains, lower costs, and profit expansion. As the simple narrative of geopolitical convergence gives way to the complex one of divergence, it is fair to expect trade architecture to adjust again, along with economic knock-on effects. In the popular telling, globalization is giving way to deglobalization, offshoring to reshoring. The benefits that were gained are supposedly to be lost.

But trade is a perfect example of treacherous extrapolation and the simplification that occurs when translating geopolitical forces to economic outcomes, about which we warned in the preceding two chapters. Consider that despite (nearly) a decade that has seen Brexit, trade wars, and decoupling, the volume of global trade has continued to climb. And as we will demonstrate in this chapter, the popular claim that trade intensity (that is, trade as a share of world GDP) has fallen does not add up. This should make leaders skeptical of widespread talk of trade reversal and the gloomy predictions that come with it.

What drives the gap between narrative and reality? For one, resilient trade volumes are consistent with a changing composition of trade. The former reflects both the enduring desire to trade and the economic benefits of trade; the latter reflects an architecture that is slowly shifting in response to new geopolitical objectives and realities. As has often been observed, geopolitical calm encouraged a system that optimized efficiency and low-cost production. But geopolitical turbulence encourages trading patterns that deliver greater reliability, which very plausibly comes at a higher cost.

How should leaders think about this shift? The architecture of resilience is only in the process of being written, so we should not rush to conclusions and certainly not the darkest ones. What we can do is sketch the future architecture, which will determine cost and economic impact. As we argue in this chapter, the macroeconomic consequences of shifting to a resilient trade architecture are far less obvious than may appear. Though there is little doubt that the price of resilience is lower long-run growth potential, equating higher cost with all things bad is too simplistic. Above all, greater domestic investment will contribute to the era of economic tightness we have described elsewhere in this book. Other benefits include greater global capacity, higher wages for some, and the desired resilience in supply chains—while not textbook net gains, these gross gains still matter. Though in flux, the future of trade is not as bad as you might think.

The Curious Claim of Retreating Trade

Over the past decade or so, a powerful narrative of deglobalization has emerged.[1] Pointing to trends in world trade data, the narrative argues that global trade is in retreat. Yet a closer examination shows that this account involves an unwarranted extrapolation from geopolitical narratives to economic realities. The evidence points to resilience more than decay—thus far.

There is little doubt that the turbocharged era of trade growth in the 2000s—when trade grew considerably faster than world GDP—came to a halt with the global financial crisis of 2008. Deep recessions and sluggish recoveries in the West, along with strategic reorientation away from export-led growth and toward inward investment in the East, meant trade grew more slowly. In 2016, the Brexit referendum appeared to prove that the

FIGURE **19.1**

Trade data can be deceptive, making the case for declining trade difficult to uphold

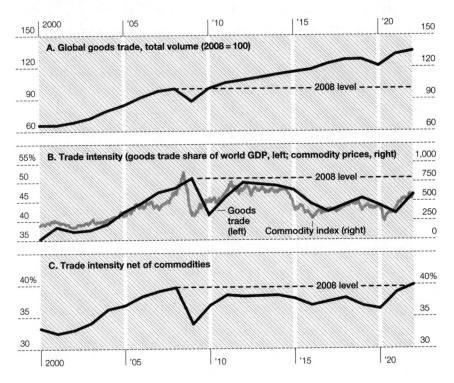

Note: Data through 2022. Commodity prices based on S&P GSCI. Net of commodities means excluding mining and fuels.
Source: World Trade Organization, Standard & Poor's, IMF, analysis by BCG Center for Macroeconomics

growth of trade might actually be reversed. Later that same year, the election of Donald Trump signaled that the United States would launch trade wars. In 2020, the pandemic delivered previously unthinkable physical disruption to cross-border commerce. The confluence of all these forces drove a narrative of decoupling and then de-risking—all underpinning gloom about the future of trade. But this gloomy narrative overshot.

We must be careful not to conflate the geopolitical trajectory and narrative with economic realities on the ground. Consider that the total volume, or real value, of trade has been growing almost every year and is well above its 2008 level, as shown in figure 19.1A. Deep cyclical downturns dent this line, but they are poor signals of geopolitical friction changing the slope of this trajectory.

We also consider the claim of receding trade intensity to be a false alarm. The declining share of trade in world GDP, as shown in figure 19.1B, is often cited to demonstrate falling intensity. Proponents will argue that a falling intensity is still consistent with growing volumes if world GDP grows faster than trade—which is exactly right. But is world GDP really growing faster than trade? Is trade becoming a less important driver of world growth? Figure 19.1B also highlights commodity prices, and their swings line up with the changing share of trade in world GDP. In other words, falling trade intensity is significantly driven by lower commodity prices—which would be weak evidence of deglobalization. The deglobalization thesis alleges less trade integration, not merely swings in commodity prices.

Figure 19.1C puts the thesis to the test, stripping out mining and fuels from global goods trade. Once these are removed, the decline in trade intensity disappears. Our point is not that commodities trade isn't real trade—it is—but rather that swings in commodity prices say little about the health of global integration. If commodity prices doubled in the next year and the share of trade in world GDP surged, should a reglobalization narrative replace the fashionable one about deglobalization? No.

There are additional reasons to be skeptical of a narrative of retreating global trade. Trade was never strictly global—but always significantly regional. The popular narratives of nearshoring capture an important point but overlook the fact that trade has long been concentrated among neighbors.[2] About 70% of Europe's total trade has been within the bloc for many years. In East Asia, 50% of trade is regional; in North America, 40% is.[3] And while North America may look less regionalized, if trade between states such as California or Texas and the rest of the United States were counted the way trade between Germany and France is today, North America would post a much higher figure. Thus, even if very long global value chains shrink in response to geopolitical friction, there remains scope for growth in regional trade.

Of course, escalating geopolitical rivalry involving aggressive sanctions and even military conflict could reduce trade materially. But even in the extreme case of great-power war, the impact on trade is surprisingly uncertain. Looking at figure 19.2, which shows global trade between 1870 and

FIGURE **19.2**

Depression—not war—has damaged trade most severely

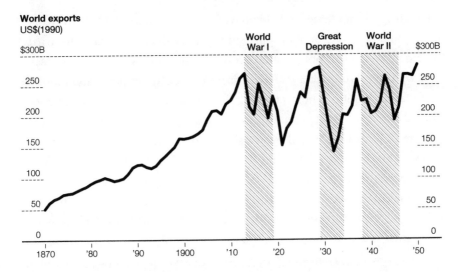

Source: *The Cambridge Economic History of the Modern World*, vol. II; analysis by BCG Center for Macroeconomics

1950 in constant dollars, we see that trade continued throughout the two World Wars—there was no sudden stop. When trade did decline owing to global conflict, it fell to levels that only years earlier would have been record strength, as seen by the trough in World War I that exceeded the level of 1900. And in World War II, trade continued at stronger levels than much of the prior three decades. Remarkably, figure 19.2 also shows that the weakest years for global trade came not from the World Wars—as destructive and violent as they were—but from an economic crisis. The impact of the Great Depression on trade was bigger than that of either military conflict.

Should one be surprised by trade's resilience? We think not. Trade is hard to stop because it promises mutual advantage. Though it can certainly experience volatility because of geopolitical crisis, we should be wary of the assumption that geopolitical stress will damage trade permanently or that the trade order will completely unwind. Note that even at its interwar trough, trade was never meaningfully below its 1900 level. And the average was on par with the 1909 level.

Toward a New Trade Architecture

Though aggregate trade has held up well, its composition is likely to change in response to new geopolitical pressures. This will happen gradually, partly because government policy often evolves incrementally. For instance, candidate Trump promised a trade war during his 2016 campaign and imposed some tariffs, but it was not until 2022 that the Biden administration imposed an embargo on the sale of advanced semiconductors to China. The architecture of global trade will evolve slowly for another reason, too. It takes time for businesses to decide on the location of (and then building of) the next generation of production.

These choices regarding incremental capacity will be critical for the marginal cost of production and will reverberate gradually through the world economy. As the architecture of global trade shifts to prioritize resilience, how much will costs increase? The answer depends on the extent of remodeling the architecture ultimately needs. Cosmetic tweaks to a building cost little. Foundational changes cost a lot—even more so if done quickly.

As geopolitical convergence gives way to divergence, a dichotomous, bipolar system of world trade seems plausible (for many types of trade) and likely (at least for certain types of trade). This is often captured in a narrative about decoupling between the Chinese and the US economies.[4] This view has a hard, all-or-nothing ring to it and a concomitant implication of abrupt cost surges. Yet decoupling will play out along a spectrum where some shifts are significant and others less so. When pondering the potential cost of divergence, we need to consider two questions. Neither has a foregone answer, and neither is entirely new:

- *Degree of separation:* How porous or sealed will the two sides be?

- *Degree of alignment:* Outside China and the United States, the two poles of the new bipolar world, how can other economies align themselves?

Regarding the degree of separation, a hard cut with two hermetically sealed hemispheres is not likely. Even during the depths of the Cold War, the two blocs were not sealed off. West Germans built gas pipelines from the Soviet Union under Willy Brandt in the 1970s.[5] Pepsi sold fizzy drinks in the Soviet Union and was paid in scrap metal.[6] China is far more integrated into the world economy than the Soviet Union ever was, so these sorts of interchanges will likely remain more plentiful. The multitude of stakeholders that have traded with China for decades have strong incentives to maintain links. This is well illustrated by the limitations of reshoring predictions.[7] Existing value chains are rarely dismantled outright. Rather, gradual decisions are made to situate incremental capacity closer to home. There is no certainty about the extent of geographical separation.

Which industries will separate the most is also uncertain. The trade in cutting-edge electronics was seen only a handful of years ago as a success of globalization. Now it's seen by geostrategists as a crucial weak point and the subject of a chip war.[8] Export restrictions have been around for decades; what changes is what's on the list. Here too, there can be no certainty about the composition of acceptable trade in the future.

The second dimension, that of alignment in a divided world order, also defies prediction. We can't rule out forced alignment, where some economies have to choose sides. But that seems unlikely to be attempted and even less likely to be successful—except in specific products and circumstances. Again, the Cold War suggests that flexibility will remain. It was during the Cold War, after all, that the Non-Aligned Movement was formed. Its members made a point of engaging with both superpowers—and the superpowers tolerated it. Remember, trade exists because it is mutually advantageous—its resilience comes from mutual interests more than shared values.

The power of realism over idealism could also be seen in the context of the Ukraine War. One-quarter of United Nations member states declined to condemn Russia's invasion. And Russia continues to maintain commercial and military linkages with much of the world. Hermetically sealing trade flows in an integrated world remains unlikely.

Despite these limits to the likely reordering of trade, the prioritization of resilience over efficiency will impose higher costs on businesses. Though there is no reason to assume that a resilient trade architecture will produce the worst-case scenarios, it is likely that higher costs will result. Specifically, shifting production facilities to nearer or friendlier geographies comes at a price. So does maintaining higher inventories and building back-up capacity. Put simply, building resilience comes down to creating options. And optionality typically costs money.

Macroeconomic Outcomes May Surprise

Even as the future architecture of trade resilience—and thus its cost—remains uncertain, public discourse rushes to survey the economic damage. Some common extrapolations include a future of slower growth, more-modest profits, lower real incomes, higher inflation, and the emergence of trade disruptions. Many of these concerns have a degree of merit, but the economic implications and cyclical risks will be more nuanced than "higher cost is bad." Just consider the common assumption that new localized capacity will *replace* existing offshore capacity, when evidence points to reshoring being mostly about projects that *add to* existing global capacity and thus incrementally enhance it.

To be sure, a step back from ever closer trade integration and cost savings must equate to the loss of upside potential for the global economy—in the long run—as the benefits of trade remain unrealized. It represents a downgrade of potential output relative to what could have been—though not necessarily an absolute fall.

Even so, in the short and medium run, the effect will likely be the opposite. We see four calibrations to the overwhelmingly negative framing of the future of trade.

> *Economic tightness.* For partial decoupling and nearshoring to take place, a significant amount of investment must be pushed into economies closer to home. As public subsidies and private investment are deployed to repatriate global value chains and to build strategic capacity, we should expect a macroeconomic tailwind. After nearly a decade of slack, this delivers additional stimulus that will reinforce economic tightness—at least in the short to medium term (longer term, it may expand supply-side capacity; see below). Hence, reshoring should be seen as an additional argument for a structurally tighter economy, which is linked to innovation and productivity gains (see chapter 8).[9] An additional benefit of tightness can include stronger real-wage gains across the income distribution (particularly at the low end, where wage growth tends to outstrip inflation the most in tight markets).

> *Inflation impact: mixed, modest, and gradual.* The reversal of the disinflationary benefits of trade has been a popular narrative, particu-

larly as it coincided with the postpandemic inflation spike. Efficient value chains helped anchor a very low inflation regime, goes the argument, so dismantling them will lead to higher inflation. We do expect that the extra investment necessitated by the shifting trade architecture will contribute to upside cyclical pressure (chapter 13). But trade was never the cornerstone of the inflation regime (monetary policy was and is), and we should not assume a structural break. Trade is not large enough as a share of most economies, certainly not of the United States, to precipitate an inflationary spiral. Moreover, shifts will take place at the margin: where to build the next plant only incrementally changes the distribution of production, so any price pressure will emerge gradually. And, as already mentioned, there is little evidence so far that new productive capacity is systematically *replacing* existing capacity. If investments *add to* the supply side, they should ease inflationary pressures in the longer run. New investments may also bring opportunity: being made at the technological frontier, say, with a greater degree of automation, they may deliver productivity gains that help offset the higher costs of producing in rich economies. Finally, as argued in chapter 12, delivering price stability remains the job of the central bank, which can offset inflationary pressures—and will protect the inflation regime—by raising rates.

Cyclical risk. The pandemic-era supply-chain disruptions have given trade's role in cyclical conditions outsize attention. Will the rejiggering of trade architecture deliver further supply shocks that shape the cycle and trigger recessions? Here, too, we are skeptical. Trade is more a force that influences the long-term productivity of an economy than a driver of cyclical outcomes. Brexit can serve as a mini–case study here. When Britain tore up its relationship with the EU, its most important trading partner, the cliff-edge cyclical disaster that was widely predicted did not materialize. Instead, a cumulative loss of potential is unfolding over time. The ability of trade architecture to define the cycle is, we think, modest.

Winners and losers. It's tempting to cast any downgrade in trade as a negative, much in line with textbook arguments. But that is looking only at aggregates. Disaggregate impacts are also of interest: just as expanding trade boosts aggregate prosperity but generates losers (think of the worker at a shuttered Ohio auto assembly line), so shrinking trade will result in aggregate losses but also disaggregated winners (think of the worker in upstate New York in a new Micron semiconductor factory). More manufacturing jobs and more investment will help some economies, sectors, and communities even as the economy's potential trajectory is diminished.

Remember, Trade Is Here to Stay

Leaders can expect a march of headlines that will highlight the strains in trade. These strains will matter, but they will more likely reflect an evolution in the trade architecture, not a rapid breakdown. Trade has persisted during hot wars and cold. It can be disrupted. Its composition and flows can change. But it is remarkably resilient. The trade architecture of the future will be shaped by the search for mutual advantage, viewed through a geopolitical lens that considers risks as well as costs. The new trade architecture may not achieve textbook efficiency, but neither is it a global unwinding:

- *Be skeptical of declining-trade narratives.* The trend toward unfettered trade has long stalled, and uncertainties have risen, but real volumes keep climbing and even trade intensity (i.e., noncommodity trade as a percent of GDP) has remained resilient. The nature of trade remains mutually beneficial, which is why it has historically proven resilient even through hot and cold wars. What is changing is the who, what, and where of trade.

- *Accept the new complexity of trade.* The simple era of "cheaper is better" is over. It's followed by an era of *more complex* trade, not *less* trade. New policy objectives as well as risk of conflict will change the architecture of global trade. This demands attention and will come with (uncertain) costs.

- *Think in terms of global capacity.* The steady stream of announcements about new production capacity in high-cost, developed economies is too easily equated with deglobalization and inflationary cost. Ask if new capacity replaces or adds to existing capacity and realize that incremental changes to the geographic mix of capacity moves average cost slowly.

- *Don't forget the impact on economic tightness.* A changing trade architecture will bring (gradually) greater cost and suggests a long-run loss of economic potential. But in the short and medium run, higher cost implies greater investment, suggesting growth tailwinds and tighter economies where value chains are repatriated, reinforcing the era of tightness.

Trade will continue to be an adjustment variable in times of geopolitical flux and will continue to invite negative extrapolations and foregone conclusions. While changes to the trade architecture will represent challenges for economies and firms, they can also represent opportunities. Trade is not as bad as it often sounds.

CHAPTER 20

The False Alarms of Dollar Death

Over the past 50 years or so, the false alarm of the dollar's death has sounded over and over. Starting with the Nixon shock of 1971 that finished off the remaining facade of the gold standard, obituaries for the greenback have been written many times. In recent years, the surge in US government borrowing needed to finance the pandemic stimulus brought a new wave of obituaries.[1] Yet over the decades, the dollar's share of world reserves has been dominant, with no other currency even coming close to dethroning it (see figure 20.1B). And despite the elevated debt, significant external borrowing, and large foreign liabilities (see figure 20.1C), in 2023 the greenback traded near record high valuations (see figure 20.1A).[2]

The arguments for dollar death extend beyond debt and into geopolitics, as the Ukraine War and its aftermath demonstrate. Consider Russia's push to create a new currency among the BRICS (Brazil, Russia, India, China, and South Africa) economies to rival the dollar or efforts to build a competitor to the SWIFT payment system. Such initiatives predated the Ukraine War but gathered pace as the aggressive use of US financial sanctions fueled urgent desire by some US adversaries to develop alternatives to the dollar-based payments system.

FIGURE

The dollar's long history of remarkable resilience

A. Long-run dollar valuation (REER) index

B. Currencies' share of allocated global reserves

USD

2nd-largest-currency share

Renminbi

C. US current account balance (left) and net foreign assets (right)

Current account balance (left scale)

Net foreign assets (right scale)

Note: Panel A through April 2023. Panels B and C through Q4 2022. Dollar valuation based on real narrow effective exchange rates (REER); 2020 average = 100. Allocated global reserves are the portion of the reserve portfolios where the currency positions are known. Current account as a % of US GDP; net foreign assets are the net international investment position, % of US GDP.
Source: BIS, IMF, BEA, NBER, analysis by BCG Center for Macroeconomics

How should leaders think about the dollar's future? Is this time different—or another false alarm? In this chapter, we add a financial dimension to our discussion of geopolitics and global divergence, and we do so with an analytical reflex that will be familiar to readers by now. A prediction of inexorable decline and decay, a gloomy narrative about the cracking of a linchpin in the economic order, data that appears to back it all up—they cry out for the antidote of sober and structural analysis. Once we look at how reserve-currency dynamics work, and how unlikely structural inflection is, dollar obituaries will continue to look premature.

Too often the dollar's role is viewed through the lens of the so-called exorbitant privilege, the idea that reserve-currency status is a lucky windfall of geopolitical clout.[3] But that tells only half the story. This is not only a privilege that must be earned and maintained, as currencies compete for the world's trust and savings, but it is also a burden, often a significant one, that the issuer of the reserve currency must be willing and able to shoulder.

The dollar's reserve status is not set in stone. In theory, some challenger to the US-led financial order could earn that privilege and accept the burden. But as this chapter shows, in practice, other major economies are unlikely to do what it takes to create a currency that foreign sovereigns or private actors find more attractive than the dollar. The bar is high, and dollar death remains a long way off.

A Privilege Earned

In 1965, French Finance Minister Valéry Giscard d'Estaing famously summed up a frustration with dollar hegemony, calling the dollar's position as the world's cornerstone currency an "exorbitant privilege."

The benefits to which he referred included being able to pay for imports in one's own currency, issue debt in one's own currency, and pay lower interest rates than would otherwise be the case: due to the dollar's centrality in global trade and finance, everyone wants (or is forced) to hold and transact in it.

Though the benefits of reserve-currency status are undeniable, its description as an exorbitant privilege never told the full story. Portraying that privilege as only a by-product of geopolitical heft cuts a few analytical corners. Issuing the reserve currency is not a perk won in a lottery but one that must be earned and maintained. There are at least four overlapping enablers of reserve-currency status, all of which are open to competition:

- *Economic footprint:* To even have a shot at issuing the primary reserve currency, an economy must be large in terms of output, trade, and finance. With this criterion, most countries and currencies are already out of the running. The United States has sustained a surprisingly stable and significant share of world output over the past half-century and a meaningful—but not dominant—position in trade flows; it also remains the world's key financial center.

- *Deep, open, and safe markets:* The reserve currency must have markets that can create reserve assets the world wants to buy: deep, liquid, credit-worthy debt instruments that must be able to absorb large inflows and outflows. The US Treasury market—despite political shenanigans around debt ceilings and technical default—credibly supplies the world's cornerstone safe asset. In contrast, Europe's lack of a significant unified government debt market has been a limiting factor in its ascent—once widely predicted—to being the primary reserve asset.[4]

- *Credible institutions:* Related to the point above, the reserve currency must be backed by institutions with a history of stability and credibility. This includes both financial institutions, such as the central bank, and legal institutions, such as independent courts that fairly adjudicate disputes between creditors and debtors. These underpin faith in the rule of law and the belief that foreigners can sell their reserve assets without friction or doubt. The United States has built a reputation of legal security and essentially unfettered capital mobility. Any other economy can strive to build such worldwide credibility, but it is hard.

- *Geopolitical clout:* Political alliances can influence reserve-currency allocations—although we view this as the least important factor.[5] The geopolitical role the United States has played for more than the past half-century has anchored the dollar in the portfolios of its allies—including large reserve portfolio holdings in the Middle East and in Japan. It is possible, albeit not simple, for those with a limited history of friendly alliances to build such relationships over time and thereby build demand for their currency. But the chief reason for foreigners to hold dollar assets is that these are liquid and reliable, not that the United States is the leading wielder of hard power.

It is important to note that each of the four enablers above is a competitive concept—there are no absolute targets in the race to be a significant reserve currency. And to be the *primary* reserve currency, a currency must be seen as *relatively* better than its competitors.

. . .

To illustrate the relative nature of currency competition, consider a crucial moment in dollar history that saw an absolute downgrade in the dollar's attractiveness, yet no relative loss in its primary-reserve status. In 1971, President Nixon unilaterally put an end to the convertibility of dollars to gold. The reneging on prior commitments led to expectations that, as one German newspaper put it at the time, "the dollar [had] collapsed as a leading currency."[6] But this proved wrong—even if during the 1970s the dollar lost value against other currencies and saw its share in reserve portfolios decline. Despite its diminished stature, the dollar maintained an overwhelming lead against any currency that was at one time or another its nearest rival (see figure 20.1B). An absolute downgrade in dollar attractiveness had occurred, but in a relative sense there was a lack of a viable alternative. Germany, France, and Britain may not have liked it, but their inability to offer something better left the dollar's position unscathed. Ultimately it is the relative competition that matters.

The dollar is not without its challenges—true then, today, and in the future. Its footprint in output and trade isn't what it was when the dollar order was formalized in 1944 at the Bretton Woods Conference in New Hampshire. Dollar markets have hiccups around liquidity, even in the Treasury markets. And the credibility of American institutions is not what one might wish it to be. Yet even if US fundamentals are far from perfect, it remains far from clear that anyone can do better.[7]

A Burden Accepted

As mentioned earlier, earning the privilege of issuing the reserve currency is only half the story. The United States' willingness to shoulder the burden of issuing the world's reserve currency is as much a prerequisite of dollar dominance as is the relative attractiveness outlined above. While many— both friend and foe—would like to see the United States lose its benefits as the reserve-currency issuer, few are able or willing to take on the associated burdens.

These burdens come down to having to absorb capital flows. If surplus economies want to invest their savings, those savings often end up in reserve-currency assets. This puts pressure on the reserve-currency issuer to accept inflows by selling assets (for instance, Treasury bills, real estate, stocks, and bonds). The upshot is that the reserve issuer has relinquished control over capital flows via a credibly open capital account. Several overlapping burdens can arise:

- *Trade deficit:* The inflow of global savings invested in reserve-currency assets often finance debt. The flip side of debt financing is increased borrowing and consumption by the reserve-currency issuer. The additional consumption will be partly of imports, which will generate a trade deficit (though capital inflows can also be invested, internally or externally, by the reserve-currency issuer).

- *Interest rates:* When global savings push their way into reserve-currency assets, they put downward pressure on interest rates (bidding up the price of government bonds, which lowers their yield). While this may not seem to be a burden—and it can be a benefit—it can complicate the central bank's ability to influence long-term interest rates. Too-low interest rates, in turn, feed into financial-stability risks, as lower rates encourage borrowing and bubbles.

- *Higher currency valuation:* Because of large-scale capital inflows, the reserve currency is going to experience a higher currency valuation than would otherwise be the case. This favors imports at the expense of exports. Manufacturing and other export-oriented sectors will be less competitive—encouraging outsourcing and leaving a smaller export-oriented sector, adding to the challenge of a trade deficit.

- *Losing demand:* Particularly in a world with weak demand and excess savings, those global savings can pull demand out of the reserve-currency country through higher exports to the reserve issuer. This shifts demand away from, in this case, US domestic producers. And global savers can accumulate reserves to explicitly hold down their currencies and aid their export-led growth.

False alarms about dollar collapse often result from ignoring the burdens of reserve-currency status and the unwillingness or inability of challengers to pick up these burdens. Some readers may intuitively object to the idea of a burden: Isn't the trade deficit evidence of a nation living beyond its means, paying for its imports by borrowing capital from foreigners? But this is a misreading of trade deficits that feeds into the idea that the dollar must fall.

In this view, surely the trade deficit is telling us that the era of dollar hegemony must be coming to a close.

However, seeing the trade deficit as a sign of US profligacy is too narrow. In another sense, the trade deficit is a sign that the United States is a dumping ground for the world's savings. It is foreigners' huge appetite for dollars that drives the currency's value above the level needed to balance the country's trade account. Remember that the balance of payments requires capital inflows to be matched by corresponding outflows, some of which are likely to contribute to a current account (trade) deficit.[8] In this light, the trade deficit is proof of the US success in rising to the challenge of supplying a dependable reserve asset the world wants to hold. We favor this reading over the idea of profligacy.

. . .

To appreciate the resilience of the dollar's role in the global financial system— and the point about capital dumping—consider the false alarm in the run-up to the global financial crisis. That episode had all the ingredients for dollar doom. After all, the subprime-mortgage crisis was made in America; it was a sign that US financial markets might not be so credible and dependable after all. The crisis coincided with a large and growing US trade deficit, and at the time the euro appeared to be the up-and-coming challenger to dollar hegemony. Sure enough, a slew of predictions of dollar collapse followed. Nouriel Roubini of New York University said the deficits (fiscal as well as external) presented a "twin financial train wreck" that would leave the dollar crashing and the economy in trouble.[9] He is often credited with having predicted the global financial crisis on the basis of these pronouncements.

Yet when the financial crisis came, foreigners did not dump dollars. To the contrary, they continued to clamor for them. And even as the crisis faded, no evidence emerged of the dollar having lost its primary reserve-currency position. Instead, it lost the most viable competitor, the euro, as a byzantine polity flirted with breakup.[10] If anything, the dollar's reserve-currency status was strengthened.

The assumption that underpinned gloomy predictions was that deficits signaled profligacy—America living beyond its means by pulling in foreign capital. That assumption ignored the evidence that the key driver was not profligacy but capital "dumping." Export-oriented economies had held down the value of their currencies and boosted their competitiveness by buying dollar assets.

Those who remain unconvinced should consider the evidence embedded in interest rates. If America were an irresponsible borrower—that is, if America were *pulling in* capital—we should expect to see high interest rates on US debt. But in the run-up to the global financial crisis, when external deficits were exceptionally large, the opposite was true. Long-term interest rates were low because savings were pouring in from Asia, notably into US agencies' mortgage bonds (e.g., Freddie Mac and Fannie Mae) and US Treasuries. Indeed, long-term rates remained low even as the Fed raised the short-term rate—a phenomenon that came to be known as the "Greenspan conundrum."[11] This is compelling evidence of capital dumping, and it's not farfetched at all to suspect that this contributed to the housing bubble, as this influenced mortgage rates and spurred a search for yield that helped lower credit standards.

Of course, the burdens of reserve-currency status vary over time and with context. They are particularly consequential in a global economy with weak demand and high savings. The details of how markets respond, how interest rates move, who ends up borrowing, and if a bubble emerges (and what it looks like) will always be situational.

Everyone would like the privilege, but few want to shoulder the burdens, of reserve-currency primacy. Seen in this light, it is understandable why dollar supremacy is more durable than commonly thought.

Remember, Dollar Obituaries Will Remain Premature

Dollar doom will never go out of fashion.[12] The latest page added to the book of dollar obituaries followed the imposition of Western financial sanctions on Russia. Observing how the dollar had been weaponized, the BRICS group of leading emerging economies redoubled their ambitions to create an alternative, complete with a rival to the Western-controlled SWIFT payment system.[13] When these sorts of ambitions surface, there is always a prominent voice to announce the greenback's death. Economists James Stock and Angus Deaton supported the idea that "weaponizing dollar finance is likely to lead to a significant shift away from the dollar as the dominant international currency."[14]

When hearing claims like this, executives should always return to the principles that underpin a reserve currency:

- *Frame it as privilege and burden.* Undoubtedly, there will be efforts to challenge the dollar at the margin. There will be concerted efforts to chip away at dollar invoicing, for example. But competitors must supply a more attractive store of value for everyone to rely on (a privilege earned) and accept the downsides of being a reserve-currency issuer (a burden accepted).

- *Don't forget it's a competition.* Reserve-currency privilege doesn't come from pushing others to use an alternative currency. It arrives when others want to use it because it is to their own advantage. Asking trade partners to invoice in one's currency can help make some inroads, but if the currency lacks a credible reserve asset and open capital accounts, accumulated balances won't be held in size in such a currency. And that matters more.

- *Ask who could do it.* The current contenders to the dollar's throne lack a combination of deep debt markets, credible institutions, and open capital markets. None of these crucial shortcomings are likely to be overcome quickly—leaving the dollar as the dominant reserve currency for the foreseeable future.

- *Don't confuse reserve currency and currency value.* Reserve currency status is not a prediction about the dollar's value—which will fluctuate, including materially to the downside. Rather, it is a statement about the dollar's position at the center of the global economic and financial system—a position that is likely to remain for a long time.

!

CONCLUSION

CHAPTER 21

Good Macro in an Era of Tightness

Our last chapter is not a traditional synthesis of what was said in prior ones. The book's first objective—*how* to analyze true macroeconomic risk—was already summarized within the preceding 18 chapters. Readers should look there for conclusions on the eclectic mix of frameworks and methods we used to analyze real, financial, and global risk, and they can refer to chapter 2 for a summary of our approach to macroeconomics.

Here we look forward. This chapter strings together and concludes our second objective: determining *what* the future of the macroeconomic system could look like. We stated in the introduction that good macro, the economy's mostly benign operating system of the past 40 years or so, was at risk. Considering the landscape of real, financial, and global risks we traversed, will good macro give way to something less favorable to business? Could good macro even turn into bad macro?

Our take on the future is advanced with due humility. We discussed at some length the fallacy of viewing economics as a predictive machine, and extolled the virtues of viewing it as an eclectic collection of narratives that facilitate judgment. Point forecasts must give way to perspective, theory to narrative, and certainty to judgment, we said. Consequently, we see little value in narrow predictions about the 2020s and much value in rendering a strategic narrative.

Shocks, crises, and false alarms will continue to hit. When they appear, we will revert to and rely on the analytical foundations outlined in this book to interpret them and—if warranted—adjust our narrative. As we said in chapter 2, we'd be quite surprised if the future agreed with all our views (the *what*), but we'd be disappointed if the approaches we laid out in this book didn't help us make sense of changing facts and context (the *how*).

In the following pages, we lay out—without the interruption of detailed arguments, data, and charts—our high-level strategic narrative of the US economy in the 2020s and, arguably, beyond. We also anticipate some objections that readers might have and strive to answer them. We then ask who wins and who loses (firms, workers, policymakers) in the world we envision.

Good macro, we believe, will persist—though it is in flux. The 2020s are an era of tightness that will deliver a growth boost. Such real-economy strength will result in financial strains—*good* strains that demand more-disciplined capital allocation. The shifts from convergence to divergence in the global economy will reinforce tightness in the years ahead. While we appreciate a variety of risks, even ugly ones, we are unwilling to anchor them at the center of our assessment. In contrast to the doomsayers who often have the loudest voices in the (public) debate, we remain rational optimists.

The macro environment will be different—challenging, too. But despite all the volatility, we think the next decade or so will feature a good-macro story. And those with the right analytical tools will be prepared for it.

Real Economy: Growth Boosts Beat Growth Risks

In the years ahead, we think growth boosts will shape the real economy more than growth risks. The cornerstone of this view is that we already find ourselves in an era of tightness, one that will persist. Strong utilization of labor and capital will amount to an inversion of the lackluster 2010s, delivering upward pressure on cost, wages, and prices that will push firms to embrace technology and transformation in search of productivity gains. Risks to cyclical growth—recessions—remain but will not overshadow better growth across cycles, in our view.

A confluence of three drivers underpins this era of tightness:

Structurally tight labor markets. Often misread as a repercussion of the pandemic and ensuing stimulus, labor-market tightness was already in place by 2017, well before Covid (see chapter 13 and figure 13.3 in particular).[1] The pandemic was a brief interruption, not the cause of, the era of tightness. Unlike the 2010s, when the corporate playbook centered on easily and cheaply available labor and deprioritized capex investment, the 2020s will be shaped by relative labor scarcity and stronger capex (chapter 13).

Strategic investments demand. Investments related to the geopolitically driven reallocation of productive capacity as well as to climate change and decarbonization will reinforce the era of tightness. As new productive capacity and supply chains are built, both labor and capital will be more fully employed (chapter 19). These forces will likely accelerate, adding to tightness across cycles.

A new generation of technology. Led by generative AI, new technologies will drive yet more investment, further pushing up demand for capital. Over time, resulting productivity effects will allow companies to do more with less (chapter 8). However, we do not believe such productivity gains will come swiftly and significantly enough to undermine tightness in the labor market.

Taken together, we see stronger resource utilization not as marginal but as the major theme shaping the real economy in the 2020s. The present decade will come to be seen as having more in common with the 1950s and 1960s or 1990s than with the 2010s, an era marred by structural slack in the economy (that is, high unemployment that declined very slowly) in the wake of the global financial crisis of 2008.

. . .

We're aware of alternative views. For some, a new machine age will cause technological unemployment—the opposite of the labor-market tightness we think will prevail.[2] But the presumed link between technological progress and labor-market slack stands on shaky ground conceptually and is not borne out empirically (chapter 8). The periods of strongest US productivity growth—the 1950s, the 1960s, the late 1990s—all came with tight, not slack, labor markets. In fact, the direction of causality is the reverse: tight labor markets first nudge and then force firms to adopt laborsaving technology (chapters 7 and 8). Predictions of technological unemployment are an evergreen feature of pundits' commentary. But despite the march of automation in recent decades, the US unemployment rate has still declined to near multigenerational lows. Technology, including AI, can and will gradually displace jobs. That still won't be enough to end the era of tightness in the years ahead.

Why? As labor is displaced by AI, particularly in the service sector, it will be reabsorbed. That is not only because of the structural backdrop of strong labor demand that, again, predates the gyrations surrounding the pandemic. AI may well be a microeconomic revolution, but we see it as a macroeconomic evolution (chapter 8). The timing and size of AI's macroeconomic impact are frequently overstated. We think it will come gradually and we expect a boost to trend growth of perhaps 50 basis points, not 150. And should the pace and magnitude prove much bigger, so too would technology's regenerative impact on employment. Remember, the macroeconomic story of productivity happens on the cost side: lower costs deliver lower prices, which boost real incomes, creating new demand and new employment (see chapter 7 for a discussion of the cost-price-income cascade).

. . .

Growth risks will persist—but not undermine—the growth boost we anticipate. To be sure, the era of tightness comes with more financial strains, and more-vigilant monetary policy to balance tightness and price pressures, as we detail in the next section. Consequently, the risk of monetary policy-induced recessions will be greater in the 2020s than in the 2010s, when sluggish growth and inflation made the risk of a hawkish policy error exceptionally low (chapter 13).

Yet such recession risk does not automatically equate to systemic resets that inject structural slack into the labor market. Not all recessions do: labor markets can snap back to tightness—or take years to recover (chapter 4). The economy's cyclical risk profile and recession types provide some guidance on the distribution of such risk (chapter 3). As we discuss below, risks of a systemic nature—specifically, an inflation regime break and deep financial crises—cannot be ruled out, and both would end the era of tightness. But we do not think they are at the center of the risk distribution.

Financial Economy: Good Strains over Systemic Risks

Real-economy tightness will flow through to the financial economy. Better utilization of resources will result in higher interest rates and force better capital allocation across the economy. We see these as good strains that should not be equated with systemic financial risks, though they certainly remain.

The good strains result from several drivers.

Inflation's cyclical upside bias. The real economy's greater utilization of labor and capital will drive upward pressure on costs, wages, and price—flipping inflation's downward bias of the 2010s to an upside bias in the 2020s (chapter 13). This isn't all bad: we view inflation's upside bias as a change in *cyclical* conditions that must not be confused with a pernicious break in the *structural* inflation regime, which remains unlikely (chapter 12). In fact, upside inflation bias can be preferable to an economy that flirts with too-low inflation, as was the case with chronic demand deficiencies and structural slack in the 2010s.

Higher but healthy rates. Cyclical inflation's upward bias will demand monetary policy vigilance and, with it, higher but healthy rates (chapter 14). Remember, the interest rate environment can shift higher both for bad reasons (inflation expectations, risk premia) and for good reasons (underlying real-economy strength). Higher rates in the 2020s, we expect, fall in the latter category. Moreover, let's not forget that the ultralow rates of the 2010s were an anomaly, not a benchmark. They were the product of monetary policy created to spur demand of *any* kind, as the economy struggled with underutilization in the shadow of the global financial crisis of 2008. The 2020s are likely much the opposite—even if rates need not be as high as in similar tight periods, such as the 1990s, given a lower neutral rate (again, see chapter 14).

More-disciplined capital allocation. In the 2010s, demand scarcity and capital abundance led to undisciplined capital allocation. In the

2020s, stronger demand and scarcer capital will force more-disciplined capital allocation. That will trigger adjustments across the economy, particularly for firms. But we think greater financial strains will be the warranted cost of the tighter, stronger economy we sketched above—a set of essentially good drivers, even if debilitating for some.

Systemic risks *always* remain. Some fear that, in an economy saddled with high debt, the interest rates required to keep inflation in check and capital allocation disciplined will be inconsistent with financial stability (chapter 15). But remember that when rates were very low in the 2010s, the worry was that low rates would inflate bubbles and undermine financial stability: the grass is always greener on the other side.

Though reflexive doomsaying doesn't make systemic crisis more likely, consideration of three sources of systemic risks is warranted, as they each could end the era of tightness that underpins our story:

> *Risks from (private and public) debt.* Tighter—sometimes restrictive—monetary policy to manage economic tightness augurs more corporate bankruptcies and fewer zombie firms, as firms and investors scrutinize investments more closely. Some see this as a systemic risk. But bankruptcies can be a healthy process for an economy that reallocates resources to better uses—they need not create a debilitating cascade of defaults. In fact, the ingredients of such a cascade are generally lacking.[3] Similarly, on the side of public debt, the obsessive focus on debt *levels* to warn about debt sustainability will remain misguided. We expect nominal rates (r) to remain below nominal growth rates (g): it is the spread between the two variables that shapes the sustainability of debt, not the amount of debt (chapter 15). That said, rates may well rise by more than growth in the era of tightness, which suggests less favorable debt dynamics than the extremely favorable dynamics of the 2010s when r was far below g.

> *Inflation regime break.* A collapse in the inflation regime would end the era of tightness by delivering stagflation: high unemployment (slack), high inflation, and more-frequent recessions. Higher rates would result not from the good forces of tightness but from bad forces of inflation expectations and risk premia. This has been a popular

narrative in the post-Covid years, yet one we find misguided (chapter 12) and have rejected since the onset of postpandemic inflation. Such disaster cannot be ruled out, but again, it is a very different risk than cyclical inflation (chapter 13). A structural break comes when long-term inflation expectations become unanchored. But an inflation regime break—a *bad-macro* regime—requires not just a single error by central banks but persistent error, as inflation expectations gradually crack, crumble, and collapse. We do not expect modern and mostly independent central banks to be consistently wrong for an extended period. The bar for this scenario is far higher than is commonly portrayed.

Deep financial crisis. A crisis would end the era of tightness via crippled banks and broken credit intermediation, forced deleveraging, and ravaged balance sheets—leaving in its wake structural slack in the labor market. This too cannot be ruled out, but we believe this scenario is far from likely. Remember that systemic risk comes primarily, but not solely, from the inadequacy of banking capital (chapter 16). And the banking system's capital should be adequate to absorb many real-economy defaults, particularly from marginal firms.[4] One of the few positive legacies of the global financial crisis was the push by regulators to strengthen the capital foundation of the banking system. Regulation remains far from perfect and the "right" level of capital is not easy to determine, but sustained bias toward more capital has lowered the risk of systemic crisis—even as hiccups in the banking system will remain.

When a big crisis does hit, remember that systemic risks are only half the story—the other half is how the economy and policy, in particular, respond (chapter 4). Stimulus is a critical backdrop to the modern economy and, while its use has been compulsive (chapter 9) and *tactical* stimulus is more constrained in an era of tightness (chapter 11), we remain confident that the ability and willingness for *existential* stimulus remains strong (chapter 10). While big crises do happen, they need not be systemic if policy is up to the task of meeting them with sufficient force and speed.

None of this is to say the financial system will always operate smoothly or without surprise. In fact, we think the proclivity for bubbles (inside and outside the financial system) will remain, especially as expansions age, and we expect such proclivity to persist even in a higher-rate environment, as was true of the 1990s (chapter 16). And because the financial system, with all its complexity and opaqueness, will remain prone to surprises, so will episodic volatility.

Our view of the macro environment does not belittle systemic risks; in fact, we've given its analysis much space throughout this book. But we're unwilling to say that systemic risks will take precedence over the good strains in the years ahead.

Global Economy: Costs and Gains of Divergence

Though the unfolding geopolitical shift from convergence to divergence will be a drag on the economy's potential in the long run, we see it as rein-forcing the era of tightness in the years ahead, therefore contributing to stronger growth. A gradually emerging and uncertain headwind, divergence will not be the dominant narrative of the 2020s economy, though further geopolitical downside risk remains.

Our view rests on four insights.

> *Underestimated resilience.* So far, the popular case that trade is in decline looks like an overstatement. Despite a decade of supposed deglobalization, trade volumes are still growing, the decline in trade intensity (that is, trade as a share of world GDP) is modest, and—correcting for falling commodity prices—trade intensity is essentially unchanged.[5] The who, what, where, and how of trade may be chang-ing, but trade is not in decline. Ironically, as "resilience" has become the buzzword to describe the shift in trade architecture, global trade has already been remarkably resilient (chapter 19).

> *New architecture adds to tightness.* Rejiggering the trade architecture in response to geopolitical needs comes with higher costs. Recall that in the phase of convergence, the global allocation of production capacity (that is, physical capital) was placed in the hands of busi-nesses. This delivered a powerful structural force of cost optimization at the firm level and deflationary impulses at the macroeconomic level. In the era of divergence, governments instead seek to influence

the allocation of global capacity in line with geopolitical objectives and risks (and firms often share that risk assessment). Whether through incentives or control, the emphasis on reliability will lower long-run economic potential as some specialization and benefits of trade are sacrificed. Yet, the shift in trade architecture also drives greater investment and more demand for labor in rich economies. Put simply, repatriating global production capacity will reinforce the era of tightness in the years ahead (chapter 19).

Cost and price impacts will be gradual. Although we agree that global divergence will raise production costs, thereby putting pressure on prices, we disagree with those who fear that this threatens the structurally anchored inflation regime—the cornerstone of good macro. First, trade is a relatively small share of GDP, so the inflation pressures from global divergence will not likely dominate. Next, production shifts will take place at the margin: incremental decisions affect where to build the next plant but don't change the distribution of existing ones, so any price pressure will emerge gradually. Third, so far there is little evidence that the reallocation of capacity systematically *replaces* existing capacity. If incremental builds are adding to global capacity, boosting the supply side, they should ease inflation pressures in the longer run. Last, if new capacity is built at the technological frontier or even pushes it outward—say, with a greater degree of automation—the resulting productivity gains can offset (some of) the cost increases that come with shifting production to rich economies.

Global financial imbalances remain. In the realm of global financial capital, we expect the flows of global savings to continue to look for safe destinations (chapter 20). The United States will continue to attract global capital flows, making capital more abundant (that is, cheaper) than it would otherwise be—and keeping risks from external deficits at bay. The dollar will remain the reserve currency, though obituaries will continue to be written. Fluctuations in the dollar's value, even when materially lower, will not undermine the dollar's fundamental advantages over its competitors anytime soon (chapter 20).

Of course, there are structural downsides in geopolitics, too. Great-power conflict is increasingly debated but remains essentially unpredictable; narratives of inevitability remain unwarranted in our view (chapters 17 and 18). Whatever its likelihood, great-power conflict shouldn't be dismissed with any comfort because the consequences would be tragic. In macroeconomic terms, however, the impact of conflict is difficult to gauge (and can make for uncomfortable analysis). Looking across decades of geopolitical risk, macroeconomic impact is often absent, rarely linear, and occasionally the opposite of what could intuitively be expected (chapter 18).

If great-power conflict were to happen, the greatest economic impact would come from sharp changes to the rules of the business environment, not from economic collapse. When economies are subordinated to the objectives of war, resource utilization spikes and labor markets turn incredibly tight. But it would be disingenuous to call this a tight labor *market*—prices, production, supply, and demand would be controlled or significantly influenced by the state in its pursuit of a military objective. However, note that a milder version of conflict—such as a proxy war or a contained conflict—could also drive tightness but without a radical rewriting of the rules of the marketplace.

There remains one category of residual risks that are outside the realm of the real, financial, and geopolitical dimensions discussed above. These are mostly exogenous shocks, and as such, can never be ruled out or predicted. On reflection, a range of highly unlikely but truly disruptive risks come to mind—including solar flares that cripple the electromagnetic infrastructure or a new global pandemic. But long lists of extreme risks don't help, as our inclusion of a pandemic in our own 2020 outlook reminds us.[6] General awareness of any such shock gives you little foresight—neither the probability nor the consequences are easily predicted.

Separately, endogenous shocks, including those to the political system, could also undermine the business environment. Liberal market democracy looked like an unassailable socioeconomic model only a short while ago (chapter 16), but now the consensus is in flux. As economic pains translate into internal rifts, disruptive shifts in politics cannot be ruled out. We think the era of tightness with its good strains—including stronger wage gains—bodes better for this type of risk than the lackluster 2010s. However, built-up frustrations will not heal quickly, and narratives often lag.

. . .

Taken together, the real, financial, and global forces we see at play in the years ahead do not amount to a bad-macro world. Rather, they deliver an era of tightness that is—though more challenging—still a good-macro environment, favorable for firms. It is different but not daunting to leaders who have the right analytical tool kit.

Who Will Win—and Lose—in an Era of Tightness?

What does the era of tightness mean for firms, consumers, and policymakers? Who stands to gain or lose from it? When the economy's resources are fully utilized and there is upward pressure on cost, wages, and prices, the economy will need release valves for these pressures; there are three such valves, each with different consequences for firms, consumers, and policymakers. Figure 21.1 offers a stylized summary of the adjustment mechanisms for cyclical tightness; it differentiates between the interests of firms (seeking profit growth), workers (seeking real income gains), and policymakers (seeking to manage inflation and growth).[7]

How will firms handle greater cost and wage pressures?

Tightness is absorbed in profit margins. In this scenario, firms lose, consumers (and workers) win, and policymakers are OK with this outcome, particularly in the short to medium run. This is an unfavorable path for firms, yet one that can still be relatively attractive for them. Consider that profit margins shrank across the economy in the late 1990s, an earlier period of sustained tight labor markets.[8] Yet it would be difficult to argue that this era was a bad environment for business. Stronger growth means that the pie is growing, so businesses may be well off even as their margins are under pressure.

Tightness is passed through to consumers (cyclical inflation). Firms can (and will) try to pass on cost pressures, carefully balancing the trade-off between price increases and giving up market share. Overall, firms are likely no better off as a result because gains are nominal. Consumers lose, as inflation erodes wage gains. Policymakers lose, as

FIGURE **21.1**

Who will win—and lose—in an era of tightness?

RELEASE VALVE		OUTCOMES FOR ...	
Tightness (cost pressures) is ...	Firms (capital)	Workers (labor)	Policymakers
... **absorbed** in profit margins	Lose	Win	Qualified success
... **passed through,** driving inflation (and recession risk)	Lose	Lose	Risk of tactical failure (policy recession) or strategic failure (inflation-regime break)
... **offset** by productivity growth	Win	Win	Success

Source: HBR, BCG Center for Macroeconomics

inflation pressures provoke monetary tightening that risks recession. If this becomes the key release valve, recessions become more likely—a scenario in which all are losers. (In the extreme, it can even lead to an inflation regime break if policymakers fail to contain the pressures over a long period, and long-term inflation expectations break; see chapter 12.)

Tightness is offset with productivity growth. Given the alternatives, incentives to strive for greater productivity growth are enormous for firms in tight economies (see chapters 7 and 8)—and such growth is also the best outcome for the economy as a whole. If the cost pressures of tightness can be offset by productivity growth, then firms, workers, and policymakers all win. Firms offset costs by more efficiently turning inputs into outputs, workers gain with higher real wages, and policymakers don't need to push back on tightness as much because the capacity of the economy is growing and thus easing inflationary pressures.

These outcomes are stylized and not mutually exclusive. In fact, we expect all three to play a role in the 2020s. Firms will feel the squeeze of higher labor costs and try to pass through those costs with partial success—the most successful will find sources of new productivity to absorb the cost pressure rather than eating into their margins. Policymakers will push back on aggregate price gains, more often seeking to balance a strong economy with price stability. Households will benefit from real wage gains and the relative ease of finding jobs. Which of the three release valves is doing the most work will vary at any point in time. And, of course, these dynamics will play out differently across industries—not least because the degree of tightness will differ. The degree to which different sectors can absorb technologies to enhance productivity will also vary—as will pricing power and the ability to absorb margin pressure.[9]

In many ways, but not all, the late 1990s are a reasonable, if imperfect, mental model for this period of good macro. The bad-macro era of the 1970s remains a poor model for the years ahead.

Remember, It's All about Judgment

We have little doubt that good macro in an era of tightness is more challenging—and more stressful—for executives and investors. Leaders should ask not only what these new challenges will be—but where they come from. When we look for the drivers of tightness, we discover they are part and parcel of a still-favorable macro backdrop. This can be easy to forget under the pressures of labor and capital scarcity, the strains of higher rates, and the disorienting uncertainties of geopolitics.

To manage these economic stressors, leaders need to exercise good judgment about macroeconomic risks. As shocks, crisis, and false alarms hit, we hope the eclectic instruments we discussed throughout this book will help readers cut through the thicket of doomsaying headlines and gyrating dataflow, and thus retain a posture of rational optimism. Remember, macro judgment is essentially about how we assess risk continuously, not forecasting what will happen.

We hope readers will remember three things.

First, master-model mentality cripples economic judgment. There is only false precision in point forecasts. When used as an answer, they obscure the narrative and the drivers while offering every chance for misinterpretation and inappropriate extrapolation, particularly at the most critical time: when crisis hits.

Second, there will be plenty of doom-mongering. In good times, recession risk will be more interesting than cyclical upside, and in times of crisis, systemic collapse more interesting than recovery. Readers will need strength to lean against the doomsayers—the analytical instruments and mindset discussed in this book can make that easier.

Third, economic eclecticism, the approach outlined in chapters 1 and 2, should always be the analytical starting point. Look to understand how things work; identify the drivers and dynamics; see what it might take for those to change structurally. This involves awareness of the macro data, to be sure, but only as a complement to a narrative that is built on context and history. Blinking dashboards can't supersede macro judgment.

. . .

To close this book, we return to Voltaire's observation about uncertainty, that doubt is not a pleasant condition, but certainty is an absurd one.[10] We still share the view that certainty is absurd: one should never expect certainty of macroeconomics. But we're not even sure that uncertainty is so unpleasant. Macroeconomics—with all its weaknesses, idiosyncrasies, history, debate, and failure—is not only inescapable but also captivating. It can even add significant value for those willing to do the work to unlock its potential.

NOTES

Chapter 1

1. Our term *good macro* refers to the structural foundation that the macroeconomy provides to the business environment. It makes no judgment about socioeconomic outcomes or challenges. Neither does it suggest there were no setbacks or challenges. It merely states that the conditions for global business interests were predominantly favorable and stable.

2. "And I don't know how long it's going to take us to get back to the 2019 per capita GDP. I would say, looking at it now, five years would seem like a good outcome out of this," said Kenneth Rogoff in "This Time Really Is Different," *Bloomberg Markets*, June–July 2020, https://www.magzter .com/stories/Investment/Bloomberg-Markets/This-Time-Really-is-Different. See also Nouriel Roubini, "The Coming Greater Depression of the 2020s," *Project Syndicate*, April 28, 2020, https://www .project-syndicate.org/commentary/greater-depression-covid19-headwinds-by-nouriel-roubini-2020 -04, and Stephen Roach, "The Dollar's Crash Is Only Just Beginning," *Bloomberg*, January 25, 2021, https://www.bloomberg.com/opinion/articles/2021-01-25/the-dollar-s-crash-is-only-just-beginning.

3. For example, an April 2021 Goldman Sachs report predicted a 1.3 percentage point increase over baseline productivity growth, which the report cites as 1.25% in the previous cycle and 2% over the long run, thus predicting productivity growth between 2.55% and 3.3% over the three years of 2020, 2021, and 2022. Jan Hatzius et al., "Productivity in the Post-Pandemic Economy," Goldman Sachs, April 25, 2021, https://www.gspublishing.com/content/research/en/reports/2021/04/26/ cfda70bf-88c0-4ad3-83e2-2cc4215c1add.html. Many others issued similarly strong forecasts. In fact, annual labor productivity growth averaged 1.43% in that period according to the BLS. Our own estimates were for very modest impact. See Philipp Carlsson-Szlezak and Paul Swartz, "Why We Shouldn't Overstate the Pandemic's Effect on Productivity Growth," World Economic Forum, October 15, 2021, https://www.weforum.org/agenda/2021/10/how-to-be-realistic-about-covids -impact-on-productivity-growth/; earlier in the pandemic, we had argued a similarly skeptical stance. See Philipp Carlsson-Szlezak and Paul Swartz, "Will COVID Be a Catalyst for Service Sector Productivity?" BCG Henderson Institute, July 2020, https://bcghendersoninstitute.com/center-for -macroeconomics/research-portal/will-covid-be-a-catalyst-for-service-sector-productivity/.

4. The prediction of contagious emerging-market (EM) crises did not play out. Individual EM economies such as Pakistan, Egypt, and Argentina, faced idiosyncratic problems in this window.

5. Nouriel Roubinin, "A Greater Depression?" Project Syndicate, March 24, 2020, https:// www.project-syndicate.org/commentary/coronavirus-greater-great-depression-by-nouriel-roubini -2020-03.

6. Philipp Carlsson-Szlezak, Martin Reeves, and Paul Swartz, "What the O-Ring Tells Us About Forecasting in the Age of Coronavirus," BCG Henderson Institute, April 14, 2020, https:// bcghendersoninstitute.com/what-the-o-ring-tells-us-about-forecasting-in-the-age-of-coronavirus/.

7. It's worth considering this quotation from John Maynard Keynes, *The General Theory of Employment, Interest and Money* (London: Palgrave Macmillan, 1936): "Practical men, who believe themselves to be quite exempt from any intellectual influences, are usually the slaves of some defunct economist. Madmen in authority, who hear voices in the air, are distilling their frenzy from some academic scribbler of a few years back."

8. "[T]he more prominent the individual concerned, the more often the forecaster is reported by the media, the more frequently consulted by politicians and business leaders, the less credence should be placed on that individual's prognostications," suggested political scientist Philip Tetlock, in John Kay and Mervyn King, *Radical Uncertainty: Decision-Making Beyond the Numbers* (Washington, DC: National Geographic Books, 2021), 221.

9. We acknowledge that all journalists have to deal with headline writers and editors who may push them toward more flashy titles.

Chapter 2

1. We are reminded of comments made by former Federal Reserve Bank of New York President William Dudley, "Wall Street economists try to synthesize an abundance of information into material that's useful for the person who's trying to figure out the world that we live in. A research economist is trying to push the frontier of knowledge outward, so that's a very different goal." From "Hey, Economist! Outgoing New York Fed President Bill Dudley on FOMC Preparation and Thinking Like an Economist," Liberty Street Economics, June 1, 2018, https://libertystreeteconomics.newyorkfed.org/2018/06/hey-economist-outgoing-new-york-fed-president-bill-dudley-on-fomc-preparation-and-thinking-like-an/.

2. S. G. Tallentyre, ed., *Voltaire in His Letters* (New York: G.P. Putnam's Sons, 1919), 232.

3. Although even in hard sciences—those with stationary properties—the statement "follow the science" crumples under the reality of David Hume's is–ought problem. Science can help attempt to discover what trade-offs there are, but it cannot answer the question of which trade-offs to make. Or as Ludwig von Mises said in *Human Action* (1949), "Science never tells a man how he should act; it merely shows how a man must act if he wants to attain definite ends."

4. Hayek argued that the Nobel Prize in Economics Sciences was a mistake because it encouraged economists to pronounce confidently on matters beyond the limits of their expertise. He argued instead that economists should be required to take an oath "never to exceed in public pronouncements the limits of their competence"—a nice idea but not likely to happen. Friedrich Hayek, "Banquet Speech," The Nobel Prize 1974, https://nobelprize.org/prizes/economic-sciences/1974/hayek/speech/. And Hayek wasn't the first to make the observation about the risks of trying to make economics more like natural sciences. Ludwig von Mises, in his book *Human Action* (1949), wrote:

> No such constant relations exist in the field of human action outside of physical and chemical technology and therapeutics. For some time economists believed that they had discovered such a constant relation in the effects of changes in the quantity of money upon commodity prices. It was asserted that a rise or fall in the quantity of money in circulation must result in proportional changes of commodity prices. Modern economics has clearly and irrefutably exposed the fallaciousness of this statement. Those economists who want to substitute "quantitative economics" for what they call "qualitative economics" are utterly mistaken. There are, in the field of economics, no constant relations, and consequently no measurement is possible.

5. The term "physics envy" was coined by Philip Mirowski; see Philip Mirowski, "Do Economists Suffer from Physics Envy?" *Finnish Economic Papers* 5, no. 1 (Spring 1992): 61–68.

6. ". . . even more fundamentally, the Standard Models left out both banks and the shadow banking system, central to the determination of the flow of credit, which in turn is central to the determination of aggregate demand." Joseph E. Stiglitz, "Rethinking Macroeconomics: What Failed, and How to Repair It," *Journal of the European Economic Association* 9, no. 4 (August 2011): 591–645, https://doi.org/10.1111/j.1542-4774.2011.01030.x.

7. "Epidemic forecasting has a dubious track-record, and its failures became more prominent with COVID-19." John P. A. Ioannidis, Sally Cripps, and Martin A. Tanner, "Forecasting for COVID-19 Has Failed," *International Journal of Forecasting* 38, no. 2 (2022): 423, https://www.ncbi.nlm.nih.gov/pmc/articles/PMC7447267/.

8. Robert McNamara had brought his quantitative management style from Ford to the Defense Department, and after his first visit to Vietnam in 1962 said, "Every quantitative measurement we have shows we're winning this war." Fredrik Logevall, "Rethinking 'McNamara's War,'" *New York Times*, November 28, 2017, https://www.nytimes.com/2017/11/28/opinion/rethinking-mcnamaras-war.html.

9. Milton Friedman, *Money Mischief: Episodes in Monetary History* (Boston: Houghton Mifflin Harcourt, 1994).

10. The Phillips curve began as an observation about the relationship between the rate of nominal wage growth and unemployment by A. W. Phillips in 1958. Since then, it has been widely studied and used to describe the relationship between inflation and economic tightness—yet the stability of the relationship is weak and therefore its usefulness in describing how and when inflation moves is very modest.

11. Financial-market participants typically understand forecasts to be a condensed means of expressing (and understanding) current views of the world, not a stable reality. They look across sets of forecasts—across variables and across time—to help understand someone's view. Yet even where this language is common, communicating uncertainties is a long-standing challenge. An interesting case study comes from Sherman Kent—the father of intelligence analysis and longtime member of the CIA. Kent was known for pushing people to use probabilistic language in their reporting, with the purpose of trying to tie them down to something that could convey what was meant. However, this is rather tricky to do. Not only will the assumptions about what a word like *probably* means vary enormously from person to person, it's also not obvious that probabilities around onetime idiosyncratic events are particularly meaningful. At their best, they are representations of confidence. At their worst, they are used as an excuse to take decision-making away from those responsible and seeking instead to find answers in a false scientific approach that bends to assigned probabilities. A worthwhile read is Donald P. Steury, ed., *Sherman Kent and the Board of National Estimates: Collected Essays* (Washington, DC: Center for the Study of Intelligence, Central Intelligence Agency, 1994).

12. "In physics, it takes three laws to explain 99% of the data; in finance, it takes more than 99 laws to explain about 3%," said MIT economist Andrew Lo, quoted in Emanuel Derman, "Beware of Economists Bearing Greek Symbols," *Harvard Business Review,* October 2005, https://hbr.org/2005/10/beware-of-economists-bearing-greek-symbols. "In physics you're playing against God, and He doesn't change His laws very often. In finance you're playing against God's creatures, agents who value assets based on their ephemeral opinions." Emanuel Derman, *Models. Behaving. Badly.: Why Confusing Illusion with Reality Can Lead to Disaster, on Wall Street and in Life* (New York: Free Press, 2011). Richard Feynman is claimed to have said jokingly, "Imagine if protons had feelings," after the stock market crash of 1987.

13. Letter from John Maynard Keynes to economist Roy Harrod, July 4, 1938, https://economicsociology.org/2018/04/03/what-is-economics-read-keynes-definition/.

14. We are reminded of Ludwig von Mises's words in *Human Action* (1949), where he uses *understanding* in the way we use *judgment*: "Understanding is not a privilege of the historians. It is everybody's business. In observing the conditions of his environment, everybody is a historian. Everybody uses understanding in dealing with the uncertainty of future events to which he must adjust his own actions."

15. Philipp Carlsson-Szlezak and Paul Swartz, "Economic Pessimists' Bet on a 2023 Recession Failed. Why Are They Doubling Down in 2024?" *Fortune*, December 11, 2023, https://fortune.com/2023/12/11/us-economy-pessimists-bet-2023-recession-failed-doubling-down-2024-outlook/.

16. "Where you stand depends on where you sit" is a saying often attributed to Rufus Edward Miles, who served three presidents (Dwight D. Eisenhower, John F. Kennedy, and Lyndon B. Johnson).

17. *Resulting* is a coinage attributed to decisions strategist Annie Duke. It highlights the tendency to evaluate decisions based on outcomes (results). Just because the result was bad doesn't

mean the decision was. We must evaluate the decision separately—particularly idiosyncratic, one-off decisions.

18. Arguably in the long run—in economics and finance—the optimists have won out, even if not everywhere. See Elroy Dimson, Paul Marsh, and Mike Staunton, *Triumph of the Optimists: 101 Years of Global Investment Returns* (Princeton, NJ: Princeton University Press, 2002).

19. "A 'sound' banker, alas! is not one who foresees danger and avoids it, but one who, when he is ruined, is ruined in a conventional and orthodox way along with his fellows, so that no one can really blame him." John Maynard Keynes, *Essays in Persuasion* (London: Macmillan, 1931).

20. See chapter 11 of John Kay and Mervyn King, *Radical Uncertainty: Decision-Making Beyond the Numbers* (Washington, DC: National Geographic Books, 2021): "The job of the court is always to establish 'what is going on here' in a unique case. And that is a narrative, not a statistical question."

21. The demand for bold point forecasts will not end. Contrarian approaches will not be popular, but popularity is overrated. In his 1974 Nobel Prize acceptance speech, Hayek suggested that popularity should be feared in the social sciences. Quoting the economist Alfred Marshall, Hayek said, "Students of social science, must fear popular approval: Evil is with them when all men speak well of them."

Chapter 3

1. Philipp Carlsson-Szlezak and Paul Swartz, "The Yield Curve and Its Three False Friends," Sanford C. Bernstein, January 14, 2019. Reprinted in *An Economic History of Now*, vol. 2, September 2019.

2. "In 1900, the top 3 causes of death were infectious diseases—pneumonia and flu, tuberculosis, and gastrointestinal infections," Rebecca Tippett, "Mortality and Cause of Death, 1900 v. 2010," *Carolina Demography*, June 16, 2014, https://www.ncdemography.org/2014/06/16/mortality-and-cause-of-death-1900-v-2010/.

3. One weakness of this analogy is that recession risk—unlike mortality risk—works with an exceedingly small sample size. However, like mortality risk, recession risk can have multiple drivers that overlap. In each area, it remains useful to consider the dominant driver as a tool for thinking about the risk profile.

4. Philipp Carlsson-Szlezak and Paul Swartz, "What Penicillin, Heart Disease, and Cancer Tell Us about the Business Cycle and Recession Risk," Sanford C. Bernstein, August 3, 2018. Reprinted in *An Economic History of Now*, November 2018.

5. Based on GDP by Industry accounts from the Bureau of Economic Analysis. Depending on how one slices the economy, by classifying services, this can be higher or lower. See https://www.bea.gov/data/gdp/gdp-industry.

6. While policy has always been a factor in the economic cycle, its active role was limited before the early 20th century, as policymakers took a relatively hands-off approach. Policy-induced recession introduced a new type of risk into the cycle, but well-executed policy can play a key role in reducing and offsetting risk (both real and financial)—reducing risk overall.

7. This risk is two-sided: interest rates could be set too high, pushing the economy into recession, or rates could be too low, leading to inflation and eventually higher rates and tighter financial conditions.

8. The law passes in 1913; the bank begins operations in 1914.

9. In a speech honoring Milton Friedman on his 90th birthday, Ben Bernanke said, "Regarding the Great Depression. You're right, we did it. We're very sorry. But thanks to you, we won't do it again." Ben S. Bernanke, "On Milton Friedman's Ninetieth Birthday," remarks at the Conference to Honor Milton Friedman, University of Chicago, November 8, 2002, https://www.federalreserve.gov/boarddocs/speeches/2002/20021108/.

10. Philipp Carlsson-Szlezak and Paul Swartz, "Longest Ever . . . Why the Expansion Has Lasted This Long and Can It Last Longer?" Sanford C. Bernstein, June 4, 2019. Reprinted in *An Economic History of Now*, vol. 2, September 2019.

11. A soft landing occurs when policy tightens and inflation is brought down without a con-comitant rise in the unemployment rate. We think of a soft landing as having three stages during which the economy continues to grow: (1) rapidly rising rates, (2) restrictive rates ($r > r^\star$), (3) rates moving toward a more neutral stance. Despite widespread pessimism, 2023 saw the move from stage 1 to 2 and expectations rose about moving successfully to stage 3. Philipp Carlsson-Szlezak and Paul Swartz, "Economic Pessimists' Bet on a 2023 Recession Failed. Why Are They Dou-bling Down in 2024?" *Fortune*, December 11, 2023, https://fortune.com/2023/12/11/us-economy -pessimists-bet-2023-recession-failed-doubling-down-2024-outlook/.

12. The term "emperor of all maladies" is a common phrase to describe cancer and was fur-ther popularized in Siddhartha Mukherjee, *The Emperor of All Maladies: A Biography of Cancer* (New York: Scribner, 2010).

13. See also discussion in chapter 16. There is a long-running debate over whether the makers of monetary policy should try to spot and pop financial bubbles before they burst, or if they should let them run and then clean up the damage afterward. For example, in 2002 Ben Bernanke argued that policymakers would have great difficulty spotting bubbles and that monetary policy was too blunt a tool for the job. Instead, they should focus on building resilience into the financial system (e.g., higher capital requirements)—as has happened since the 2008 crisis—making cleanup less painful. See Ben S. Bernanke, "Asset-Price 'Bubbles' and Monetary Policy," remarks before the New York Chapter of the National Association for Business Economics, New York, October 15, 2002, https://www.federalreserve.gov/boarddocs/speeches/2002/20021015/default .htm.

14. Philipp Carlsson-Szlezak, Paul Swartz, and Martin Reeves, "Assessing the Current Risks to the U.S. Economy," hbr.org, March 14, 2022, https://hbr.org/2022/03/assessing-the-current -risks-to-the-u-s-economy.

15. Philipp Carlsson-Szlezak and Paul Swartz, "A Soft Landing Is Playing Out—but Opti-mism Needs to Be for the Right Reasons," *Fortune*, January 30, 2023, https://fortune.com/2023 /01/30/us-economy-outlook-soft-landing-optimism-inflation-labor-fed-2023-carlsson-szlezak -swartz/; Philipp Carlsson-Szlezak and Paul Swartz, "Will the U.S. and Europe Slide into Reces-sion in 2023? Here's How to Look Out When Economic Outlooks Don't," *Fortune*, December 12, 2022, https://fortune.com/europe/2022/12/12/will-us-europe-recession-2023-economic -outlook-inflation-bcg-carlsson-szlezak-swartz/.

16. Policy recessions tend to be mild when they are mistakes when balancing cyclical inflation and growth. However, when they are driven by a need to reanchor inflation or by a deflationary error, they have the potential to deliver significant structural slack.

Chapter 4

1. The rate was nearly 23% if one uses a broad measure of unemployment, which includes marginally attached workers and workers employed part-time for economic reasons. Bureau of Labor Statistics, "Employment Situation News Release," May 8, 2020, https://www.bls.gov/news .release/archives/empsit_05082020.htm.

2. Trend growth here is being used as a less technical version of potential GDP growth.

3. Greece has seen very strong growth after Covid—perhaps the end of its post–global financial crisis deflationary L-shape.

4. Ben S. Bernanke, "The Real Effects of Disrupted Credit: Evidence from the Global Financial Crisis," *Brookings Papers on Economic Activity*, Fall 2018, https://www.brookings.edu/wp -content/uploads/2018/09/Bernanke_final-draft.pdf.

5. Michael D. Bordo, Angela Redish, and Hugh Rockoff, "Why Didn't Canada Have a Banking Crisis in 2008 (or in 1930, or 1907, or . . .)?" National Bureau of Economic Research, August 2011, revised December 2011, https://www.nber.org/papers/w17312.

6. There is a strong case for intervention when the overall macro environment (e.g., Covid) is depressing demand and driving bankruptcies. But this does not apply to more normal business failures, driven by low productivity or bad management.

7. "This trifecta of risks—uncontained pandemics, insufficient economic-policy arsenals, and geopolitical white swans—will be enough to tip the global economy into persistent depression and a runaway financial-market meltdown. After the 2008 crash, a forceful (though delayed) response pulled the global economy back from the abyss. We may not be so lucky this time." Nouriel Roubini, "A Greater Depression?" *Project Syndicate*, March 24, 2020, https://www.project-syndicate.org/commentary/coronavirus-greater-great-depression-by-nouriel-roubini-2020-03.

8. Philipp Carlsson-Szlezak, Martin Reeves, and Paul Swartz, "Understanding the Economic Shock of Coronavirus," hbr.org, March 27, 2020, https://hbr.org/2020/03/understanding-the-economic-shock-of-coronavirus.

9. A deep U-shape is also possible due to sustained policy error, like during the Great Depression.

Chapter 5

1. President Trump promised 4% annual economic growth both during the 2016 campaign and at the start of his presidency, even saying we may do "substantially better than that." See remarks before the Economic Club of New York, September 15, 2016, https://www.econclubny.org/documents/10184/109144/2016TrumpTranscript.pdf. And while President Obama didn't explicitly promise 4% growth during his campaign, his 2010 budget projected real GDP growth above 4% for 2011, 2012, and 2013. See "Budget of the U.S. Government: Fiscal Year 2010," Office of Management and Budget, May 2009, https://www.govinfo.gov/content/pkg/BUDGET-2010-SUMMARY/pdf/BUDGET-2010-SUMMARY.pdf. President George W. Bush helped to popularize the goal of 4% growth with the launch of the Bush Institute's 4% Growth Project in 2011 and with a 2012 book on the topic. The Bush Institute, *The 4% Solution: Unleashing the Economic Growth America Needs* (New York: Crown, 2012).

2. Philipp Carlsson-Szlezak and Paul Swartz, "Pushing on Growth—the Future and Limits of the 'Compulsive Stimulus Model,'" Sanford C. Bernstein, May 22, 2019. Reprinted in *An Economic History of Now*, vol. 2, September 2019.

3. For example, Erik Brynjolfsson suggested "intelligent machines [are] arguably a *more* important invention than just about any other invention we've ever made" and argues for much higher labor productivity to come. See Erik Brynjolfsson and Robert J. Gordon, "Is the Great Stagnation Finally Coming to an End?" Pairagraph, October 31, 2021, https://www.pairagraph.com/dialogue/9301beaf3a5b4a14868c682a36402474.

4. This is not to say that demand doesn't matter. As we detailed in chapter 3, recessions and sustained weak demand can destroy productive capacity through the investment channel.

5. The full quotation describes the framework as "either an illuminating parable, or else a mere device for handling data, to be used so long as it gives good empirical results, and to be abandoned as soon as it doesn't, or as soon as something better comes along." Robert M. Solow, "Review of *Capital and Growth*," *The American Economic Review* 56, no. 5 (1966): 1257.

6. That said, there is another, albeit cyclical, reason for optimism on the labor side: tight labor markets pull in workers. Actual participation weakens relative to potential participation in downturns and strengthens relative to potential in expansions. Why? Because strong labor markets—due to wage gains and firms' flexibility in hiring—encourage strong participation. While this can help give extra room for growth, it cannot change the structural reality that labor will contribute less to growth than in the past.

7. Because the capital stock is measured in dollars of investment, it does not account for whether the investment is high or low impact. Thus, mechanically, the effect of changing quality of investment will show up in higher or lower productivity growth, not in capital contribution to growth.

8. This is not an argument exclusive to decarbonization technologies. Consider the example of capital stock building for the Olympics—a stadium may be a long-lived asset but will not add to output/productive capacity if it is not used.

9. We are using *Cassandra* as is often used today—to refer to someone who is constantly saying bad things are coming, when in fact they likely aren't coming. This is not strictly consistent with Greek mythology, where Cassandra warns of events that do happen but is not believed beforehand.

Chapter 6

1. To avoid any confusion, we are using *frontier* in the plain English sense of the word—to refer to countries that are at the cutting edge of development. Economists sometimes use *frontier* to describe economies that are small and less developed.

2. By one estimate, 23 countries have moved from middle-income to high-income status since 1960. "Which Countries Have Escaped the Middle-Income Trap?" *The Economist*, March 30, 2023, https://www.economist.com/finance-and-economics/2023/03/30/which -countries-have-escaped-the-middle-income-trap.

3. Labor is linked to overall economic growth but not to per capita growth. And even for overall growth, labor's importance declines as countries become richer and as population growth tends to slow.

4. This also results in higher dependency ratios, which, while not impacting labor supply directly, diverts resources to care and curtails the ability to invest and build capital.

5. Addressing Western diplomats at the Polish embassy in Moscow in 1956, Khrushchev said, "About the capitalist states, it doesn't depend on you whether or not we exist. If you don't like us, don't accept our invitations, and don't invite us to come to see you. Whether you like it or not, history is on our side. We will bury you!" "Foreign News: We Will Bury You!" *Time*, November 26, 1956, https://content.time.com/time/subscriber/article/0,33009,867329,00.html. Khrushchev later (1963) said, "I once said, 'We will bury you,' and I got into trouble with it. Of course we will not bury you with a shovel. Your own working class will bury you." *New York Times*, August 25, 1963, p. 19, https://timesmachine.nytimes.com/timesmachine/1963/08/25 /issue.html.

6. Lincoln Steffens, *The Letters of Lincoln Steffens*, Volume 1: 1889–1919 (New York: Harcourt, Brace, 1938), 463.

7. See, for example, William Easterly and Stanley Fischer, "The Soviet Economic Decline," *The World Bank Economic Review* 9, no. 3 (1995), https://academic.oup.com/wber/article-abstract /9/3/341/1666811.

8. See per capita GDP growth rates for the Soviet Union in Maddison Project Database 2020, https://www.rug.nl/ggdc/historicaldevelopment/maddison/releases/maddison-project -database-2020?lang=en.

9. In addition to running out of room for capital accumulation, the Soviet economy stopped well below advanced levels of income because of the inefficiencies of top-down direction of capital accumulation, among other factors.

10. Shintaro Ishihara, *The Japan That Can Say No: Why Japan Will Be First Among Equals* (New York: Simon & Schuster, 1991), 84.

11. This book was first published in 1989 with Sony cofounder and chairman Akio Morita as a coauthor. When unauthorized translations of the book began circulating in Washington, there was a significant backlash over the book's arguments and strident tone (e.g., the accusation that US trade demands were partly motivated by racism). Morita soon distanced himself from the book's claims, and his essays didn't appear in the official 1991 translation. See Andrew Pollack, "Akio Morita, Key to Japan's Rise as Co-Founder of Sony, Dies at 78," *New York Times*, October 3, 1999, https://archive.nytimes.com/www.nytimes.com/library/world/asia/100399obit -morita.html.

12. Ishihara, *The Japan That Can Say No*, 123.

13. Paul R. Krugman, *The Age of Diminished Expectations: U.S. Economic Policy in the 1990s* (Cambridge, MA: MIT Press, 1990), 195.

14. In 1979, Chinese leader Deng Xiaoping borrowed the term *xiaokang* from ancient Confucian philosophy to describe the goals of China's economic reforms. The term translates to "a moderately prosperous society." James Miles, "Meet 'Moderately Prosperous' China," *The Economist*, November 2019, https://web.archive.org/web/20200604040502/https://worldin.economist.com/article/17353/edition2020meet-moderately-prosperous-china.

15. "China Defends Xi Focus on Stability, Security Ahead of Reshuffle," *Bloomberg*, October 15, 2022, https://www.bloomberg.com/news/articles/2022-10-15/china-s-communist-party-congress-to-conclude-oct-22-in-beijing.

16. China has attempted to shift from investment toward consumption-led growth over the past 15 years, but this has proved difficult as household savings rates remain high (i.e., about one-third of income) and because of the prohibitive expense of creating a safety net to encourage lower savings. China has returned to investment whenever the economy slows uncomfortably, as evidenced by spending on new housing and transportation infrastructure (e.g., trains, highways, and airports). For further reading on the challenge, see Damien Ma and Houze Song, "China's Consumption Conundrum," *Foreign Affairs*, March 16, 2023, https://www.foreignaffairs.com/china/chinas-consumption-conundrum.

Chapter 7

1. Of course, software is not the only form of technological investment and was reasonably modest in the early part of figure 7.1. But the argument, though simplified, holds: as a new generation of technological investment emerges, productivity growth slumps. In the next chapter, figure 8.2 will show a more nuanced picture using investment in information processing equipment, which grew rapidly in the late 1970s and early 1980s. Aside from a boom in the late 1990s (when there was a bump in productivity) investment has moved sideways at a higher level, but productivity growth has remained sluggish. Even if we looked at all types of technological investment, the picture of sluggish productivity growth remains.

2. Capacity utilization improvements varied: in New York, from 49.5% (taxis) to 51.2% (UberX), a very modest improvement, and in Boston from 32.0% (taxis) to 46.1% (UberX), a more substantial improvement. Judd Cramer and Alan B. Krueger, "Disruptive Change in the Taxi Business: The Case of Uber," working paper 22083, National Bureau of Economic Research, Washington, DC, March 2016, https://www.nber.org/papers/w22083.

3. Productivity is commonly measured in two different ways. One is labor productivity, which corresponds to the real output per hour of work. The other is multifactor or total factor productivity (TFP), which looks to see how much real output is made after accounting for labor inputs and capital inputs. In general, we are referring to TFP measures, as we see this as a clearer indication of how economies are getting *better* at making goods and services. In other words, it's not just about getting a new machine, but about getting better at doing something, even when the costs of the machine are accounted for. In some cases, due to data limitations, we use measures that are more similar to labor productivity, such as gross value added per worker.

4. One study estimated that between 1995 and 2001, labor productivity in services-producing industries in the United States increased by 2.6% per year (compared to 2.3% in goods-producing industries). Service industries accounted for 73% of labor productivity growth in this period. The paper goes on to show that information technology (IT) primarily contributed to productivity growth through the service sector. Increased use of IT in service sectors accounted for 80% of the overall contribution of IT to labor-productivity growth. Jack E. Triplett and Barry P. Bosworth, *Productivity in the U.S. Services Sector: New Sources of Economic Growth* (Washington, DC: Brookings Institution Press, 2004), 1.

5. Philipp Carlsson-Szlezak and Paul Swartz, "The Secret of Productivity Growth Is Not Technology," World Economic Forum, August 3, 2021, https://www.weforum.org/agenda/2021/08/the-secret-of-productivity-growth-is-not-technology/.

6. To be precise—relative prices.

7. The speed and scope of price falls will be strongly influenced by the degree of competition within the sector and how widespread the increase in productivity is. It is not hard to imagine a firm that moves productivity substantially but only cuts prices marginally if they know that their competition can't compete with them. This would lead to more modest price declines. As productivity gains spread across the sector, which over time seems likely, the price declines will become more significant. It is important to remember that productivity is not nominal revenue per input, but rather real output per input, so falling prices—or even falling revenues—don't mean that productivity gains haven't happened.

8. While imports do influence this, we also see relative price declines in domestic gross value added in durable-goods manufacturing and essentially flat absolute prices.

9. Growing prices in low productivity services are impacted by the Baumol effect, where higher wages in sectors with productivity growth push up the wages (and prices) in sectors without.

10. The same can be said of internet search engines, restaurant booking apps, and other modern novelties. You may like them, but they shouldn't be credited with moving GDP unless they are changing real incomes. We would remain skeptical of any productivity claims that were primarily the result of new product innovation without any accompanying clear signs of stronger incomes. We are not alone in this view. Consider, for example, this observation from the economist Larry Summers:

> I do not base this judgment on calculations about the consumer surplus from Google or Facebook; I think those are important conceptual issues for measuring the welfare of the average citizen. I am not sure that they are important conceptual issues when quantified for measuring market GDP, as economists traditionally understand market GDP.

Lawrence H. Summers, "Reflections on the Productivity Slowdown," Peterson Institute for International Economics, Washington, DC, November 16, 2015, https://www.piie.com/sites /default/files/publications/papers/transcript-20151116keynote.pdf.

11. See Brent Moulton, "The Measurement of Output, Prices, and Productivity," the Hutchins Center on Fiscal and Monetary Policy at the Brookings Institution, July 25, 2018, https://www.brookings.edu/research/the-measurement-of-output-prices-and-productivity/, and David E. Lebow and Jeremy B. Rudd, "Measurement Error in the Consumer Price Index: Where Do We Stand?" *Journal of Economic Literature* 41, no. 1 (2003), https://www.aeaweb.org/articles?id =10.1257/002205103321544729.

Chapter 8

1. Philipp Carlsson-Szlezak and Paul Swartz, "The Secret of Productivity Growth Is Not Technology," World Economic Forum, August 3, 2021, https://www.weforum.org/agenda/2021 /08/the-secret-of-productivity-growth-is-not-technology/.

2. "Tesla under US Criminal Investigation over Self-Driving Claims, Sources Say," *The Guardian*, October 26, 2022, https://www.theguardian.com/technology/2022/oct/26/tesla -criminal-investigation-self-driving-claims-sources.

3. Using numerous case studies, a 2016 book by Calestous Juma examines the backlash to new technologies, including the printing press, farm mechanization, electricity, and refrigeration, among others. Calestous Juma, *Innovation and Its Enemies: Why People Resist New Technologies* (New York: Oxford University Press, 2016).

4. Adoption of drones is limited by the FAA's beyond-visual-line-of-sight regulations for unmanned aircraft, which require that operators be able to see the drone they are operating. The regulatory process has been slow to address this barrier. The FAA established a visual-line-of-sight rulemaking committee in 2021, which issued a report with recommendations in March 2022. And while FAA officials say they are developing a Notice of Proposed Rulemaking in response to the report, this likely won't be published until early 2024. US Government

Accountability Office (GAO), "Drones: FAA Should Improve Its Approach to Integrating Drones into the National Airspace System," GAO-23-105189, January 26, 2023, https://www.gao.gov /products/gao-23-105189.

5. Big regulatory resets in US history were driven by popular backlash, typically stoked by journalists and activist writers. Ida Tarbell's work contributed to the breakup of Standard Oil (1911), Upton Sinclair paved the way for the creation of the FDA to regulate food safety (1906), and Rachel Carson's work is associated with the creation of the EPA (1970). In each case, regulators responded rather than drove the agenda. Philipp Carlsson-Szlezak and Paul Swartz, "Popular Outrage, not Economics, Will Determine the Fate of Big Tech," *Fortune*, August 18, 2021, https://fortune.com/2021/08/18/big-tech-breakup-antitrust-popular-outrage-facebook-google -standard-oil-microsoft/. We argued that significant changes in policy come not from forward-looking policymakers but from politicians reacting to popular outrage.

6. Laura Tyson and Jan Mischke, "Productivity after the Pandemic," Project Syndicate, April 20, 2021, https://www.project-syndicate.org/commentary/productivity-after-the-pandemic -by-laura-tyson-and-jan-mischke-2021-04.

7. Philipp Carlsson-Szlezak and Paul Swartz, "Will Covid Be a Catalyst for Service Sector Productivity?" BCG Henderson Institute, July 2020, https://bcghendersoninstitute.com/center-for -macroeconomics/research-portal/will-covid-be-a-catalyst-for-service-sector-productivity/, and Philipp Carlsson-Szlezak and Paul Swartz, "Why We Shouldn't Overstate the Pandemic's Effect on Productivity Growth," World Economic Forum, October 15, 2021, https://www.weforum .org/agenda/2021/10/how-to-be-realistic-about-covids-impact-on-productivity-growth/.

8. Robert M. Solow, "We'd Better Watch Out," *New York Times Book Review*, July 12, 1987, http://digamo.free.fr/solow87.pdf.

9. Daniel Susskind, *A World without Work: Technology, Automation, and How We Should Respond* (New York: Metropolitan Books, 2020). Philipp Carlsson-Szlezak (host), *A World without Work with Daniel Susskind*, BCG Henderson Institute audio podcast, October 27, 2020, https://bcghendersoninstitute.com/a-world-without-work-with-daniel-susskind/.

10. Joel Mokyr, Chris Vickers, and Nicolas L. Ziebarth, "The History of Technological Anxiety and the Future of Economic Growth: Is This Time Different?" *Journal of Economic Perspectives* 29, no. 3 (2015): 31, https://www.aeaweb.org/articles?id=10.1257/jep.29.3.31.

11. "Difference Engine: Luddite Legacy," *The Economist*, November 4, 2011, https://www .economist.com/babbage/2011/11/04/difference-engine-luddite-legacy.

12. Philipp Carlsson-Szlezak, Paul Swartz, and François Candelon, "Why We Need to Be Realistic about Generative AI's Economic Impact," World Economic Forum, August 31, 2023, https://www.weforum.org/agenda/2023/08/generative-ai-realistic-economic-impact/.

Chapter 9

1. While President Kennedy's tax cuts—which were signed into law in 1964 by President Johnson and which reduced the top marginal income tax rate by 20 percentage points—can arguably be considered a stimulus, they were modest from a modern perspective in terms of their impact on public debt.

2. Or at least that debt-to-GDP ratios should fall afterward—if not literally pay off the debt in nominal terms. President Eisenhower believed that paying down the debt was a moral issue. For example, according to Eisenhower biographer Stephen Ambrose, Eisenhower "thought of deficit spending as almost sinful and immoral, except in wartime." Bill Buzenberg, "A Half Century Later, Another Warning in Eisenhower Address Rings True," the Center for Public Integrity, January 17, 2011, https://publicintegrity.org/accountability/a-half-century-later -another-warning-in-eisenhower-address-rings-true/.

3. In January 1980—just before submitting its FY1981 budget—the Carter administration announced a 50% upward revision in the Office of Management and Budget's forecast for the

FY1980 budget deficit. Along with soaring inflation, this drove markets into a tailspin, and Carter was forced to send a revised budget to Congress in late March. W. Carl Biven, *Jimmy Carter's Economy: Policy in an Age of Limits* (Chapel Hill, NC: University of North Carolina Press, 2003), 8.

4. This did come at the cost of a significant economic downturn, with unemployment reaching a peak of 10.8% in December 1982.

5. James M. Poterba, David Stockman, and Charles Schultze, "Budget Policy," in Martin Feldstein, ed., *American Economic Policy in the 1980s* (Chicago: University of Chicago Press, 1994), 23.

6. *Morning in America* refers to a 1984 Reagan campaign ad that is considered one of the most effective in history and has become a metaphor for economic renewal.

7. Of course, financial bubbles are not new (think of the Tulip bubble of the 17th century) and they have been macroeconomically significant (Mississippi bubble in the early 18th century). But it can be said that the late 20th-century and early 21st-century bubbles were more significant macroeconomically than their more-recent postwar counterpoints—including the Nifty Fifty bubble in the 1960s and early 1970s.

8. Remember that Ross Perot's deficit-reduction message helped earn him 19% of the popular vote in the 1992 presidential election.

9. Lower them by compressing elevated term premia.

10. The ability of policymakers to stop bubbles in any reasonable way is debatable (see chapter 16). During a 1996 speech to the American Enterprise Institute, Fed Chair Alan Greenspan seemed to suggest that the stock market was overvalued, asking "[H]ow do we know when irrational exuberance has unduly escalated asset values, which then become subject to unexpected and prolonged contractions as they have in Japan over the past decade? And how do we factor that assessment into monetary policy?" The stock market briefly dropped in reaction to the speech, but soon continued its ascent for another three years. Alan Greenspan, "The Challenge of Central Banking in a Democratic Society," remarks at the Annual Dinner and Francis Boyer Lecture of the American Enterprise Institute for Public Policy Research, December 5, 1996, https://www.federalreserve.gov/boarddocs/speeches/1996/19961205.htm.

11. Ron Suskind, *The Price of Loyalty: George W. Bush, the White House, and the Education of Paul O'Neill* (New York: Simon & Schuster, 2004), 291.

12. Ben S. Bernanke, "The Global Saving Glut and the U.S. Current Account Deficit," remarks at the Sandridge Lecture, Virginia Association of Economists, March 10, 2005, https://www.federalreserve.gov/boarddocs/speeches/2005/200503102/default.htm. Even when monetary policy tried to tighten rates, a global savings glut kept long rates very low (Greenspan's conundrum).

13. Some went so far as to suggest that a new bubble was necessary to replace the Nasdaq bubble. Paul Krugman, "Dubya's Double Dip?" *New York Times*, August 2, 2002, https://www.nytimes.com/2002/08/02/opinion/dubya-s-double-dip.html.

14. Alan Greenspan was keenly aware of the potential wealth effects of a stock market crash, as evidenced by his 1977 New York University PhD dissertation, titled "Why Central Banks Must Fight Bubbles." See Sebastian Mallaby, *The Man Who Knew: The Life and Times of Alan Greenspan* (New York: Penguin Press, 2016).

15. Testifying before the Senate Banking Committee in July 2008 about plans to stabilize Fannie Mae and Freddie Mac, Treasury Secretary Hank Paulson said, "If you've got a squirt-gun in your pocket, you may have to take it out. If you've got a bazooka, and people know you've got it, you may not have to take it out." Stephen Labaton and David M. Herszenhorn, "Opposition, from Both Parties, Over Bailout Plan," *New York Times*, July 16, 2008, https://https://www.nytimes.com/2008/07/16/business/16fannie.html. In a 2009 interview with the Financial Crisis Inquiry Commission, Ben Bernanke said, "I honestly believe that September and October of 2008 was the worst financial crisis in global history, including the Great Depression." Ben Bernanke (interviewee), Financial Crisis Inquiry Commission, November 17, 2009, http://fcic-static.law.stanford.edu/cdn_media/fcic-docs/FCIC%20Interview%20with%20Ben%20Bernanke,%20Federal%20Reserve.pdf.

Chapter 10

1. Philipp Carlsson-Szlezak, Martin Reeves, and Paul Swartz, "Understanding the Economic Shock of Coronavirus," *Harvard Business Review*, March 27, 2020, https://hbr.org/2020/03/understanding-the-economic-shock-of-coronavirus.

2. Philipp Carlsson-Szlezak, Martin Reeves, and Paul Swartz, "The U.S. Is Not Headed Toward a New Great Depression," hbr.org, May 1, 2020, https://hbr.org/2020/05/the-u-s-is-not-headed-toward-a-new-great-depression.

3. Treasury Secretary Andrew Mellon is quoted saying, "Liquidate labor, liquidate stocks, liquidate the farmers, liquidate real estate . . . It will purge the rottenness out of the system." Herbert Hoover, *The Memoirs of Herbert Hoover: The Great Depression, 1929–1941* (New York: Macmillan, 1952), 30.

4. Ben Bernanke's efforts in 2008 show that he followed through on his promise to Milton Friedman not to do it again. See Bernanke's speech honoring Friedman on Friedman's 90th birthday, in which Bernanke said, "Regarding the Great Depression. You're right, we did it. We're very sorry. But thanks to you, we won't do it again." Ben S. Bernanke, "On Milton Friedman's 90th Birthday," remarks at the Conference to Honor Milton Friedman, University of Chicago, November 8, 2002, https://www.federalreserve.gov/boarddocs/speeches/2002/20021108/.

5. In 2003, the Nobel Prize–winning economist Robert Lucas went so far as to write about macroeconomics: "Its central problem of depression prevention has been solved, for all practical purposes, and has in fact been solved for many decades." Robert E. Lucas Jr., "Macroeconomic Priorities," *American Economic Review* 93, no. 1 (2003), https://www.aeaweb.org/articles?id=10.1257/000282803321455133.

6. Poul M. Thomsen, "The IMF and the Greek Crisis: Myths and Realities," International Monetary Fund, September 30, 2019, https://www.imf.org/en/News/Articles/2019/10/01/sp093019-The-IMF-and-the-Greek-Crisis-Myths-and-Realities.

7. In July 2012, then-European Central Bank President Mario Draghi pledged that "within our mandate, the ECB is ready to do whatever it takes to preserve the euro. And believe me, it will be enough." This promise alone helped to calm markets, bringing bond yields down and arguably helping save the eurozone. Mario Draghi, "Speech at the Global Investment Conference," London, July 26, 2012, https://www.ecb.europa.eu/press/key/date/2012/html/sp120726.en.html.

8. Uncertain variables include the natural rate of interest, the state of real rates, inflation, the state of financial conditions, and many other factors.

9. Edmund L. Andrews, "A New Role for the Fed: Investor of Last Resort," *New York Times*, September 17, 2008, https://www.nytimes.com/2008/09/18/business/18fed.html.

Chapter 11

1. Philipp Carlsson-Szlezak and Paul Swartz, "The U.S. Economic Stimulus Machine Is Sputtering, but It Isn't Broken," *Fortune*, March 3, 2022, https://fortune.com/2022/03/03/inflation-stimulus-machine-interest-rates-tax-cuts/.

2. UK Chancellor Kwasi Kwarteng lasted only 38 days in office, and UK Prime Minister Liz Truss resigned after only 45 days.

3. "Fed put" is used to describe the tendency of monetary policy to ease when risk assets—particularly the stock market—fall in value. The easing helps the market to recover. Thus it has often provided a form of insurance against downdraft, thus the "put option" language.

4. Matthew Yglesias, "A House Republican Explains Why Deficits Don't Matter Anymore," *Vox*, September 28, 2017, https://www.vox.com/policy-and-politics/2017/9/28/16378854/mark-walker-deficit.

5. Philipp Carlsson-Szlezak and Paul Swartz, "Will Bidenomics Transform America's Economy? Not So Fast," *Fortune*, May 23, 2021, https://fortune.com/2021/05/23/biden-economic-agenda-bidenomics-long-term-impact-new-deal/.

6. Philipp Carlsson-Szlezak and Paul Swartz, "The Premature Obituary of the Bond Vigilantes ('Deficits Don't Matter' and All That)," Sanford C. Bernstein, November 2, 2018. Reprinted in *An Economic History of Now*, November 2018.

7. Philipp Carlsson-Szlezak and Paul Swartz, "When Deficits Matter—How to Think about Budgetary Risks from Debt and Deficits and the Risk for Equities," Sanford C. Bernstein, October 29, 2018.

8. Carville joked, "I used to think if there was reincarnation, I wanted to come back as the president or the pope or a .400 baseball hitter. But now I want to come back as the bond market. You can intimidate everybody." James Carville, "The Vigilante," *The Atlantic*, June 2011, https://www.theatlantic.com/magazine/archive/2011/06/the-vigilante/308503/.

9. Ron Suskind, *The Price of Loyalty: George W. Bush, the White House, and the Education of Paul O'Neill* (New York: Simon & Schuster, 2004), 291.

10. Philipp Carlsson-Szlezak and Paul Swartz, "Long-Term Interest Rates Are Spiking. Could They Deliver a Recession—or Are They a Sign of Strength for the U.S. Economy?" *Fortune*, October 12, 2023, https://fortune.com/2023/10/12/long-term-interest-rates-spiking-could-recessionor-us-economy-carlsson-szlezak-swartz/.

11. Philipp Carlsson-Szlezak, Paul Swartz, and Martin Reeves, "Who Will Win—and Lose—in the Post-Covid Economy?" hbr.org, June 1, 2021, https://hbr.org/2021/06/who-will-win-and-lose-in-the-post-covid-economy.

12. Philipp Carlsson-Szlezak and Paul Swartz, "10 Years On—Policy Effectiveness and the True Legacy of the Great Recession," Sanford C. Bernstein, September 10, 2018. Reprinted in *An Economic History of Now*, November 2018.

13. Universal Basic Income (UBI) would provide all citizens with a set payment, regardless of their labor-force participation. Proponents believe that UBI would be more efficient to implement than the traditional means-tested social safety net and would receive stronger public support. People would also be free to work less and be protected from automation risk. However, critics say that UBI is too costly, that it is poorly targeted for those in need, that it disincentivizes work, and that it comes with the risk of inflation. Proponents of Modern Monetary Theory (MMT)—such as Stephanie Kelton of Stony Brook University—argue (in part) that government deficits should be the size needed to reach full employment and that deficits should lower interest rates because they expand the money supply. Critics—such as Paul Krugman, who would not disagree with the power and importance of deficit spending—argue that expansionary fiscal policy will increase interest rates unless they are stuck at the zero lower bound. See, for example, Paul Krugman, "Running on MMT (Wonkish)," *New York Times*, February 25, 2019, https://www.nytimes.com/2019/02/25/opinion/running-on-mmt-wonkish.html. Philipp Carlsson-Szlezak and Paul Swartz, "MMT, AOC, OMG—What Investors Should Know about Modern Monetary Theory," Sanford C. Bernstein, April 9, 2019. Reprinted in *An Economic History of Now*, vol. 2, September 2019.

Chapter 12

1. Volcker's successor as chair at the Federal Reserve, Alan Greenspan, was also essential to completing the journey of taming inflation and anchoring expectations based on credible central bank policy, a process that continued into the 1990s.

2. The end of price controls was also a factor.

3. The backdrop for interest rates is complicated by the continuation of World War II–based monetary policy that was holding down rates. For example, in 1942—at the request of the Treasury Department—the Federal Reserve committed to pegging the interest rate on short-term Treasury bills to 3/8%, maintaining this peg until the Treasury–Federal Reserve Accord of 1951. John Mullin, "A Look Back at Financial Repression," Federal Reserve Bank of Richmond, First Quarter 2021, https://www.richmondfed.org/publications/research/econ_focus/2021/q1/economic_history.

4. Philipp Carlsson-Szlezak and Paul Swartz, "Think Trump vs. Powell Is Ugly? Try Jackson vs. Biddle for a Taxonomy of Political Pressure," Sanford C. Bernstein, March 1, 2019. Reprinted in *An Economic History of Now*, vol. 2, September 2019.

5. The Treasury–Federal Reserve Accord of 1951, which freed the Fed from the cap on interest rates that had been in place since World War II, was fiercely resisted by the White House and President Truman—who saw the Korean War as reason for the arrangement to persist. Truman lost the battle with the Fed but thought he had scored a victory by pushing out the chairman and replacing him with his own man—William McChesney Martin. But Martin proved to be an able chair early in his tenure and successfully checked inflation. When Truman saw him years later, he simply said, "Traitor."

6. Persistent errors are typically conceptual, driven by mistakes about economic dynamics and trade-offs or political forces that deprioritize inflation and price stability. In the 1940s, war finance was an overwhelming driver of the low-interest-rate policy. In the 1960s, policymakers believed that monetary/fiscal coordination was appropriate, that policy was tight when it wasn't, that there was a sustained trade-off between inflation and employment, that unemployment could go lower, and that it wasn't the place of monetary policymakers to harm the economy in order to bring down inflation, all of which contributed to sustained errors. The modern central bank seems less prone than its predecessors to make such conceptual and political errors.

7. Paul A. Volcker and Christine Harper, *Keeping at It: The Quest for Sound Money and Good Government* (New York: PublicAffairs, 2018).

8. "Inflation is a monetary policy phenomenon, not a monetary phenomenon." Angel Ubide, *The Paradox of Risk: Leaving the Monetary Policy Comfort Zone* (Washington, DC: Peterson Institute for International Economics, 2017), 163.

9. We simplify, as 1940s inflation includes the early 1950s inflation, and 1970s inflation begins with the inflation surge in the 1960s.

10. In late 2021 we argued that those fearing a structural break in the inflation regime were likely still wrong, as the Fed would not commit sustained policy errors and would respond to elevated inflation.

11. Carlsson-Szlezak and Swartz, "The Fed Isn't Likely to Let Inflation Skyrocket, No Matter What the Doomsayers Think," Fortune, November 8, 2021, https://fortune.com/2021/11/08/inflation-fears-federal-reserve-jerome-powell/.

12. Economist Mohamed El-Erian has said that because of its late start in fighting inflation, the Fed now has "no choice but to go after inflation. That is their mandate. Because they were so late, there will be undue damage to the real economy—to employment, to livelihoods—that could have been avoided." Jennifer Sor, "The Fed Has No Choice but to Cause 'Undue Pain' for the Economy after Blowing It on Inflation, Mohamed El-Erian Says," *Business Insider*, December 21, 2022, https://markets.businessinsider.com/news/stocks/economic-outlook-fed-inflation-rate-hike-recession-risk-el-erian-2022-12.

13. Philipp Carlsson-Szlezak and Paul Swartz, "For the Fed, Fighting Inflation Is Imperative, but Slamming the Economy Would Be Premature," *Fortune*, April 8, 2022, https://fortune.com/2022/04/08/inflation-interest-rates-federal-reserve-recession/.

14. The real hourly wage at the 10th percentile grew by 9% overall from 2019 to 2022. Elise Gould and Katherine deCourcy, "Low-Wage Workers Have Seen Historically Fast Real Wage Growth in the Pandemic Business Cycle," Economic Policy Institute, March 23, 2023, https://www.epi.org/publication/swa-wages-2022/.

15. Larry Summers, "Secular Stagnation or Secular Stagflation," Speech at the London School of Economics, June 20, 2022, https://www.lse.ac.uk/Events/Open/202206201845/secular-stagnation-or-secular-stagflation.

16. Philipp Carlsson-Szlezak and Paul Swartz, "How to Break Inflation Expectations and the Equity Market," Sanford C. Bernstein, June 15, 2018. Reprinted in *An Economic History of Now*, November 2018.

17. The Federal Reserve believed that monetary policy was already tight at the time and that the Fed was only moving toward less, but still tight, status. Ben S. Bernanke, *21st Century Monetary Policy: The Federal Reserve from the Great Inflation to COVID-19* (New York: W. W. Norton & Company, 2022).

18. Arthur F. Burns, Milutin Cirovic, and Jacques J. Polak, "The Anguish of Central Banking," the 1979 Per Jacobsson Lecture, Belgrade, Yugoslavia, September 30, 1979, http://www .perjacobsson.org/lectures/1979.pdf.

19. For example, in December 1965 President Johnson summoned Fed Chair William McChesney Martin Jr. to his ranch to express his displeasure over the announcement of a rate increase. Johnson even reportedly shoved him and yelled, "Boys are dying in Vietnam, and Bill Martin doesn't care." Sebastian Mallaby, *The Man Who Knew: The Life and Times of Alan Greenspan* (New York: Penguin Press, 2016), 104. More recently, President Trump repeatedly called on Fed Chair Jerome Powell, both on Twitter and in interviews, to not raise rates. Emily Stewart, "Trump Makes Last-Ditch Effort to Pressure the Fed ahead of Interest Rate Meeting," *Vox*, December 18, 2018, https://www.vox.com/policy-and-politics/2018/12/17/18144497/trump -tweet-fed-reserve-Jay Powell.

Chapter 13

1. For example, see Olivier Blanchard, "In Defense of Concerns over the $1.9 Trillion Relief Plan," Peterson Institute for International Economics, February 18, 2021, https://www.piie.com /blogs/realtime-economics/defense-concerns-over-19-trillion-relief-plan.

2. Milton Friedman originally said a version of this line in a 1963 lecture in India, and it served as a challenge to the economics field, which had come to be largely dominated by Keynesian thought in the post–World War II years. Milton Friedman, "The Counter-Revolution in Monetary Theory," Institute of Economic Affairs, 1970, https://miltonfriedman.hoover.org /internal/media/dispatcher/214480/full.

3. The basis of the monetarist argument is that $MV = PQ$, or that money times velocity equals price times quantity (output). If money grows faster than output, prices rise—however, this relies on an assumption that velocity is stable and not influenced by changes in money, which is a weak assumption (at best).

4. For an overview on the usefulness of the Phillips curve, see Peter Hooper, Frederic S. Mishkin, and Amir Sufi, "Prospects for Inflation in a High Pressure Economy: Is the Phillips Curve Dead or Is It Just Hibernating?" working paper 25792, National Bureau of Economic Research, Cambridge, May 2019, https://www.nber.org/papers/w25792.

5. See John Cochrane, *The Fiscal Theory of the Price Level* (Princeton, NJ: Princeton University Press, 2023). While fiscal policy certainly plays a role in inflation dynamics (at a minimum through the demand channel), the idea that the present value of future deficits can meaningfully provide insight into the path of inflation strikes us as uncredible. Even if it were true, what could be done? It also doesn't seem credible that inflation can be successfully managed primarily through fiscal policy. As for greedflation, aside from the implausibility of being able to measure greed in any way that would inform one about inflation, it seems unlikely that firms have gone from being ungreedy when inflation was persistently low to being excessively greedy when inflation was too high. While a popular lens for the politics of inflation, it is an exceedingly weak lens for understanding and responding to inflation. Market concentration seems likely to play a role in the level of prices and profit margins, but it seems much less likely to be useful for understanding the dynamics of cyclical inflation. Was market concentration low when inflation was undershooting the Fed's target? Did it change meaningfully to mirror the surge in inflation or the shift in composition of inflation? No.

6. The Fed provided the conclusions to its monetary-policy review in August 2020 and announced a new policy of targeting 2% inflation on average over time. The idea was to lean against the deflationary bias by making it possible to remain easy even if inflation popped above

the 2% mark. Federal Reserve, "Federal Open Market Committee Announces Approval of Updates to Its Statement on Longer-Run Goals and Monetary Policy Strategy," FOMC press release, August 27, 2020, https://www.federalreserve.gov/newsevents/pressreleases /monetary20200827a.htm.

7. Charles Goodhart and Manoj Pradhan, *The Great Demographic Reversal: Ageing Societies, Waning Inequality, and an Inflation Revival* (London: Palgrave Macmillan, 2020).

8. Formerly known as NAIRU, the nonaccelerating inflation rate of unemployment.

9. When tight (u < u*), inflationary pressures may be building; when loose (u > u*), pressure may be easing.

Chapter 14

1. Paul Schmelzing, "Eight Centuries of Global Real Interest Rates, R–G, and the 'Suprasecular' Decline, 1311–2018," staff working paper 845, Bank of England, January 3, 2020, https://www.bankofengland.co.uk/working-paper/2020/eight-centuries-of-global-real-interest-rates-r-g-and-the-suprasecular-decline-1311-2018.

2. This lays the groundwork for understanding the environment of the risk-free rate, which is a reference point for all other rates. The ecosystem of interest rates extends far beyond that, to corporate bonds, high-yield corporate debt, mortgages, and many other things. We like to joke that we strive here to give an approach to interest rates in roughly 3,000 words—the cornerstone books on interest rates (for example, Fabozzi's *The Handbook of Fixed Income Securities* and Homer and Sylla's *A History of Interest Rates*) have nearly 3,000 pages between them.

3. Why don't these call out specific quantitative levels of rates? Because the level of rates won't tell us the nature of the regime. For example, a 10-year rate of 3% could be associated with multiple regimes. Instead, what matters (in an anchored inflation regime) is the level of the policy rate (r) relative to the neutral rate of interest (r*). The policy stance helps signal the type of regime. And since r* also changes over time—which will impact the level of rates—the rate levels are less interesting and can even be misleading when one is trying to understand the interest-rate regime.

4. This can be thought of as policy rates (r) being higher than views of the neutral rate (r*).

5. Philipp Carlsson-Szlezak and Paul Swartz, "Is This the End of Low Interest Rates?" *Fortune*, June 7, 2022, https://fortune.com/2022/06/07/inflation-interest-rates-higher-but-healthy-bcg/.

6. This will remain true even when monetary policy is able to moderate from a very restrictive stance and cut rates to a restrictive stance.

7. The 10-year government bond rate is the benchmark for many other rates, from mortgages to corporate bonds. The 10Y can be decomposed into the average short rate over the next 10 years and a term premium. The average short rate is influenced significantly in the near term by the current policy position and its near-term path, while in the out years, it is significantly influenced by the views around r*.

8. Even if it is not as low as it was commonly thought to be in the late 2010s.

9. The April 2023 IMF World Economic Outlook estimated that the natural rate declined by about 2 percentage points in most advanced countries from the late 1970s to the late 2010s. It estimates that the neutral rate in the United States will remain below 1% (below 3% in nominal terms) over the next 30 years (due to the aging population and weak productivity growth). By contrast, the economist Larry Summers has suggested that r* could be in the range of 1.5% to 2% (presumably 3.5% to 4% in nominal terms), driven in part by increased government borrowing and investments into the green economy. While higher than other estimates, this is still lower than rates in the pre-global-financial-crisis era. See "The Natural Rate of Interest: Drivers and Implications for Policy," chapter 2 in *World Economic Outlook: A Rocky Recovery* (Washington, DC: International Monetary Fund, April 2023), https://www.imf.org/en/Publications/WEO/Issues/2023/04/11/world-economic-outlook-april-2023. See also Rich Miller, "IMF Disagrees with Summers over Where Interest Rates Will Settle," *Bloomberg*, April 10, 2023, https://www.bloomberg.com/news/articles/2023-04-10/imf-disagrees-with-summers-over-where-interest-rates-will-settle.

Chapter 15

1. Lionel Shriver, *The Mandibles: A Family, 2029–2047* (New York: HarperCollins, 2016).

2. We spoke with Lionel Shriver on BCG's *Thinkers and Ideas* podcast in 2021 about *The Mandibles*. At that time, she told us that she sees literature as a "safe space to explore your worst fears." She also suggested that although the movie rights to *The Mandibles* had been sold, she feared the movie may not come out before her novel turned into reality. Philipp Carlsson-Szlezak (host), *The Mandibles: A Family, 2029–2047 with Lionel Shriver*, audio podcast, BCG Henderson Institute, February 12, 2021, https://bcghendersoninstitute.com/the-mandibles-a-family-2029 -2047-with-lionel-shriver/.

3. Joseph Patrick Kennedy was rumored to have said that during the Depression and unrest of the 1930s, he would willingly give up half his fortune if he knew he could keep the other half.

4. Peter F. Drucker, "The Changed World Economy," *Foreign Affairs*, Spring 1986, https:// www.foreignaffairs.com/articles/1986-03-01/changed-world-economy.

5. Philipp Carlsson-Szlezak and Paul Swartz, "Why High Debt Levels Don't Worry Us (Too Much)—r-Minus-g, Its Spread, and Its Quality," Sanford C. Bernstein, October 7, 2019.

6. Carmen M. Reinhart and Kenneth S. Rogoff, "Growth in a Time of Debt," *American Economic Review*, May 2010. (Note: While the authors in their academic works are more nuanced about the causal linkages, little nuance survived in the political debate around debt that this article triggered. Ultimately the debate faded as this article by Reinhart and Rogoff was found to have mechanical errors.)

7. Risk premia stayed elevated, as it took time for markets to be convinced that inflation risk was durably slayed. This gave way to the antideficit stimulus of the early Clinton years, where reducing deficits led to reduced term premia and rates and therefore more stimulus, as discussed in chapter 10.

8. Ron Suskind, *The Price of Loyalty: George W. Bush, the White House, and the Education of Paul O'Neill* (New York: Simon & Schuster, 2004), 291.

9. Other stock effects, such as asset purchases and currency mismatches, will influence debt levels as well.

10. If financial repression or fiscal dominance takes precedence, the economy will underperform its potential as resources are poorly allocated and inflation will rise sooner or later and undermine economic health.

11. Philipp Carlsson-Szlezak and Paul Swartz, "10 Years On—Policy Effectiveness and the True Legacy of the Great Recession," Sanford C. Bernstein, September 10, 2018. Reprinted in *An Economic History of Now*, November 2018.

12. We're referring to substantive but not technical default (for instance, debt ceiling). The United States often flirts with technical default when at the debt ceiling—most recently in spring 2023—and it could return as an issue in 2025. Regarding currency blessings, if you're more concerned about manufacturing competitiveness and external balances, a strong currency can be seen as a negative.

13. Philipp Carlsson-Szlezak and Paul Swartz, "Is U.S. Debt 100%, 1,000% or 2,000% of GDP . . . ? It's Up to You, Sort Of," Sanford C. Bernstein, September 9, 2019.

Chapter 16

1. The Nasdaq rallied from 2,688.18 on October 19, 1999, to 5,048.62 on March 10, 2000—an 88% increase (300% annualized rate).

2. Using Robert Shiller's CAPE (Cyclically Adjusted Price to Earnings ratio), the S&P 500 multiple was 10.36 in September of 1925 and 32.56 in September 1929.

3. Often considered the first speculative bubble in history, Dutch Tulipmania refers to the run-up in prices of tulip bulbs (which had only spread to Western Europe in the mid-16th century) starting in 1634, before collapsing in February 1637. See Peter Garber, "Tulipmania," *Journal of*

Political Economy 97, no. 3 (1989): 535, https://www.journals.uchicago.edu/doi/10.1086/261615. In 1716 the Scottish economist John Law—who was in exile in Paris for a murder conviction in a duel and was a friend of the French regent—helped create the Banque Générale, a private bank that brought paper money to France and provided credit based on land values. Then in August 1717 Law founded the Mississippi company, which was granted a monopoly on trade in North America. Law issued shares in the company in exchange for public debt securities. This eventually led to a stock market bubble that burst in 1720. See Janet Gleeson, *Millionaire: The Philanderer, Gambler, and Duelist Who Invented Modern Finance* (New York: Simon & Schuster, 1999). The Railway Mania was a classic stock-market bubble in the United Kingdom in the 1840s (and not the only bubble in railroad stocks). As railway share prices increased, speculators moved in pushing prices to unsustainable levels, followed by a collapse. Regarding the tech bubble, see Michael Lewis, *The New New Thing: A Silicon Valley Story* (New York: W. W. Norton & Company, 2000).

4. Regarding cryptocurrencies, we realize that many will disagree, and perhaps not all pockets of crypto are a bubble. But we should be able to agree that dogecoin was evidence of froth. Regarding NFTs, digital assets are likely to be real, but the $2.9 million paid for the digital rights to the first-ever tweet from Jack Dorsey seems off. Regarding bankrupt stocks, Hertz, JCPenney, Pier 1, and Whiting Petroleum (among others) experienced temporary sharp rallies in 2020.

5. Walter Bagehot—the editor in chief of *The Economist* from 1861 to 1877—once said, "John Bull can stand many things but he cannot stand 2%." John Bull was not an actual person, but a stand-in for the everyday investor. The idea is that instead of accepting a low return, investors will put their money into more risky, speculative investments. Edward Chancellor, *The Price of Time: The Real Story of Interest* (New York: Grove Atlantic, 2022).

6. We recognize that fracking had meaningful impact in terms of US oil production, which benefited economic activity, external balances, and so on, but its bubbly state was reflected in some of the poor investment return—as seen, for example, in Chesapeake Energy's bankruptcy.

7. It's not too much of a stretch to suggest that the Mississippi bubble played a role in the forces that started the French Revolution, illustrating the most extreme potential effects of bursting bubbles.

8. Supreme Court Justice Potter Stewart said this in his 1964 concurring opinion for the *Jacobellis v. Ohio* case.

9. Ben S. Bernanke, "Monetary Policy and the Housing Bubble," speech at the annual meeting of the American Economic Association, Atlanta, January 3, 2010, https://www.federalreserve.gov/newsevents/speech/bernanke20100103a.htm.

10. Keynes went so far as to argue that "the government should pay people to dig holes in the ground and then fill them up"—a silly illustration to make the point that any stimulus can be worthwhile in the context of a depression.

11. Philipp Carlsson-Szlezak and Paul Swartz, "The Death of the Well-Behaved Drawdown—What Investors Need to Know about Modern Volatility," Sanford C. Bernstein, June 24, 2019. Reprinted in *An Economic History of Now*, vol. 2, September 2019.

12. Ben S. Bernanke, "Asset-Price 'Bubbles' and Monetary Policy," remarks before the New York Chapter of the National Association for Business Economics, New York, October 15, 2002, https://www.federalreserve.gov/boarddocs/speeches/2002/20021015/default.htm.

13. Ben S. Bernanke, Timothy F. Geithner, and Henry M. Paulson Jr., *Firefighting: The Financial Crisis and Its Lessons* (New York: Penguin, 2019).

14. "Bank Failures in Brief—Summary 2001 through 2023," Federal Deposit Insurance Corporation, https://www.fdic.gov/bank/historical/bank/, and *The First Fifty Years: A History of the FDIC 1933–1983* (Washington, DC: Federal Deposit Insurance Corporation, 1984).

15. Philipp Carlsson-Szlezak and Paul Swartz, "How We Can Learn to Stop Worrying and Love Market Bubbles," *Fortune*, July 13, 2021, https://fortune.com/2021/07/13/stock-market-bubbles-investing-spacs-positive-legacies-economy/.

16. Strictly speaking, Chuck Prince was commenting on financing leveraged buyouts in a July 2007 interview with the *Financial Times*, "When the music stops, in terms of liquidity, things will be complicated. But as long as the music is playing, you've got to get up and dance. We're still dancing." Growing fears about the subprime mortgage market had raised concerns about liquidity for buyouts. Michiyo Nakamoto and David Wighton, "Citigroup Chief Stays Bullish on Buy-Outs," *Financial Times*, July 9, 2007, https://www.ft.com/content/80e2987a-2e50-11dc-821c-0000779fd2ac.

Chapter 17

1. "History repeats itself, first as tragedy, second as farce," Karl Marx; "History doesn't repeat itself, but it often rhymes," often attributed to Mark Twain; "What is history but a fable agreed upon," Napoleon Bonaparte but also Bernard Le Bovier de Fontenelle.

2. William Faulkner, *Requiem for a Nun* (New York: Random House, 1951).

3. With respect to the past being over, in the wake of the collapse of the Soviet Union, Francis Fukuyama identified "Western liberal democracy as the final form of human government." To be fair, Fukuyama didn't argue that all significant historical events had ended, but that in the long term, liberal democracy would become only more prevalent. Francis Fukuyama, *The End of History and the Last Man* (New York: Free Press, 1992).

4. The term—popularized by Graham Allison—comes from fifth century BC Athenian historian Thucydides's explanation for the inevitability of the Peloponnesian War: "It was the rise of Athens and the fear that this instilled in Sparta that made war inevitable." In his 2017 book, Allison says that over the last 500 years, war has broken out in 12 of the 16 cases when a rising power has challenged the established one. Allison suggests that the United States and China may be headed in this direction. Graham Allison, *Destined for War: Can America and China Escape Thucydides's Trap?* (Boston: Houghton Mifflin Harcourt, 2017).

5. To be clear, convergence does not mean that there wasn't stress. For example, see the 1995 US intervention in the Bosnian War, the 1990s US involvement in drug wars in Latin America, and a general fear of the threat from nonstate actors. But overall, these were smaller conflicts (at least compared with past wars). In contrast to Fukuyama's argument for the end of history, Samuel Huntington expected future conflicts to continue, but arising from tribal hatreds and cultural differences. Samuel P. Huntington, *The Clash of Civilizations and the Remaking of World Order* (New York: Simon & Schuster, 1996).

6. Gary Gerstle, *The Rise and Fall of the Neoliberal Order: America and the World in the Free Market Era* (New York: Oxford University Press, 2002).

7. The Washington Consensus is an informal set of policy recommendations aimed at promoting economic development in less developed countries. Recommendations include such things as fiscal discipline, trade liberalization, privatization, and liberalization of foreign direct investment inflows. John Williamson, "What Washington Means by Policy Reform," Peterson Institute for International Economics, November 1, 2002, https://www.piie.com/commentary/speeches-papers/what-washington-means-policy-reform.

8. Keynes once wrote, "If economists could manage to get themselves thought of as humble, competent people on a level with dentists, that would be splendid." John Maynard Keynes, *Essays in Persuasion* (New York: Norton, 1931).

9. J. William Fulbright, *The Arrogance of Power* (New York: Random House, 1966).

10. On May 1, 2003—only six weeks after the launch of the Iraq War—President Bush landed in a navy fighter jet on an aircraft carrier, the USS *Abraham Lincoln*. In front of a banner saying "Mission Accomplished" Bush declared, "Major combat operations in Iraq have ended. In the battle of Iraq, the United States and our allies have prevailed." But the Iraq War continued for eight years, with US troops finally withdrawing in 2011.

11. Robert Barsky and Matthew Easton, "The Global Saving Glut and the Fall in U.S. Real Interest Rates: A 15-Year Retrospective," *Economic Perspectives*, Federal Reserve Bank of Chicago, March 2021, https://www.chicagofed.org/publications/economic-perspectives/2021/1.

12. In Greek mythology Cassandra was a Trojan priestess to the god Apollo—cursed to tell accurate prophecies that were never believed. We assert a modern usage in reverse—someone who inaccurately predicts doom and is too often believed.

13. For an example of this, consider Ray Dalio, *Principles for Dealing with the Changing World Order: Why Nations Succeed and Fail* (New York: Avid Reader Press, 2021).

14. Adopted by China in 2013, the Belt and Road Initiative is an infrastructure-development strategy whereby China finances infrastructure projects to connect Asia, Africa, and Europe through both land and sea routes. Launched in 2016 and headquartered in Beijing, the Asian Infrastructure Investment Bank is a multilateral development bank that finances infrastructure projects in Asia and is seen as a rival to Western-led institutions like the IMF and the World Bank.

15. For an example of this, consider Dalio, *Principles for Dealing with the Changing World Order: Why Nations Succeed and Fail.*

Chapter 18

1. Philipp Carlsson-Szlezak and Paul Swartz, "Would a War Drive Equities Lower and Volatility Higher? How to Think about Geopolitics and Equity Markets," Sanford C. Bernstein, September 3, 2019. Reprinted in *An Economic History of Now,* vol. 2, September 2019.

2. When Germany marched through France the following year, equity markets sold off as more pessimism took hold.

3. George F. Kennan, *Memoirs: 1950–1963* (New York: Pantheon Books, 1967), 218.

4. Norman Angell, *The Great Illusion* (New York and London: G. P. Putnam's Sons, 1910). The work was first published as a pamphlet in 1909, and then as a book a year later. Angell was a British journalist, author, and (briefly) member of Parliament for the Labor Party. He was a public advocate for internationalism and a supporter of the League of Nations, and in 1933 he became the only person to win the Nobel Peace Prize for writing a book. *The Great Illusion* argued that growing interdependence between states made war economically futile. The outbreak of World War I undermined the idea that such conflict was impossible.

5. Niall Ferguson, Barry Eichengreen, and Hélène Ray, "Earning from History? Financial Markets and the Approach of World Wars," The Brookings Institution, Spring 2008, https://www.brookings.edu/bpea-articles/earning-from-history-financial-markets-and-the-approach-of-world-wars/.

6. Marko Papic, *Geopolitical Alpha: An Investment Framework for Predicting the Future* (Hoboken, NJ: Wiley, 2020).

7. George F. Kennan ("X"), "The Sources of Soviet Conduct," *Foreign Affairs,* July 1947, https://www.foreignaffairs.com/russian-federation/george-kennan-sources-soviet-conduct. Kennan was a US diplomat and historian best known for his promotion of a policy of containment against Soviet expansion after World War II.

8. Philip E. Tetlock, "Theory-Driven Reasoning about Plausible Pasts and Probable Futures in World Politics: Are We Prisoners of Our Preconceptions?" *American Journal of Political Science* 43, no. 2 (1999): 335, https://www.cambridge.org/core/books/abs/heuristics-and-biases/theorydriven-reasoning-about-plausible-pasts-and-probable-futures-in-world-politics/DA30926CF20DE839ADFF065C614024DE.

9. Paul Barnett, "If What Gets Measured Gets Managed, Measuring the Wrong Thing Matters," *Corporate Finance Review,* January/February 2015, https://static.store.tax.thomsonreuters.com/static/relatedresource/CMJ--15-01%20sample-article.pdf.

10. Dario Caldara and Matteo Iacoviello, "Measuring Geopolitical Risk," *American Economic Review* 112, no. 4 (2022): 1194, https://www.aeaweb.org/articles?id=10.1257/aer.20191823.

11. At this point in time the Federal Reserve had only just been created (December 1913) and a traditional gold standard was still in effect, meaning that fears of capital flight could lead to a credit crunch. The legacy of the Panic of 1907 motivated the closing of the stock market (as well as the creation of the Federal Reserve).

12. Ferguson, Eichengreen, and Ray, "Earning from History?"

13. A version of this quote was first attributed to the Italian Renaissance philosopher and writer Niccolò Machiavelli and has been repeated (in various forms) by many politicians over the years, including Winston Churchill.

14. Dwight D. Eisenhower, "Remarks at the National Defense Executive Reserve Conference," The American Presidency Project, November 14, 1957, https://www.presidency.ucsb.edu /node/233951. Note that Prussian Field Marshal Helmuth von Moltke the Elder wrote something similar in 1871: "No plan of operations extends with any certainty beyond the first encounter with the main enemy forces." This has often been shortened to "No plan survives first contact with the enemy."

Chapter 19

1. See, for example: Adam S. Posen, "The End of Globalization?: What Russia's War in Ukraine Means for the World Economy," Foreign Affairs, March 17, 2022, https://www .foreignaffairs.com/articles/world/2022-03-17/end-globalization; "Is This the End of Globalization?" Foreign Policy, Spring 2020, https://foreignpolicy.com/2020/04/03/coronavirus-end -globalization/; and "Slowbalisation: The Future of Global Commerce," The Economist, January 24, 2019, https://www.economist.com/weeklyedition/2019-01-26.

2. Nearshoring refers to the process of businesses shifting their supply chains to nearby countries to reduce risks of disruption.

3. Shannon K. O'Neil, The Globalization Myth: Why Regions Matter (New Haven, CT: Yale University Press, 2022), 7.

4. Keith Johnson and Robbie Gramer, "The Great Decoupling," Foreign Policy, May 14, 2020, https://foreignpolicy.com/2020/05/14/china-us-pandemic-economy-tensions-trump -coronavirus-covid-new-cold-war-economics-the-great-decoupling/.

5. Susanne Schattenberg, "Pipeline Construction as 'Soft Power' in Foreign Policy. Why the Soviet Union Started to Sell Gas to West Germany, 1966–1970," Journal of Modern European History 20, no. 4 (2022), https://doi.org/10.1177/16118944221130222.

6. Mark Stenberg, "How the CEO of Pepsi, by Bartering Battleships and Vodka, Negotiated Cold War Diplomacy and Brought His Soda to the Soviet Union," Business Insider, November 11, 2020, https://www.businessinsider.com/ceo-of-pepsi-brought-soda-to-the-soviet-union-2020-11.

7. A 2022 Goldman Sachs report found that US companies have engaged in limited reshoring so far, as they look to strengthen supply-chain resilience. Instead, companies have focused on inventory overstocking and broadening their supplier base. Jan Hatzius et al., "Strengthening Supply Chain Resilience: Reshoring, Diversification, and Inventory Overstocking," Goldman Sachs, March 27, 2022, https://www.gspublishing.com/content/research/en/reports/2022/03/28 /a69df56c-b50e-4af5-9295-7fc7be33e096.html.

8. Chris Miller, Chip War: The Fight for the World's Most Critical Technology (New York: Scribner, 2022).

9. Of course, the local impact depends on the degree of reshoring versus nearshoring.

Chapter 20

1. Stephen Roach, "The Dollar's Crash Is Only Just Beginning," Bloomberg, January 25, 2021, https://www.bloomberg.com/opinion/articles/2021-01-25/the-dollar-s-crash-is-only-just -beginning#xj4y7vzkg.

2. Using BIS (Bank for International Settlements) Narrow Real Effective Exchange Rates— an index based on a trade-weighted average of bilateral exchange rates and adjusted by consumer prices.

3. Barry Eichengreen, Exorbitant Privilege: The Rise and Fall of the Dollar and the Future of the International Monetary System (Oxford: Oxford University Press, 2011).

4. For example, a 2005 paper by two prominent economists suggested that—under certain scenarios—the euro could overtake the dollar as the top reserve currency by 2022. Menzie Chinn and Jeffrey Frankel, "Will the Euro Eventually Surpass the Dollar as Leading International Reserve Currency?" working paper 11510, National Bureau of Economic Research, Cambridge, August 2005, https://www.nber.org/papers/w11510.

5. Neutral Switzerland has a currency that people want to hold. If there were more Swiss franc instruments available, the franc would possibly be a major global reserve asset, and neutrality wouldn't matter.

6. The paper was *Suddeutsche Zeitung*. See Jeffrey E. Garten, *Three Days at Camp David: How a Secret Meeting in 1971 Transformed the Global Economy* (New York: HarperCollins, 2021), 250.

7. There is one unearned benefit the incumbent does have—inertia. A new currency being incrementally better across the four enablers is not enough, as network effects play a role in keeping the status quo in place. The fact that the dollar is used for reserves, international banking, and trade makes it more likely that it will continue to be used. A marginally better option would struggle to overcome the incumbent's advantage.

8. The balance of payment identity says: Current account = capital + financial account. It's an identity, and by definition must always balance/offset. But it doesn't show you the driving forces (for instance, which part of the identity is pushing which around). For additional reading, consider Matthew C. Klein and Michael Pettis, *Trade Wars Are Class Wars: How Rising Inequality Distorts the Global Economy and Threatens International Peace* (New Haven, CT: Yale University Press, 2020).

9. See the Nouriel Roubini profile by Stephen Mihm, "Dr. Doom," *New York Times*, August 15, 2008, https://www.nytimes.com/2008/08/17/magazine/17pessimist-t.html. Note: Roubini's other dark call, on US housing, came out right—but the "dual train wreck" of fiscal deficits and external deficits did not create economic problems.

10. In 2007 former Fed Chair Alan Greenspan said that it was "absolutely conceivable that the euro will replace the dollar as reserve currency." Reuters Staff, "Euro Could Replace Dollar as Top Currency—Greenspan," *Reuters*, September 17, 2007, https://jp.reuters.com/article/greenspan-euro-idUSL1771147920070917.

11. Greenspan called this a conundrum. Ben Bernanke, then the Fed chair, said it was not so much a conundrum as a consequence of a "global savings glut."

12. Niall Ferguson, "The Dollar's Demise May Come Gradually, but Not Suddenly," *Bloomberg*, April 22, 2023, https://www.bloomberg.com/opinion/articles/2023-04-23/dollar-may-fall-to-yuan-crypto-but-not-soon-niall-ferguson.

13. Huileng Tan, "China and Russia Are Working on Homegrown Alternatives to the SWIFT Payment System. Here's What They Would Mean for the US Dollar," *Business Insider*, April 28, 2022, https://www.businessinsider.com/china-russia-alternative-swift-payment-cips-spfs-yuan-ruble-dollar-2022-4.

14. Chicago Booth—Kent A. Clark Center for Global Markets, "Ukraine Survey," March 8, 2022, https://www.kentclarkcenter.org/surveys/ukraine-2/.

Chapter 21

1. Tight labor markets are seen when the unemployment rate (u) is below the neutral rate of unemployment (u★).

2. See, for instance, Daniel Susskind, *A World without Work: Technology, Automation and How We Should Respond* (London: Penguin, 2020); David H. Autor, David A. Mindell, and Elisabeth Reynolds, *The Work of the Future: Building Better Jobs in an Age of Intelligent Machines* (Cambridge, MA: MIT Press, 2022); Erik Brynjolfsson and Andrew McAfee, *The Second Machine Age: Work, Progress, and Prosperity in a Time of Brilliant Technologies* (New York: W. W. Norton, 2016); David G. Blanchflower, *Not Working: Where Have All the Good Jobs Gone?* (Princeton, NJ: Princeton University Press, 2021); Martin Ford, *Rise of the Robots: Technology and the Threat of a Jobless Future* (New York: Basic Books, 2015); and Malcolm Frank, Paul Roehrig, and Ben Pring, *What to Do When*

Machines Do Everything: How to Get Ahead in a World of AI, Algorithms, Bots, and Big Data (New York: John Wiley & Sons, 2017).

3. First, corporate credit—and in particular low-quality or high-yield credit—does not reside on the asset side of bank balance sheets in a meaningful way. This limits contagion, as private debt that is outside of the banking system poses far smaller risks (see chapter 15). Second, corporate defaults need not cascade in the same way that defaults in other debt markets can. Consider that if a mortgage defaults, the asset is sold, depressing the price of homes and making the odds of credit problems in the neighborhood more likely. Yet if a retailer goes bust, the remaining competition will benefit from new demand, new labor supply, and potentially cheaper rents— making them more profitable and their credit stronger. And third, perhaps most significantly for the concern that higher rates will trigger a cascade, rates can be lowered if economic problems arise as long as inflation risks are contained (most importantly if long-term inflation expectations are anchored—remember they never showed signs of unanchoring during the postpandemic inflation spike). If higher rates are the problem, in many scenarios they can be walked back.

4. Additionally, monetary policymakers have a broader tool set than just a single policy rate—and while they do not have the capacity to quickly solve problems of capital, their liquidity tools are powerful against many of the strains created by higher rates.

5. See figure 19.1C. When global goods trade is looked at, excluding mining and fuels (which are meaningful influences by price, albeit not entirely), the drop in trade share of global GDP disappears.

6. Philipp Carlsson-Szlezak and Paul Swartz, "Outlook 2020—Keep Calm and Carry On (and Watch Your Back)," Sanford C. Bernstein, December 9, 2019.

7. Philipp Carlsson-Szlezak, Paul Swartz, and Martin Reeves, "Who Will Win—and Lose— in the Post-Covid Economy?" hbr.org, June 1, 2021, https://hbr.org/2021/06/who-will-win-and -lose-in-the-post-covid-economy.

8. Measured as economywide profits as a percentage of gross value added.

9. Consider, for example, the differences between a software company and a hotel chain. The software company will see relatively less tightness and have great opportunities for productivity gains; margin pressure will likely remain modest, and the company will not contribute much to inflation. In contrast, the hotel chain will be under a great deal of stress, as competition for low-wage labor remains fierce and opportunities to automate hard to implement. The hotel chain will therefore suffer sustained cost pressure; at the same time, because competitors within the hotel industry will face the same pressures, each may have the scope to push up prices. While this may add to inflation, the effect on the overall price level may be small—in which case, the central bank will not need to sharply raise interest rates and risk a policy recession.

10. S. G. Tallentyre, ed., *Voltaire in His Letters* (New York: G.P. Putnam's Sons, 1919), 232.

LIST OF FIGURES

INTRODUCTION

PART ONE

REAL ECONOMY

Growth Risks and Growth Boosts

PART TWO

FINANCIAL ECONOMY

Good Strains and Systemic Risks

PART THREE
GLOBAL ECONOMY
From Convergence Boom to Divergence Gloom

CONCLUSION

INDEX

ACKNOWLEDGMENTS

Though our research process naturally involves a lot of writing, it is as much—if not more—about conversation and debate. Many of our arguments and narratives are developed through countless discussions with executives and investors. Their questions often shape our research agenda. And our research output spurs the next round of conversations. This flywheel keeps us on our toes, forces us to evolve, and allows us to paint on a canvas that has no real edges. This book benefits from years of covering global macro in this way. Therefore, we start by thanking the hundreds of clients that have been our counterparts in these discussions.

Of course, none of this would be possible without a formidable platform to stand on. We're indebted to Rich Lesser and Martin Reeves for inviting us to make our professional home at BCG and for their support; to Christoph Schweizer, François Candelon, Sharon Marcil, Tawfik Hammoud, Rohan Sajdeh, Kilian Berz, and Carol Liao for encouraging us to write this book; and indeed to the wider BCG partnership, with its unparalleled ability to engage leaders across the entire spectrum of the real and financial economy around the world. We are also indebted to our former colleagues at Sanford C. Bernstein for imbuing us with their differentiated research ethos, for the countless meetings with savvy institutional investors, and for letting us utilize some of our work from those days.

But a book will not grow on research and debate alone. Once that edgeless research canvas is transformed into a coherent manuscript, it needs critical eyes. Here too we have benefited greatly from fine minds. We thank Sebastian Mallaby, Kathleen Stephansen, John McDonald, Jeffrey E. Garten, Rafael Ziegler, as well as our editor at Harvard Business Review Press, Jeff Kehoe, and four anonymous reviewers for making the final manuscript better.

Turning a manuscript into a physical book is far more complex than we thought. For ensuring a smooth process and a high-quality product, we'd like to thank Anne Starr and the entire production team at the Press. At BCG, we'd like to thank Amanda Wikman and her team for their formidable operations and marketing support.

Writing this book did not fit into our normal work schedules. Hence, we have run up a considerable debt with our families, who accepted our shorter weekends and longer evenings. Philipp would like to thank Teresa and his daughters, Clara and Nora, who like to joke that economist, communist, and ecologist all sound much the same to them. Paul would like to thank Rebecca and Cara, without whom he might have decamped long ago to a cabin in the woods full of books and a Bloomberg terminal.

Although a printed book has a certain finality to it, looking ahead we know it will be the beginning of new debates and thus new research. For that we remain immensely grateful.

ABOUT THE AUTHORS

Philipp Carlsson-Szlezak is Global Chief Economist at BCG and a managing director and partner in the firm's New York office. He also runs the Center for Macroeconomics at the BCG Henderson Institute. Prior to BCG, Carlsson-Szlezak was Chief Economist at Sanford C. Bernstein, where he covered the economy and markets for institutional investors in the global asset management industry. Earlier in his career, he spent more than 10 years advising financial institutions and governments at BCG, the Organisation for Economic Co-operation and Development (OECD), and McKinsey & Company. With longtime collaborator Paul Swartz, he regularly publishes technical research for clients and is a frequent contributor to *Harvard Business Review*, *World Economic Forum*, *Fortune*, and other business publications. He studied at the London School of Economics and earned a PhD from the University of Oxford.

Paul Swartz is a senior economist at the Center for Macroeconomics within the BCG Henderson Institute and an executive director in BCG's New York office. Prior to BCG, Swartz worked with Carlsson-Szlezak at Sanford C. Bernstein. Earlier in his career, he worked at Goldman Sachs' Investment Strategy Group, where he used a macro lens for tactical asset allocation. He also spent time at the Council on Foreign Relations' Greenberg Center for Geoeconomic Studies, where he contributed to the Emmy Award–winning *Crisis Guide: The Global Economy*, established the blog *Geo-Graphics*, and published in outlets including the *Wall Street Journal*. He began his career at Bridgewater Associates. Swartz studied at Syracuse University and serves as the vice chair to the College of Arts and Sciences' Dean's Advisory Board.